PAUL NEWMAN

Books by Lawrence J. Quirk

Robert Francis Kennedy

The Films of Joan Crawford

The Films of Ingrid Bergman

The Films of Paul Newman

The Films of Fredric March

Photoplay Anthology

The Films of William Holden

The Great Romantic Films

The Films of Robert Taylor

The Films of Ronald Colman

The Films of Warren Beatty

The Films of Myrna Loy

The Films of Gloria Swanson

The Complete Films of Bette Davis (Update from 1965)

The Complete Films of Katharine Hepburn (Update from 1970)

Claudette Colbert: An Illustrated Biography

Lauren Bacall: Her Films and Career

Jane Wyman: The Actress and the Woman

The Complete Films of William Powell

Margaret Sullavan: Child of Fate

Norma: The Story of Norma Shearer

Some Lovely Image (A Novel)

Fasten Your Seat Belts: The Passionate Life of Bette Davis

Totally Uninhibited: The Life and Wild Times of Cher

The Great War Films

The Kennedys in Hollywood

Paul Newman

Paul Newman

Lawrence J. Quirk

TAYLOR PUBLISHING COMPANY

Dallas, Texas

Published by Taylor Publishing Company
1550 West Mockingbird Lane
Dallas, Texas 75235

Library of Congress Cataloging-in-Publication Data

Quirk, Lawrence J.
    Paul Newman / Lawrence J. Quirk.
        p.   cm.
    Filmography: p. 337
    Includes bibliographical references and index.
    ISBN 0-87833-962-0
    1. Newman, Paul, 1925–   . 2. Motion picture actors and
actresses—United States—Biography. I. Title.
PN2287.N44Q52   1997
791.43'028'092—dc21
    [B]   96-37451
                                                                          CIP

Printed in the United States of America

10   9   8   7   6   5   4   3   2   1

This book has been printed on acid-free recycled paper.

For James E. Runyan

CONTENTS

INTRODUCTION

ARMED WITH GOOD LOOKS, DISARMING CHARISMA, AND A limited but often rigorously applied talent, Paul Newman has been in the public eye for over four decades, zealously guarding his privacy and refusing autographs to any and all comers.

He is a man of contrasts: An often befuddled if well-meaning Hollywood liberal who can be as close minded as any Moral Majority type when it comes to opinions that differ from his own. A down-to-earth lover of male camaraderie and boozing who can bond with virtually any (drinking) man except his own son, who wound up killing himself. An artist who can direct sensitive, gentle studies such as *Rachel, Rachel* and *The Glass Menagerie* yet who is still embarrassed by what to him is the unmanly profession of acting and races cars and chooses superbutch roles to compensate. A husband who professes to adore his wife but won't lift a finger to help her raise their three children (or her two surviving stepchildren). And an activist who espouses the liberal causes of the nineties yet as a husband and father is still trapped firmly in the 1950s.

Although Newman comes from a fairly privileged background with a genteel, educated upbringing and is often surrounded by creative people of all stripes, he oddly prefers the company of grease monkeys and drivers on the racing circuit. He has always tried to come on modest, unassuming, and self-deprecatory—he claims his stardom is the result of good looks and the "Newman Luck," and he just may be right—but one coworker deemed him "the most monstrously narcissistic and egomaniacal person I have ever known."

Newman has been a movie star for most of his life, and that sets him apart from the sea of humanity. He can be so self-absorbed that it is impossible for him to relate to the average person—even if they are literally related *to* him—on any deep or serious level. Despite his stabs at analysis with various therapists, there is reason to suspect, as this book will examine, that Newman has gone all his long life without adequately understanding and facing the complex inner processes that have kept his outlook on life rather fuzzy and self-deceptive, not to say contradictory.

Previous biographies and articles on the actor—with a few exceptions—tend to go easy on Newman, as if he were somebody you didn't dare say anything bad about. The question is why. Newman is only a movie star, not someone who has discovered a cure for cancer. Movie stars are no different from "ordinary" human beings and often turn out to have feet of clay, if not much worse.

As an actor Newman always had narrow range, but through quiet persistence and channeled energy, he managed to expand the horizons of his talent to the point where, on some occasions, the mannered, gimmicky style of his early years gave way to a more mellow, balanced technique of underplaying. He tended to get lost and confused in splashy epics (like *Exodus*), but when handed a more intimate story (such as *The Hustler* or *Cat on a Hot Tin Roof*), came off much better. But his forays into certain character portrayals as he got older were often disappointing if not downright disastrous. His directorial efforts have occasionally won acclaim, but this acclaim has been accompanied by feelings in certain critical circles that Newman mostly directs the actors and leaves the technical, cinematic side to his editors and cinematographers, who practically function as codirectors.

A very different era existed when I wrote the first-ever book about Newman over twenty-five years ago. *The Films of Paul Newman* was meant in part as a tribute to a major movie star. The publisher preferred illustrated write-ups on movies and a generally admiring tone toward Newman instead of the much more frank approach of today. But many of the films in which the public so loved Newman's performances have not worn at all well in the intervening years.

Therefore, this volume not only explores Newman's private life but also reevaluates many of his most famous films and roles. Comments made about Newman from many of his coworkers during my more than fifty years in the entertainment field are included, as well as material from my own private interviews with Newman and new interviews with many who know or have worked with him.

What has emerged is, I believe, a fair and honest portrait of a man who is, as is true of any of us, only human.

1

SECOND SON

WHEN THERESA FETZER NEWMAN PROUDLY SHOWED HER husband Arthur the bouncing baby boy with the vivid blue eyes, neither of them had any idea that he would grow up to become a famous movie star and international sex symbol. For now, on January 26, 1925, he was simply Paul Leonard Newman, their pride and joy, the second of their two sons.

The eight-pound baby was quickly rushed home to 2100 Renrock Road in Cleveland Heights, a suburb of Cleveland, Ohio, for neighbors and relatives to fuss over. Soon, however, baby Paul was on his way to yet another location, the more upscale neighborhood of Shaker Heights. It was at 2983 Brighton Road that the blue-eyed baby grew into the handsome young man who would star in dozens of movies and set millions of hearts aflutter.

Paul Newman did not have an impoverished, difficult, terrible, or especially dramatic childhood. Most of the drama was internal, in his head. His father, Arthur S. Newman, was a partner in a highly successful sporting-goods retail business, Newman-Stern. Arthur and his brother Joe had originally sold radios—the first in Cleveland to do so way back in 1915—but because of World War I and its ban on private radio broadcasts, Art and Joe instead switched to sporting goods, where they made a killing. Later Joe became a well-known Ohio poet and journalist and left the running of the business to his brother and associates.

Arthur Newman was far too busy being secretary and treasurer of Newman-Stern to be much of a father to Paul. Paul admitted years later that he never felt close to his father and, in turn, was never as close as he should have been to his own son, Scott. "I think [my father] always thought of me as pretty much of a lightweight," Newman said. "He treated me like he was disappointed in me a lot of the time."

Paul's older (by one year) brother, Arthur Jr., was no parent substitute: Although the two siblings had a problematic relationship, they worked out their differences years later and brother Arthur eventually became a production manager for a motion picture firm Paul started. But in their younger days, they were rivals for their father's affections. Arthur Jr. was better at sports, bigger, taller, seemingly everything Paul wanted to be in his father's eyes.

Paul enjoyed a much closer relationship—comparatively speaking—with his mother, who had been born in Hungary. She had grown up in relative poverty and at times seemed more interested in the material things her husband's success had acquired than in her children. Theresa loved the theater and would see play after play at the Hannah Theatre in Cleveland, then come home to regale her son with stories of what she had seen on the stage. People who knew her felt that Theresa was a frustrated would-be actress.

Theresa had been raised a Catholic—her husband Arthur was a German Jew—but she converted to Christian Science when Paul was five years old. Paul became a Christian Scientist, too, although the household never stuck too rigidly to the religion's tenets; there was no aversion to doctors and medical checkups, for instance.

A primary influence on young Paul was Uncle Joe, who became a kind of surrogate father. Paul knew that Arthur Jr. was his father's favorite, but Uncle Joe never slighted him. As Paul watched with envy the perhaps imaginary camaraderie between his father and brother, Joe would encourage him to read, lending books he thought the boy would be interested in. Above all Joe was a pal to young Paul. (Later Paul would claim that he stopped reading as soon as he got interested in girls.)

Uncle Joe also inadvertently encouraged Paul in his thespian pursuits. When Paul was seven, he was cast as a court jester in a school play about Robin Hood and got to sing—with the rest of the cast—a song that had been written especially for the occasion by no less than Joseph F. Newman. Uncle Joe and the rest of the relatives beamed with pride as little Paul made his entrance, said his one or two lines, then made a hasty exit. Paul's memory of the experience? "I felt as uncomfortable and disturbed then as I do now when I'm onstage." Paul has never completely gotten over his stage fright.

Still, this minor experience, despite whatever trauma it engendered, must have awakened something in the fledgling actor. As Paul got older, he would turn more often toward the kind of artistic fulfillment and thrilling ego-gratification that only acting could bring.

Part of Paul's trouble in youth was that he was not as tall or muscular as many of his peers. His interest in sports was not matched by his ability, although no one could say he didn't try. Nor was he an instant success onstage. He was disappointed when he didn't get the role of First Gravedigger in the Shaker Heights Senior High School's production of *Hamlet* and had to settle for mere stage manager instead. He stage-managed other productions and got smaller roles, but no one would ever have considered the possibility that someday he might become a major movie star.

Not that he didn't look the part. The blue-eyed baby had developed into a strikingly handsome high-school youth, and the ladies were beginning to notice. At first, girls were just something to play jokes on—Paul and his friends would hold jack-o-lanterns up to female classmates' bedroom windows late on Halloween night and hope to hear screams—but later he couldn't help but notice that certain young women (and not a few older ones) were looking at him in a particular way. "In a way it was a shame to waste such beauty on a boy," his mother said.

Eventually Paul's good looks would prove an embarrassment to him, but during his youth, he was more interested in being the neighborhood cutup and class clown than the resident lover boy. His mother would recall how Paul was "always into some mischief," always taking part in skits and tomfoolery and playing gags on people, acting out parts and playing the fool. By high school he was already a ham. He was also extremely accident prone, coming home with all manner of bruises and contusions on a nearly constant basis.

The gang that Newman palled around with during his high-school days was a reckless, irresponsible crew—by 1940s Ohio standards at any rate. One night Paul went on a joyride in a car that one of his buddies had borrowed from his father. The car wound up nearly wrapped around a tree on this buddy's front lawn. Understandably, when the father came out, he got hysterical and threatened to call the police, until he saw his own son was involved. Instead he phoned all the other boys' fathers. Paul was grounded for awhile, but eventually it all blew over.

Paul graduated in 1943 and promptly enlisted in the navy for flight training. Since it might have been some time before he was called for service, he went to Ohio University in Athens for a few months, majoring in "beer drinking," he later commented. There, two events of singular importance occurred. He met a young lady who became the first real love of his life, and he decided to attend auditions for a play entitled *The Milky Way*, which was being staged by the speech department. In a moment of weird foreshadowing, he was cast as a middleweight champ, Speed McFarland, little knowing that he would make his mark playing a boxer in the movies many years later. He did not, however, make as much of a mark on the young lady who had raised his blood pressure, although he was not to learn this until sometime later. For now, they were hot and heavy.

In June Paul had to bid a reluctant farewell to his lady love. The navy was calling, specifically a V-12 program that would begin with training on the grounds of Yale University. Paul had wanted to be a pilot—his head flying with the dreams all young men had of glory, heroism, and patriotism in the wake of Pearl Harbor—but these plans were stymied when his first test revealed that he suffered from color blindness. Although he argued vociferously against the decision, he was told he couldn't stay in the program if he couldn't distinguish one ground object from another using color as a differential. His dreams of being a courageous pilot were shot to hell. He had to settle for being a radioman, third class.

Boot camp was uneventful, despite the fact that one of his instructors was a man who would become a famous actor himself, Robert Stack, now solving *Unsolved Mysteries* on television. Although years later movie publicity people would try to cast Paul as "Ironjaw" Newman, the Allied Beast of the Pacific, he had a relatively quiet time as "a back seat man on a Navy torpedo plane." By his own admission, Newman never saw any combat. "Most of the time we cruised around in readiness for action that simply did not happen."

Paul spent the war bumming around such "awful" spots as Saipan, Guam, and even beautiful Hawaii, reading countless books and consuming as much liquor as he could get his hands on. For awhile, the only negative note struck was when his lady love in Athens sent him a Dear John letter, which positively floored him. She had found someone else—someone who was *around*—and the woman who might have become the first Mrs. Paul Newman changed the course of Hollywood history by marrying another.

Perhaps the only outré incident occurred on a troopship in the Pacific Ocean. Newman was up on the deck skimming Nietzsche when a navy chaplain came over and started a conversation. In his Ohioan naiveté, Paul assumed the chaplain was simply being kind to a homesick sailor, but it wasn't long before the older man, smitten with Newman's striking good looks, made a rather flagrant pass. Shocked, Paul rebuffed the man and darted off. Years later, when he recalled the incident to Gore Vidal, he said, "Now *that* really put me off." When Vidal asked him if it put him off Christianity or homosexuality, Newman replied, "Neither. Nietzsche."

What he refers to as the Newman Luck carried him through every possible danger during World War II. At one point his squad was supposed to report to practice simulated aircraft carrier landings. But only five of the six three-man crews in the squadron could transfer to the aircraft carrier because Newman's pilot had developed an ear infection that not only grounded the pilot but also Newman and the other man in the crew. The other fifteen men on the carrier were among those in the ready room when Japanese kamikaze pilots attacked. There was no time to launch any planes for an effective counterattack. Hours later Newman learned that all of his friends in the squadron had been killed. He couldn't get over how if it hadn't been for his pilot's earache . . . .

Newman returned to civilian life in 1946, still feeling

worthless in his father's eyes and inferior to his older brother. There had been no combat heroism, his girlfriend had left him flat for another man, and he was facing a dull future in his father's business. But at least he was *alive*, and for that he was undoubtedly grateful. Still stinging from his ex-girlfriend's rejection, he decided to go to an all-male college, Kenyon, in Gambier, Ohio. His family was pleased: The girl at Athens had distracted him from his studies. Despite his earlier efforts at amateur dramatics, he had no particular interest in professional acting and at this time never thought seriously of a career in the theater.

Along with his naval days, he was happiest at Kenyon. He seemed to enjoy all the male camaraderie, which apparently made up for the absence of females and almost made up for the fact that he hated what he was studying. He had thought that majoring in economics would please his father—it was still very important for him to do that—but he had no interest in the subject; banks and money just bored him. He wanted desperately to make the football team—Dad and Arthur Jr. would sure be impressed by that. Although he was afraid he might weigh too little (he was 150 pounds at the time) and have too slight a build, he managed to make the second-string team.

Thrilled at even this consolation prize. Paul and some buddies went out skirt chasing one night. There was a notorious (again, by 1940s Ohio standards) nightclub some miles outside of Gambier, in nearby Mount Vernon. There were girls there—and lots of beer.

Paul and his football friends drank and drank and drank and had words with some young men from Mount Vernon. Oaths and epithets were flung back and forth. Eventually the words turned into shoves and pushes. Drinks were thrown and finally punches. A full-fledged, wild barroom brawl of the more crashing variety erupted. Bottles and mirrors and faces were smashed; chairs were thrown; girls were screaming. The manager did his best to quell the disturbance but had to throw up his hands and call the police. When the Mount Vernon officers arrived, they found the nightclub in a shambles and quickly subdued the ones responsible, including Paul Leonard Newman.

For the first—but not the last—time in his life, Newman found himself in a jail cell. He spent the night sleeping off his drunkenness and lying in his own vomit, as his buddies did the same. When morning came, he got a dose of cold reality. The dean sent an emissary to the courtroom to watch the proceedings, then made his own judgment. Two of the men involved in the brawl were immediately expelled from Kenyon. Newman and three of his friends were put on suspension and thrown off the football team. Newman might have been crushed by his decision were it not that he was supremely relieved to escape expulsion. He also knew deep down that he wasn't a very good football player. No one could see how bad he was if he never got to play.

The story made headlines in the *Cleveland Plain Dealer*, and Paul braced himself for his father's reaction. Paul had already been arrested three times for other minor offenses, such as public drunkenness and disturbing the peace, but this was a bit more serious. And because of the damned papers, the whole world knew about it. He knew his father would be furious and felt a wrenching dismay at having let down the one person in the world whose love and approval he sought more than anyone else's. He had gone out with the guys and gotten involved in the brawl because it was *what college boys did* if they were *men*. Paul, with his thin frame and pretty boy features, having failed to distinguish himself overseas, needed to prove to himself and his father that he was a man.

And he succeeded in part. After his father's initial rage subsided, Paul realized that his father was in some way proud his errant son had at least been bloodied off campus if not in combat. Besides, Arthur and Theresa figured that Paul would have been expelled if he had been one of the prime instigators in the tavern fight.

There was a happy side effect of the whole incident in any case. Not having football to fill his extracurricular needs, Paul decided to try out for the Kenyon production of *The Front Page*. He got the plum role of Hildy Johnson, and his college theatrical career was launched. There were nine more productions in which he appeared, including *RUR* (*Rossum's Universal Robots*), *Charley's Aunt*, *The Taming of the Shrew*, and *The Alchemist*. He even mounted his own musical with male classmates in drag, which he wrote and directed, giving himself the lead role of the dean (who loved it). He threw himself into acting and the whole theatrical experience with much more enthusiasm than he ever could have mustered for football.

Whether Newman was ever *seriously* interested in athletics, for which he betrayed no particular talent, is debatable. There are curious indications that he felt it was all part of being a man, that he sought excellence in sports as a way of compensating for what he felt were his overly pretty features and slight (as compared to a quarterback) frame. In many ways, he is still of this mind-set, which contributed to his racing fanaticism decades later.

In 1959 I was interviewing Newman when he suggested that I might want to join him and his ball team in Central Park that weekend. There had been some rough patches to the interview, and I replied a bit testily that sports "were for lunkheads who never crack a book." To my surprise, a look of almost startled respect came into his eyes, and he said, "Oh, but in some respects a guy has to go along, keep up appearances, don't you think?"

"Why?" I asked him.

He lowered his eyes and said, "Forget I said it. It's just me . . ."

Whatever the case during his days at Kenyon, he didn't think much of his acting, either. "I was probably one of the worst college actors in history. I didn't know anything about acting. I had no idea what I was doing. I learned my lines by rote and simply said them, without spontaneity, without any idea of dealing with the forces around me onstage, without knowing what it meant to act and to react. I didn't really learn about any of that until I got into the Actors Studio." He did enjoy all the recognition he got from being in the plays, however.

Newman had no thought of becoming a professional actor after graduation. He had no real idea of what to do with himself, only a vague notion that he would make a living *teaching* dramatics. In his junior year, he changed his major from economics to English and speech. To himself, at least, he was making it very clear that he wanted no part of his father's sporting-goods business.

He would have little to say about that, however, when the time came.

2

PANIC

PAUL'S PARENTS DID NOT TAKE IT WELL WHEN HE SWITCHED majors from economics to speech and English. His father had proven that money could be made through *business* and hard work. That money could also be made through talent and artistry was not as certain. Even Theresa was worried about what would happen to Paul. Whatever her own ambitions, she was never a typical stage mother. Prancing around the neighborhood making kids laugh and appearing in college plays was one thing; doing it for a living was another. Paul assured them both that he planned on becoming a *teacher*, not an actor. There was nothing for them to worry about. But his father, who had always intended his sons to follow him in the family business, was not so easily placated.

Conversely, Arthur Newman did not like the idea of his sons battening off of him. They had never gotten any special privileges; when they'd helped him out in the business over the summer, they'd done the same menial work any beginner would have. Their father never even let them have free samples of all the athletic equipment he sold. Paul was given very

little spending money while at Kenyon, even though his
father could certainly have afforded it, and whatever meager
allowance Arthur may have given him was certainly cut off as
soon as news of his drunken high jinks hit the papers.

So Paul hit upon a scheme to enrich his coffers, a
scheme so cleverly simple that it indicated he might have
been quite a businessman had he chosen to follow that path.
He hit the streets of Gambier until he found a small shop on
a good street that was available for a modest rent. He had
managed to save up enough money—service pay and the
like—to convert the shop into a laundry. What made Paul's
laundry stand out from all the others in town was that his
offered free beer to customers. Naturally the place was soon
packed with college students armed with bags of soiled
shirts and underwear, anxious to partake of the suds pouring from the large keg Paul bought each week for twelve
dollars. On an average week he would take in sixty dollars,
often more. "I didn't like working on the side," he said years
later, "but at home they couldn't tell me what to do if I had
money of my own."

Despite having all those soused college kids as customers, the Newman Luck held right up until he sold the
joint in his senior year; there was never any trouble with the
police. That wasn't the case with the next owner, a friend of
Paul's, who found himself out of business the very first day he
took over when a customer imbibed too much brew and
drunkenly began masturbating a horse that was hanging
around on the street. When the horse took off down the
block with the drunken student still holding on to its massive
member, the police were called in to put an end to the
shenanigans. The town figured that any business that encouraged acts of bestiality, as it were, on public streets, was a business that Gambier could do without.

To Paul's chagrin, his father seemed to blame him for

this inauspicious end to the business he had started single handedly. The sheer vulgarity of the stories that circulated about what had killed the laundry ensured that Arthur Newman would never take the business and Paul's success at it seriously. Once again Paul had failed to please or impress his father.

After his junior year, in the summer of 1948, Paul did work in summer stock at Plymouth, Massachusetts. At the Priscilla Beach Theater, he performed in such plays as *All My Sons* and *Dear Brutus*. Even at this early stage, he was interested in doing character parts, in disguising the good looks that proved an embarrassment to him. When people would compliment him on his blue eyes, he'd either freeze up or turn red in the face. To him "pretty" equaled effeminate. Even worse was the occasional incident similar to the one on the troopship with the chaplain—men would assume he was "that way" and make suggestive remarks or gestures. He would handle it by pretending he didn't know what they were talking about or by walking out of the room in a hurry. These incidents only added to his self-doubts.

During his last year at Kenyon, there was another confrontation with his parents. Just before graduation, he was offered a room-and-board scholarship with a summer stock company in Williams Bay, Wisconsin, and determined to take it. His father thought this acting business was a lot of nonsense. Paul countered that if he was going to teach drama, he had better get some experience and know what he was talking about. Caught in the middle, Theresa tried to see both sides of the argument but held little influence over her husband.

Wanting his son to have the stability of a job in the family business, Arthur Newman allowed Paul to go to Williams Bay, and even supplemented the room and board with some cold cash, on the condition that Paul would give up this foolishness and join Newman-Stern with his brother Art if things didn't work out after a few months. One thing was for certain: There would be no more handouts. If Paul was determined to stick with the theater, he would have to live on what he made as an actor. Cocky, young Newman, bolstered by his campus fame as a handsome thespian, wasn't worried. On this matter he was sure he knew better than his hardheaded father.

On June 13, 1949, at two in the afternoon, Paul went to the podium with the other graduates and accepted his diploma. He barely had time to kiss his proud mother, shake hands with Dad, and say good-bye to a few select classmates before he was running to the depot to catch a four o'clock train to Williams Bay. Young and eager and glad to be free of Shaker Heights and parental influence for the nonce, he didn't look back.

At this time Paul wasn't necessarily thinking seriously of becoming a professional actor. Summer stock was more like a paid vacation, a chance to put off the dreaded day when he had to be under his father's thumb and watch Arthur Jr. do a better job and win all of dad's praise. Anything was better than working for Newman-Stern doing something dull and predictable. He really didn't know what he wanted to do with his life. There was still the vague idea of teaching drama and speech, but other than that, his future was a blank slate.

At Williams Bay he got good parts right off the bat. First he was cast as the soldier in Norman Krasna's *John Loves Mary*. Then he got the role of the gentleman caller in Tennessee Williams's *The Glass Menagerie*, little dreaming that one day he'd not only become acquainted with the playwright himself but also become one of the foremost interpreters of Williams's work.

The summer in Williams Bay went by too quickly as far as Newman was concerned. Soon it was autumn, and he had to face the tough decision of returning to Cleveland and security—and deadening dullness—or taking on the challenge, excitement, and amusement of the stock company actor's vagabond life. He still had some of his father's money left, so unlike the other stock players, he would not have to struggle to survive. He phoned home and got more lectures, but his mind was made up. Soon he was on another train bound for Chicago, where he would make his way to Woodstock, Illinois, for a longer season of winter stock.

Paul appeared in, did props for, and even directed some of the sixteen plays during the season, all of which were mounted in the town hall: *Our Town, Mister Roberts, Born Yesterday, See How They Run, Cyrano de Bergerac,* and *Meet Me in St. Louis* among many others. As the winter progressed, he began to know and like an attractive fellow player named Jackie Witte. A Wisconsin native, Jackie had been bitten by the acting bug while studying at Lawrence University in Appleton. She was a very pretty blonde with brown eyes and a good sense of humor, and she was very different from the kind of girls—including the one who'd jilted him—that Paul had known before.

Other young women had always seemed to size him up as a "prospect," with one eye on his father's blooming business and the other on the likelihood of his following in his father's footsteps and becoming an equally good provider. Jackie seemed to understand that a man could be a success by striking out on his own and taking a different route from his forebearers. As they co-starred in *Dark of the Moon,* kissed on the sly in dark backstage corners, and fell slowly in love with each other, it occurred to Paul that she wouldn't pester him to become the conventional husband. On that point he was sadly wrong, but the Jackie Witte of 1949 was a different creature from the Jackie Witte of several years to come. He asked her to marry him.

Many of Newman's associates, then and now—perhaps even Newman himself—have wondered why he ever took a wife at that time. No matter how much he may have been in love and regardless of how financially undemanding Jackie was, his future was utterly uncertain. Jackie was not pregnant, or at least couldn't have known she was, at the time of their wedding in December 1949. (Their first child was born exactly nine months later.) The most likely answer is that Paul saw marriage as yet another escape—escape from his stifling family and what they represented, escape from nagging self-doubts and insecurities. In the 1940s even more than today, actors were generally thought of as sexually ambiguous mountebanks, an attitude that Paul knew his father shared. Paul may have been a failure as a son, but he would not be a failure as a husband and father. Paul was no different from many men. Marriage, starting his own family, was a way of escaping the disapproval of his immediate family.

There was another factor. Paul was a victim of homosexual panic, which afflicts heterosexual as well as homosexual men. In his younger days he may have been afraid that he was or would become homosexual. Now he was afraid that others would *perceive* him as homosexual. First he was good looking, too pretty as even his own mother had suggested. Next he had been a complete washout at sports. Finally, he had chosen—at least for the time being—an occupation that was in itself "suspect." During his time in summer stock, he had met many more homosexuals than he had in the navy, or at least the gays were more apparent in the theater than in the services, where they couldn't be so open (naval chaplains excluded).

So for a variety of reasons, and because Jackie was attractive and attentive and fun to be with, Paul took the plunge and got married. Even this didn't please his father, who felt Paul had no business marrying when he could barely support himself on what he was earning. Acting brought in so little, even with two salaries, that he was forced to work days as a laborer on a farm. Getting up early to till the soil, dig dirt,

and perform other barnyard chores may have helped keep
him in shape physically, but it left him in no shape to act in
the evenings—although that didn't stop him. Jackie often
went to bed in her nightie unfulfilled as new hubby snored
away from sheer exhaustion. But there was no choice. Paul
would not beg his father for money, and he would not have
sent it in any case. If Paul wanted money, all he had to do was
come home and join the family business. Stubbornly,
admirably, Newman resisted and put up with the calluses and
the long hours. Jackie just put up.

The farm work didn't last long. In April 1950 Paul got
word that his father was seriously ill and that he had better
come back to Cleveland. Of course Paul had enough feelings
for his father—and his worried mother—to be concerned,
but more troubling was the thought that what he had wanted
to put off indefinitely could be put off no longer. With his
father ill, they would need more help—family help—at the
sporting-goods store. For her part, Jackie, who now knew she
was expecting a little one, felt a certain relief. The "romantic"
life of artistic poverty was wearing thin, and a steady income
would mean a lot when there'd soon be three mouths to feed.
Paul returned to Shaker Heights and the sporting-goods
store, hoping his father would recover and that the situation
would be a temporary one.

It was not. The following month Arthur Newman died.
Paul could not really feel much for a man he had never
been close to. Thinking of the child that was on the way, he
and Jackie decided, after much soul searching, to stay in
Cleveland. Paul Leonard Newman became a company man,
going off to the store each morning to work with Uncle Joe
(who relegated his writing pursuits to spare time as he assist-
ed in the business), his brother Art, and a cousin. Jackie kept
Theresa Newman company as the two hatched plots to keep
Paul from getting the wanderlust again.

For awhile Paul seemed to accept his lot in life. Jackie

seemed to accept it, too—why shouldn't she?—and this certainly influenced his decision to buy a house in nearby Bedford. Jackie and Paul moved into their new house after the baby was born, Alan Scott Newman, a handsome child with his father's devilish grin. Paul dutifully reported for work and mastered the running of the business as well as he had mastered the running of the laundry, although he did not pass out beer mugs to the customers. Uncle Joe was back writing again as Paul and brother Art took care of everything. All was proceeding quite nicely.

Except that it wasn't. On the surface Paul Newman seemed to have it all, wife, child, steady employment, money in the bank, but inside he was going quite *crazy*. He hated this existence. This was exactly the kind of safe, conformist, stultifying life that he had been trying to avoid by traipsing from one stock company to another. There was something missing in his life, something that success in business just couldn't supply. He was now living his father's life, as if he had taken over from him after his death, and that was exactly what he had never wanted to do. He began to feel another kind of panic, a panic that was no less crushing because it had come upon him slowly. Finally one day he couldn't take it anymore. He went into his brother's office and announced that he wanted *out*.

This made no sense to Art, who knew as well as Paul did that Paul was terrific at his job. "I was very successful at being something that I was not, and that is the worst thing that can happen to a man!" Paul said many years later. One way or another Paul cajoled Art into taking over the business completely, running the whole operation on his own with help from the cousin, other employees, and on occasion, Uncle Joe.

Jackie and Theresa were not thrilled with Paul's decision. To them it was as if he had taken leave of his senses. The final straw was when Art decided that if Paul wasn't interested, neither was he, and Newman-Stern went up for sale. While they waited for takers, Paul tried a variety of odd jobs. He knew he had to do *something*, but he wasn't ready to make his move yet. His first position was as a manager at a golf range, which had him digging in the grass for lost balls and washing them off so they could be reused later on. As he washed these balls, his hands filthy with mud and chilled from the cold water, Paul must have contemplated that running his father's business was a whole lot better than managing somebody else's.

For awhile he got back into acting—of a sort. He went over to the local radio station and inquired if there might be a use for his rather rich, striking, theatrically trained baritone voice. He showed the powers-that-be lists of his credits, which undoubtedly impressed them to no end, and was hired to do on-air commercials for the Ohio Bell telephone company and the McCann-Erickson advertising agency. But it wasn't the answer to his prayers and he knew it.

Finally Paul got the news he had been waiting for. Newman-Stern had been sold, and he was entitled to a chunk of the action. One afternoon he told everyone—including a startled though relatively supportive Jackie—what his plans were. He now had the money and could afford to take the kind of risky step that most people were only able to dream about.

"Jackie," he said, "we're going to New Haven."

He had decided to go for his master's degree at no less than Yale University.

Escape!

3

"YOUNG ACTORS NEED FREEDOM"

The Newman clan found themselves in New Haven in the fall of 1951, living on the top floor of an old, unattractive wooden house with two other families below them. The floors creaked, everyone worried about fires, and there were enough screaming babies and hollering children to drive a saint to distraction, but Paul was where he wanted to be and that was all that mattered. He was twenty-six years old.

At the Yale School of Drama, Paul specialized in directing. When he wasn't in classes, he sold encyclopedias door-to-door and made more money as a salesman than expected, undoubtedly because his charming manner and good looks were not lost on all the housewives he called on. He recalled making nine hundred dollars in one ten-day period, although he did not make out so well every week. (Judging from how he set female hearts afire once he became a movie star, one might wonder how many women bought a set of encyclopedias from Paul when they already owned one.) Money was not really that much of a problem, however. His share of the family business was large—over four thousand dollars—and if worse came to worst, he could always dip into the savings that were left over after paying university fees. Despite the crowded surroundings he came home to, his was not a life of real struggle by any means.

Newman's directing professor, Frank McMullan, saw a certain potential in Paul as actor if not as stage director. McMullan thought Paul had a "magnetic presence" and determined to use him in a student production when the occasion arose. The occasion materialized when another student handed in a script for an original play on Beethoven. McMullan thought Newman would be perfect for the part of Beethoven's nephew, Karl, and cast him in the role when he decided to mount a production of *Beethoven* in the spring of 1952. Newman did not have to be talked into it.

However, there were problems. Newman was not and never would be comfortable in period pieces, and *Beethoven* was no exception. Karl was "a very formal guy," in Paul's opinion, just the thing Newman was not. McMullan helped Paul smooth over the rough stretches, but Newman got by essentially on that "magnetic presence" McMullan had noticed.

On opening night this presence wasn't lost on the audience, which included the husband-and-wife agenting team, Audrey Wood and William Liebling. Wood handled playwrights—Tennessee Williams was among her famous clients—while husband Bill represented actors. Wood disappointed *Beethoven*'s playwright—she didn't think much of the play or of his chances—but Liebling went backstage to have a chat with Paul. He told the young man that he had real potential and suggested he drop by his office if he ever decided to embark upon a professional career. Newman told him that if he was ever in New York, he would do just that.

Secretly, he wondered what all the fuss was about. He had felt terribly awkward on stage in the play, and felt it did not showcase him at his best. Part of him wondered what Liebling might really be after.

He discussed the whole situation with Jackie, who spent most of her time taking care of Alan Scott Newman. In the midst of the terrible twos, Alan Scott indulged in fits of screaming and whining at the slightest opportunity. Now that they were far away from Ohio, she had turned back—to a certain degree—into the supportive "anything you want to do is all right with me, darling" wife that he had married. She figured there was nothing to lose if Paul tried to grab the brass ring; given their cramped, noisy quarters in New Haven, anything would be an improvement.

Not only did Paul feel there was no guarantee he could secure a teaching post after he left Yale, the thought of teaching in some backwater now held as much excitement for him as working for Newman-Stern or at a golf range. They decided that he should finish up the school year at Yale, then move to New York City where he could try to round up acting jobs with Bill Liebling's help. When summer came, Paul took the plunge.

First there was the matter of living quarters. Jackie suggested, and then insisted on, Staten Island, although Paul felt that would be too far away from the action. She told him that she had an aunt on Staten Island who could babysit little Alan Scott while the two of them were out looking for work. She announced that now that she had her figure back she wanted to become a model. She was bored staying home all day while Paul was out doing this and that, having a *life*. They located a modest apartment near Jackie's aunt that rented for sixty dollars a month. Settled, assured that their son would be looked after when they were away, Paul and Jackie made plans to take New York by storm.

Like most of the best laid plans, things didn't quite work out the way the couple wanted. For one thing, Jackie was pregnant again, and this put an end to her dreams of modeling. It also put a lot more urgency on Paul's need to secure acting jobs. They wouldn't starve—not for awhile yet—but *two* children would mean they'd need a lot more money than their by now meager savings could provide.

Bill Liebling was willing to represent Newman, but he told Paul bluntly that he would have to wait until the right major Broadway part came along before Liebling could do anything for him; the powerful agent did not traffic in bit parts or small roles. Liebling did not explain how Paul was supposed to make a living until this happened. Like many an actor before and since, Paul learned that while waiting for this perhaps mythical role to arrive, he had to basically agent himself, hitting the pavement, going dejectedly from one audition to another.

Newman would remember waking up each morning around seven, catching the Staten Island ferry to Manhattan around eight, then walking around in his one seersucker suit in the broiling sun, going from casting call to casting call, then coming back home where he'd sell more encyclopedias door-to-door from the late afternoon until early evening. Staten Island housewives were no more immune to his charm than were the New Haven ladies, so there was always food on the table. But he was frustrated. From the way people had gone on about him he'd expected almost instant success. "I had no intention of waiting around till I was old and bruised and bitter," he said years later. Just as his father had once given him a few months to make good on his own, now Newman gave himself his own ultimatum. If nothing happened within a year, it was back to school for him and the end to dreams of acting. If he could teach drama at, say, his old alma mater, Kenyon College, would it really be so bad?

Underneath this cool, *que sera, sera* attitude, Newman wanted very badly to succeed as an actor. With two powerful factors in his favor—his good looks and Bill Liebling—his success was practically preordained; it just took a short while longer than he anticipated. Before a single month was up, he was getting parts—bits, perhaps, but parts that paid. His big break would not be long in coming, either.

His first professional job was a walk-on in *The March of Time*, a live television drama about President McKinley. Paul was made up as an old man in the crowd during McKinley's inauguration. For this he received the not insignificant sum (considering the insignificance of the part) of seventy-five dollars. Once he had amassed several of these minor television credits, he decided to speak to yet another agent, one who specialized in television as opposed to stage parts, and made an appointment with Maynard Morris of the Music Corporation of America. People who worked at the agency at the time commented that Paul resembled a Greek god when he walked into the offices.

However much the face and physique had to do with it—and it was probably a lot—Morris was able to get Newman his first speaking role on television. Newman was nervous as hell on the night that the live broadcast went out over the air, even though he only had about twenty-four lines to speak as an army sergeant involved in an unnatural disaster. The story line for this episode of *Tales of Tomorrow* had to do with an enormous slab of ice forming off the west coast of the United States and presumably wreaking havoc with shipping lanes and the like; ominous sounds of ice crackling and creaking could be heard in the background, alternately giving Newman the willies or making him giggle. "It was one of the funniest shows in television history," he said about it years later, although it was supposed to be deadly serious and thought provoking. At the time Newman mostly worried about forgetting one of his lines. He got through it all right, however.

No matter what part Paul tried out for, he invariably got it. More talented actors who were less pretty could hardly get a foot in the door, but the blue eyes and solid body of Mr. Newman added up to a chemistry that most casting agents found irresistible. Paul was also likable, charming, and self-effacing when he needed to be. In short, he made himself agreeable and available. His acting was good enough for some of the junk he appeared in back in those early days—blocks of ice, indeed—and if the actor in that small part had a handsome face on top of it, what was the problem? Before long he was appearing on such shows as *The Web, The Mask,* and *You Are There* and won a recurring role on a soap entitled *The Aldrich Family.* Not exactly the stuff critics are talking about when they wax poetically about the "Golden age of television," but the assignments would eventually become more distinguished.

All during his time at Yale and now on each television studio set and at each audition, the name of the Actors Studio would invariably be invoked. If you wanted to be a "real" actor, that was the place to go—if they would have you. The other actors Paul worked and hung out with all talked about the great talents who were part of the studio—Eli Wallach, Julie Harris, Marlon Brando, Rod Steiger—and what an honor it would be to be taken under the wing of the group for serious study. Paul was intrigued—he wanted to be a "real" actor, not just a pretty boy—but didn't think he was good enough to walk among such distinguished company. As fate would have it, he was soon proven wrong.

A young actress friend of Paul's, who had already passed the required initial audition for the studio, asked if he would do a scene with her for her final audition, because the man she had partnered herself with before was unavailable. She had chosen Tennessee Williams's *Battle of Angels,* the first version of what would eventually become *Orpheus Descending.* Newman took the part of the sexy drifter, Val Xavier, who comes to a small town and works for an Italian lady who runs a shop. The young actress played the part of a free-spirited, slightly crazy townsperson who also makes a play for Xavier. (Ironically, Joanne Woodward would play this part when the play was filmed as *The Fugitive Kind* in 1959.)

Since Newman himself was not really auditioning, he wasn't too nervous the night they were to perform. Until he found that in addition to the two people who always presided over final auditions, Elia Kazan and Cheryl Crawford, such luminaries as the director Frank Corsaro, Karl Malden, and Geraldine Page were sitting in the audience. Paul was suddenly struck with a severe case of the jitters. Years later he explained that he felt Kazan and Crawford mistook his nervousness for the rage that his character was supposed to be generating. "An actor's discomfort sometimes works well for him." When the dust cleared, he found himself accepted into the Actors Studio—bypassing the initial audition in front of a larger crowd—while the poor young lady for whom he had been doing a favor was denied admission. Newman Luck again.

Studying at the Actors Studio not only honed Newman's acting style but also helped him define exactly how he worked. "I discovered that I was primarily a cerebral actor," he said, as opposed to the "instinctively emotional" who "work from the inside out." Due in part to his emotionally distant and sterile father, Paul had trouble getting in touch with his own feelings, something that has plagued him his entire life and perhaps contributed to a terrible later tragedy. Unlike those actors who were in touch with their feelings, Newman could not simply summon up emotions from within and let them work for him. A true Method actor, he would have to recreate a particular situation from his past and somehow manufacture the emotions that a character who was in a similar or related situation would be feeling.

Newman interpreted this as "cerebral" acting because he

would have to think instead of feel. Many people actually feel that the smarter an actor is, the more likely he is to disdain the Method and simply proceed on experience-cultivated, intelligence-activated instinct. In fact, many non-Method actors find Method actors a trial, the most famous anecdote having to do with an impatient Laurence Olivier sitting and abiding Dustin Hoffman "getting into" a scene for a lengthy period, then finally turning to him and saying, "Can't you just *act* it?"

Newman found an additional activity to consume his time when he wasn't acting or going out on auditions (he had finally been able to forget about hawking encyclopedias), and that was politics—of a sort. During his free time, he would stuff envelopes and do other distinctly unglamorous work for the Adlai Stevenson campaign, not the last time that he'd do favors for a politician.

But his favorite activity was simply being among his fellow actors and sharing with them the excitement of being young, being employed (most of the time), and most of all, being in New York City. While pregnant Jackie stayed back on Staten Island with the two year old and her aunt, Paul explored all the theatrical hangouts of Times Square, soaking in all the atmosphere of the Great White Way, so different from Ohio and a thousand times more fascinating than Cleveland and Shaker Heights. He would have drinks with Actors Studio classmates and coworkers, sit for hours in coffee shops watching the teeming masses swirl by on the sidewalks, trade stories with older men who had been there and back, and thoroughly revel in his lot in life. He felt more like a boy just starting out than an "old man" of twenty-seven. There were so many things he would have done, were it not for Jackie and the boy back home.

Tennessee Williams, who would eventually encounter Paul both socially and professionally, summed it up best when

he said, "Young actors need freedom." Manhattan represented freedom and hope; Staten Island represented convention-
ality and restriction. Jackie, whose modeling plans and
ambitions had come to nothing, was not thrilled at the number of hours Paul spent away from her and their child. She
didn't suspect that before too long the situation would get
much, much worse.

For late in 1952 Newman would be cast in the role
that would forever take him out of the supporting cast and
head him on the road to stardom. And he was to meet a
certain young lady who would have much more of an impact
on his life—and Jackie's—than any of them could ever have
anticipated.

4

BROADWAY PICNIC

BILL LIEBLING, SUPERAGENT, FINALLY CAME THROUGH FOR Newman. Liebling had heard from director Joshua Logan that the latter was casting a new Broadway play by William Inge, *Picnic,* and Liebling thought there was a part that might be perfect for Paul. Although it has generally been assumed that this was the part Paul eventually played, that of Alan, the protagonist's friend, he actually auditioned for the bit part of a filling station attendant nicknamed Joker.

Joker had a total of one line, when he made a pass at the heroine, Madge. Paul read for Inge and then Logan and was sure, as usual, that he'd muffed it. Instead, he found that he'd won the part. "All I had behind me was nine months at Yale and a couple of months at the Actors Studio," Newman said years later, as if that were nothing. Besides, having Liebling going to bat for him—plus the fact that Liebling's wife was Inge's agent—practically added up to a sure thing. If anything Newman was angry that the part was so laughably small. He didn't have to worry. He was to eventually get more lines without half trying.

Newman did need the work, however. He and his wife, with a second child coming, had only about two hundred and fifty dollars left in the bank (although to some actors in 1952 that would have been a small fortune). His salary in *Picnic* started at $150 a week (this included understudying the lead role) and went up to $200 when he got a bigger part.

Appearing in *Picnic* provided Newman's career with the impetus it needed. It also significantly altered the direction of his personal life. In the cast of *Picnic*, understudying two of the female roles, was a young woman by the name of Joanne Woodward.

When Paul first saw Joanne during rehearsals, he was sure that he had seen her somewhere before, but it was only when they compared notes that he remembered. Some weeks before he had gone to the MCA (Music Corporation of America) offices to talk to his agent Maynard Morris. While there, he got into a conversation with one of Morris's associates, John Foreman, who was waiting to speak to one of his clients, Joanne. The two men forgot the time and Joanne, who was impatiently sitting out in the reception area waiting for Foreman to get through. When Foreman escorted Paul out of the office, he apologized for keeping Joanne waiting and introduced her to Paul by way of a peace offering. Foreman knew any actress would not mind meeting this Greek god for herself.

Paul thought Joanne was attractive, but he wasn't bowled over. For her part, Joanne was unimpressed. He seemed like just the kind of shallow bit of handsome beefcake she had no use for, an "arrow collar" man without brains. It wasn't until after weeks of rehearsals that she warmed up to his less obvious charms and personality. Even then, it was awhile before their romance began in earnest.

Picnic was about a small town and a handsome, aging drifter named Hal who comes in and touches the lives of all the characters. The playwright, William Inge, was an alcoholic whose career was started after a short affair with Tennessee Williams. The director, Josh Logan, was a closet gay who suffered from manic-depression. In a way Paul managed to innocently secure a bigger part for himself by climbing the lavender ladder. Inge and Logan found Newman so attractive they were beside themselves.

Logan felt the actor who had been cast as college boy Alan wasn't working, but the primary trouble was that he wasn't as good looking or charismatic as Paul Newman. Logan went to Inge and asked him what he thought of putting the kid playing Joker in the part of Alan. They could even go so far as to make Alan younger, a freshman, instead of the older guy he had been originally. Logan knew that Inge, who was quite smitten with Paul, would go for the idea without any problem.

Newman played Alan for a few days of rehearsal when Inge and Logan, who enjoyed the extra time working with Paul, admitted that Paul just wasn't the seasoned actor the part required. They got yet another actor, a fellow who was the same age as the character had been originally, and put Newman back in the bit. But when this third actor didn't work out either, they decided to spend more time with Newman until he was acceptable. They could only hope the time would never come when Paul had to go on for Ralph Meeker, who had the lead.

Logan couldn't make up his mind about Newman and apparently didn't trust his own judgment—or Inge's. Although Newman begged Logan to let him stay in the part and agreed to work with Logan until all hours if he did, Logan told Paul he wanted to call in some people whose opinions he respected to see what they thought of Newman in the part. So Paul found himself in another kind of Actors Studio audition, reading lines for the likes of Tennessee

Williams, Dorothy McGuire, and once more, Elia Kazan. Logan was told by the trio that Newman could manage it—with hard work and luck. He might even do okay in the lead role if he *had* to go on.

Eventually Logan felt Newman was up to snuff, but there were other problems. For one thing, Inge and Logan battled bitterly over the ending of the play. There were essentially two romances in the script: The young couple, Hal and sexy Madge (Janice Rule), and the middle-aged couple, Howard (Arthur O'Connell) and Rosemary (Eileen Heckart). In his original draft, Inge had both these romances end with the couples breaking up. Inge did not want to write the stereotypical, puerile "happy ending," but Logan argued that it was too depressing as it stood, that the audience would feel cheated after investing so much time in these relationships. Inge wrote revision after revision, but each was worse than the last. Finally Logan convinced Inge that having Madge run off with Hal could hardly be construed as a happy ending when Hal was a penniless bum and once the thrill wore off their lives would inevitably be miserable. A man who loved misery as much as he loved drink, Inge wrote the new ending. (Years later he would rework the play as *Summer Brave* and put back in the more cynical ending he had always intended, and then, regrettably, drink himself to death.)

There was more fine tuning as *Picnic* had out-of-town try-outs. Paul still felt awkward on stage, but Logan gave him fewer notes each night, so he figured he was doing okay. In fact, in one sense he would actually save the show from disaster. Reviews for *Picnic* were not good, and when the company got to Cleveland, Logan thought he had figured out what was wrong. He overheard two men as they walked out of the performance muttering "*some* hero!" Then he realized to his astonishment that the audience thought the play's creators were unaware of Hal's flaws, that they expected the audience to see Hal as an absolute good guy. Ralph Meeker was so good swaggering around on stage, swearing and bragging and being miserable to everyone, that he dominated the show and made everyone seeing it think he was the genuine hero instead of simply the pivotal character against which the other characters reacted.

Logan put in a frantic call to Inge, who agreed that the problem needed fixing. With one or two changes, he approved of some new lines Logan had quickly drafted. "I decided the most reliable character to put across our attitude toward Hal was Alan," Logan said. "All the ladies adored Paul Newman." In the speech Paul was given, Alan told Mrs. Owens that the other boys didn't like Hal and the way he "swaggered and posed" but that Alan had found out underneath it all Hal was basically a nice, if imperfect, fellow.

When *Picnic* arrived in New York, it got rave reviews and settled in for a lengthy run. It would eventually play for 477 performances, most of which Paul participated in. Paul began to feel more at ease in front of an audience and thought there might be a chance he could make it as a professional actor after all.

Studying at the Actors Studio had shown him just how little he really knew about acting. Once he realized how much he had to learn, he lost the casual, cocky attitude he'd had previously while performing. Whatever cockiness he had left had been figuratively beaten out of him by Josh Logan, who used all the directorial skills and experience he could muster to get a Broadway-worthy performance out of Paul. Now that Paul was getting good reviews as Alan, some of his cockiness was returning. He was convinced he could do anything he wanted to do and gave no more thought to the idea of teaching drama at Kenyon or anywhere else.

And why should he have? This was the most exciting time of his life. Each night he drew applause as part of a stellar acting company in a superb drama that had become a big Broadway hit with audiences, as well as the focus of extremely positive critical reaction. Paul Newman had it made.

After their second child, a daughter named Susan, was born, Paul moved his family into a two-bedroom apartment in Queens Village on Long Island. It cost $88.50 a month, which he could easily afford. Not only was Jackie preoccupied with the new baby, but she still had her hands full with the tiny terror, Alan Scott. This was just the way Newman liked it, for the dreary domesticity of Long Island simply couldn't compare with the excitement of the Great White Way and being in a hit on Broadway.

Paul would drive his Volkswagen in from Long Island and suddenly enter a whole new world—actors and lines, glaring spotlights, the hush of the audience, the heady applause, the whole delirious theatrical experience that was so much more intense and rewarding than anything he'd been through in college or in summer stock. It was a world you had to be a part of to understand. Jackie had never been part of it, in spite of her own hopes. But there was someone else who could understand.

Joanne Woodward occasionally got to go on as Madge or her younger sister, Millie, when Rule or Kim Stanley, who was playing Millie, were indisposed, but mostly she just rehearsed with Newman for the day they would act together as Madge and Hal. One particular bit they rehearsed endlessly was the second-act slow jitterbug that Hal and Madge dance to "Moonglow." This was the sexiest moment in the whole play, and when Rule and Meeker did it, it really sizzled. Unfortunately, when Newman and Woodward did it, it just fizzled.

Logan knew that with Newman he was dealing with a very different actor, and person, than Ralph Meeker. Newman was still very much the well-bred, comes-from-money, polite-to-the-ladies college boy. That worked fine for the part of Alan—in fact in some ways Paul was typecast—but it would not work at all for Hal. As Logan watched Newman do the dance with Joanne, he told him to loosen up a bit, maybe wiggle his ass here and there. Paul was uncertain, a little embarrassed, but agreed to do it Logan's way. After awhile Logan couldn't help but notice that there was a certain sexual heat between the two understudies, and it wasn't all in the acting.

Newman didn't know it at the time, but Joanne had fallen head over heels. Paul was not the lout she had first assumed him to be. He was gentlemanly, well raised, and he was good looking enough to be exciting but not necessarily dangerous. When Joanne was in his arms during the dance number, she practically felt like melting. It took awhile longer for Newman's feelings to match hers, and she kept mum about how she felt about him—at least to Paul. To everyone else, she made it clear she intended to land him by hook or by crook.

Joanne Woodward was a woman who got what she wanted. She had been born in 1930 in a small Georgia town named Thomasville. Her father was a school administrator who later became a publishing executive with Charles Scribner's Sons. Her movie-struck mother named her Joan after Joan Crawford, but in Southern style the name eventually metamorphosed into Joanne. At nine years of age, she convinced her mother to take her to Atlanta for the premiere of *Gone with the Wind,* where, screeching, she leaped in the car where Laurence Olivier was sitting and landed on his lap. Even at twelve, she was determined to be somebody one day and kept a list on "How to Be a Fascinating Woman" on her night table. Armed with an IQ of 135 and a good measure of talent, she eventually made her way to New York where she did some modeling, small parts on television, and then wound up in *Picnic*—with Paul.

When they weren't practicing the sexy, slow jitterbug, Paul and Joanne were talking and discovering they were soul mates. Both of them were ambitious, wary of some people, anxious to have lives that were unconventional, or at least to live life on their own terms and nobody else's. Even when Joanne wouldn't have to go on for somebody, she'd generally wait around when the performance was over. The two would go out with others in the cast or crew and talk for hours over coffee or drinks, comparing notes on their dreams and what they thought of the theater in general and this play or that actor in particular. Sinking into his blue eyes, Joanne would sometimes just let him drone on after everyone else had gone home. Torn between going home to wife and kids or chatting another hour with this woman who so understood and listened to him, Paul would often choose Joanne. There was no romance just yet—or at least the romance was strictly one-sided.

Although most people involved in *Picnic* were perfectly aware of Joanne's feelings, the general consensus was that Paul did not feel the same. How could he? He was so good looking and Joanne was so, for lack of a better word, average in appearance. To put it bluntly, Paul was prettier than she was. Everyone figured if Paul cheated on Jackie, it would be with some busty beauty in a late-night bar, not this plain Jane who stimulated Paul's intellect but not his hormones.

Joanne's intelligence and the bluntness it engendered could put people off. "She was a *cunt*," one observer who was in their crowd at the time commented. A more charitable opinion might be that Joanne knew she didn't have the striking looks other women had and was aware what a disadvantage this would be in the looks-obsessed theatrical world with its "producers" and their "girlfriends." This created a defensiveness in her that some people might misinterpret as bitchiness. Joanne was never one to put up with bull. Even years later, when she and Paul became a golden couple in filmland, she was never quite of Hollywood, and this led certain people to view her as unlikeable or even hostile. Woodward probably could not have cared less.

In any case, it would be awhile before she would really snare Newman, something she would have gone to any lengths to do—and did. In the meantime, Newman was finding that his own ambitions were stymied.

Paul wanted to play Hal in the road company of *Picnic* and tried to convince Josh Logan to give him the part. Whenever he got to go on stage for an indisposed Meeker, he would call up anyone who could possibly do his career any good, as well as friends, and beg them to come see him as Hal.

Logan had to tell Newman bluntly that he'd be no good in the part. He didn't carry any sexual threat and wasn't a crotch actor. Newman interpreted this as sheer bitchiness at the time, but what Logan meant was that while Newman may have been handsome, he wasn't necessarily sexy in that dangerous low-down, vaguely sleazy way that Meeker was. It is like the difference between the grungy but hot Brad Pitt and the preppie, if not better looking, Tom Cruise. Newman was simply too well bred to be Hal and not yet a good enough actor to impersonate him.

For consolation, Paul did a lot of television work, which he always loved to do. Of all the mediums he was to work in, live television was his favorite. He explained, "It gives you everything: Having it go non-stop; rehearsals beforehand; all the excitement of the first night. Men like Tad Mosel and Paddy Chayefsky and Max Shulman were writing for television, and they made it an inventive era." Parts came quickly: *Philco, US Steel, Playhouse 90*. Whatever roles his agents didn't get him, his friends would, for Paul believed in the power of propagating friendships with people who could do for him.

Good connections also got him a couple of screen tests. Elia Kazan was doing a screen adaptation of John Steinbeck's *East of Eden* and tested both Paul Newman and another good-looking up-and-comer, James Dean. The two men tested together, switching roles, but only Dean got the part. Then Columbia bought the rights to *Picnic.* When Paul found out that the girlfriend of a stage director he knew was testing for the movie, he called him up and asked if he could get in touch with her—with an eye on doing the test with her. The director was so taken in by Newman's smooth approach that he thought Paul was trying to do the girlfriend a favor instead of just horning in on the screen test. In any case the play backfired. Paul did the test with the young actress, Carroll Baker, but Columbia was more interested in her than in him. Although Baker didn't get to be in *Picnic,* she was awarded a film contract while Newman got nothing.

Newman transferred his attentions back to Josh Logan when he found out the stage director would also be helming the film version of the play. Paul knew Logan would never cast him as Hal—William Holden eventually got the part—but he figured he was a shoo-in as Alan. Even if Logan had wanted to use Paul, he was up against Columbia's disinterest and the fact that they had plenty of contract players who could handle the part. Cliff Robertson played Alan in the movie.

After *Picnic* closed, Paul did the television work, went out for coffee with Joanne, and avoided Queens Village as much as possible. The famous acting coach Lee Strasberg, who got to know Newman at the Actors Studio, was surprised to learn that Newman was even married. To him Paul had always come off as the typical ambitious and single actor whose career took precedence over marriage. Paddy Chayefsky once joked that Newman probably kept getting Jackie pregnant (there was to be a third child) just to keep her out of his hair. "Paul's face would fall a mile if someone he was partying or schmoozing with reminded him that he'd said he would have to leave early to get home to Long Island and Jackie," Chayefsky once told me.

Josh Logan felt that if Jackie was losing hold of Paul, she had only herself to blame. Had she insisted he go back with her to Cleveland or Wisconsin where her family was, or that he get a more conventional, family-man job, he might not have been ensnared by the glamour of Broadway—or the witchery of Woodward. Jackie encouraged him in his ambitions, to her credit and everlasting regret.

But their marriage would stumble on for some years, years during which Paul would grow closer and closer to Joanne and finally find himself on the road to beckoning Hollywood and stardom.

5

THE MAN IN THE TOGA

TALENT SCOUTS FROM WARNER BROTHERS—TIPPED OFF BY his agents Bill Liebling and Maynard Morris—had seen Paul in *Picnic* and on television and wanted to bring him out to Hollywood to do a screen test for a new biblical epic entitled *The Silver Chalice*. If all went well with the test, Paul would be awarded a $1,000 a week contract with Warner. Paul told Jackie that he might be in California for at least a couple of weeks doing the test, much longer than that if he got the part.

Jackie had encouraged Paul to go after his dreams, knowing all the risks it entailed but also aware of all the rewards for her and the children if it worked out. Paul's success in *Picnic* had made it clear that he had made the right decision, but it had also taken him further and further away from her and the children. Jackie and Paul had a major quarrel—not the first or the last—when Paul announced his intentions to go to Hollywood.

Stories of Paul's close friendship with Joanne Woodward had filtered down to Jackie, and she was afraid of what might happen should her husband be away from her for too long a period. She had heard talk that Woodward was going to Hollywood, and what about all those gorgeous starlets? Jackie was still a very attractive woman in her own right, but she felt neglected by and unappealing to her own husband, as if she were just a baby-making machine who lacked the glamour and allure of all the actresses Paul inevitably encountered.

There was no way Paul wanted to have her underfoot in Hollywood, but he needn't have worried. Jackie decided to take the kids and return to Wisconsin and her parents. They would decide what to do and where to live—and indeed if they should continue to live together at all—when he found out whether or not he'd gotten the part.

The first screen test for *The Silver Chalice* was a fiasco. Virginia Mayo, who co-starred in the film and did the test with Newman, said, "The studio heads were not satisfied with the scene and wanted him to work with an acting coach— and with me. I worked with him practically every day for a couple of weeks, until he did it better." *The Silver Chalice* was a departure for Mayo, and she admits she herself would have been "floundering" without help from the coach. Nevertheless she was far more experienced in front of a movie camera than Newman was. "We did another test," she remembered. "Paul was accepted, confirmed by the studio heads, after the second test." Newman, cast as Basil in the film, signed a contract with Warner.

In the film Paul played a slave and gifted sculptor whose destiny is to make a reliquary to hold the silver chalice from which Christ drank at the Last Supper. He needs to carve the faces of famous Christians into the receptacle, but the face of Jesus eludes him until he accepts Christ as his savior at the film's conclusion. Along the way, he is tempted by the pagan beauty he met first in childhood, Helena (Virginia Mayo) and menaced by her lover, a magician named Simon (Jack

Palance). The film begins when Basil is just a boy: Newman takes over when Basil becomes a young man, which is about a third of the way into the picture.

Newman has always hated *The Silver Chalice.* To understand this overreaction—*The Silver Chalice* is not that bad a picture and Newman isn't that bad in it—one must understand his mind-set at the time. Paul had been hoping to essay the role of grungy, sexy, low-down Hal in the road company of *Picnic.* Josh Logan and others were telling him he was too much the "safe" college boy. Ralph Meeker seemed so intensely hypermasculine that Paul felt nearly effeminate in comparison. The last thing he wanted to do was dress up in Roman togas that reminded him of women's dresses. "He always called it his cocktail dress," Mayo laughed.

To make matters worse, *The Silver Chalice* was a period film, and he was never at his best in costume roles. If he had been uncomfortable in the "sissy" clothing and classical demeanor of Beethoven's nephew in the play at Yale, one can imagine his mortification in wearing the toga and adopting the attitude of artistic, sensitive Basil. That old panic of his, which was to plague him periodically no matter how old or sophisticated he got, was causing him anxiety again. He felt completely uncomfortable all through the making of the picture.

Newman was also impatient with Hollywood types telling him how to act. He was still breathing that rarefied atmosphere of "the Theatre" and felt much of the same antipathy toward the movies that many of his New York friends and associates did. Not that any of them would turn down a contract from a major studio if it were offered to them. Privately, in fact, a lot of Paul's theater friends thought Hollywood was just where he belonged.

"He had a face born for the movies," Josh Logan said. "He did his best work in films." Despite two more forays into

treading the boards, he was never a serious stage actor.
Newman would go wherever the winds pushed him, wherever
he could achieve the most success. And he wanted success
very badly.

Although he was anxious to make an impression in the
movies, Paul felt as if he had taken two steps backward. He
had to work longer hours with the coach and Mayo than he
had with Logan and Inge back in New York. His old doubts
and insecurities about his acting ability began to resurface.
He had a snobbish attitude toward pretty Mayo, who had
appeared in many musicals and light comedies and was in his
opinion a "movie" person instead of one from the theater.
The director, Victor Saville, told me that Newman made
things twice as difficult because of his rather condescending
attitude. "He was too stiff and theatrical. We tried to make
him more at ease in front of the camera. I don't think most of
the reviewers thought I accomplished much—but we tried."

To be fair, Newman is perfectly creditable as Basil, and
his first appearance in the film is impressive, though it has
perhaps more to do with his looks than with any acting ability.
In one scene Basil, now an adult, is looking at a sculpture he's
made of his adopted father with petulant sensuality and a
hint of cruelty that is a bit at odds with the boy's sweet nature.
Franz Waxman's swelling, somewhat sinister music adds to the
effect. In this, his very first screen appearance, Newman registers so much charisma and dramatic star appeal, that it's no
surprise he became a major player in Hollywood. Despite his
being compared ad nauseam later on to another famous
actor, his looks are quite unique and distinctive—another
thing in his favor.

Not everyone thought he would amount to anything,
however. According to Mayo, who had worked with many of
Hollywood's top leading men, "James Dean was wooing
actress Pier Angeli [who played Deborrah in the film] and

hanging around her dressing room. I had seen him do TV. I thought he had much more attraction and charisma than Newman did. But I brought some photos from the set home, and my housekeeper flipped when she saw Newman. He's a fabulous actor, but he doesn't like to do classical work."

Publicly Dean may have been wooing Pier Angeli, but privately his mind was on other matters. The notoriously bisexual actor had developed a crush on Paul and was pursuing a "friendship" with him. Possibly unaware—at least at first—of Dean's more intimate feelings for him, Newman eagerly embraced the friendship, for awhile. Newman had heard stories back in New York, but Dean seemed so smitten with lovely Angeli that he didn't initially give them credence.

Dean was from the theater set in New York, where they had first met, and his presence made Paul feel less homesick. They were two expatriates taking on the phony Philistines of Hollywood. They'd go off on Paul's motorcycle, which had replaced the Volkswagen in Los Angeles, and ride the highway to the beach, stopping at the occasional waterfront gin joint and talking for hours as the tide rolled in. Paul admired Dean's rebel-like attitude of not giving a damn and taking on the world. When the two were together, rebel buddies somehow "above" the crap factor of Hollywood, Paul's wife and kids back in Wisconsin seemed farther and farther away. For now he was a happy bachelor under the wing of the maverick Dean, who said and did the things Newman could only think about. Dean was a breath of fresh air for the comparatively naive college boy from Cleveland.

Then Dean, who had earlier tried making inroads on Marlon Brando, intimated that their relationship might advance to a different level. To Dean, it would just be some casual sex that didn't matter a hell of a lot in the long run, but to Newman it was more serious and frightening. He took pains to avoid Dean from then on, the fear of guilt by association uppermost in his mind. He still liked and admired many things about Dean and didn't really care that much about his proclivities, but Dean's openness and reckless attitude made him awfully nervous. He figured he did not need James Dean in his life. Dean could be what he wanted to be and do what he wanted to do, but Newman would not have people saying or assuming things about him just because the two hung out together. The late night rides and beach talks were over. Dean kept up a "cool" front as always but found Paul's rejection— not only of his advances but even of platonic friendship— humiliating and angering.

Meanwhile, work on *The Silver Chalice* proceeded. One of Newman's best scenes in the picture is when Pier Angeli asks Basil to marry her and is initially, kindly, rebuffed by him; Newman displayed a sensitivity and sweetness that may have been brought out by Angeli's quietly passionate acting. Angeli told me in 1958 that Newman was "kind and understanding— he's more sensitive and warm than most people realize." She found his acting style "different from any other actor's I worked with—very much his own," adding, "I think it took some people a little while to get used to it." Pier would make one more movie with Paul two years later.

One problem Newman faced when making *The Silver Chalice* was that except for one lively fight scene, Basil was such a passive role. He was the hero, but he was never really heroic in the cinematic tradition. Reevaluating the picture today, one would have to say that it is hardly spectacular but not as dreadful as memory, reputation, or Newman would have us believe. The dialogue, which has always been excoriated, is occasionally memorable, such as when one character defends Basil with the line: "Why does everyone belittle dreamers? What do we get from men of action? War, trouble, taxes." The bad acting from some of the minor players makes some scenes seem straight out of one of the lesser Republic serials. The theatrical, sparse, art deco sets also came under attack. "It was supposed to be highly stylized," said Mayo. "People never understood that."

Some of the other actors in the film were not pleased with Newman when he took out an ad in the trade papers many years later urging people not to watch *The Silver Chalice* when it was shown on television in Los Angeles. (The ad was surrounded by a funeral wreath.) "What right has he to criticize?" asked Mayo. Mayo, who was fine in the picture, had no reason to be embarrassed by it, and Jack Palance gave a splendid, showy, and captivating performance as Simon. The film's highlight, in fact, is when Simon dives off a tower convinced that he has genuinely developed the power of flight. After Palance lands with a thud in front of a disappointed Caesar, the emperor says with consummate understatement, "He didn't fly."

Newman didn't consider his co-stars' feelings when he took out the ad, an act of egomania that was not necessarily atypical for the actor as he climbed to the pinnacle of fame in Hollywood. What's worse, the ad wasn't even necessary, because Newman's performance was perfectly adequate and the movie reasonably entertaining. In fact, compared to some of the movies Newman would make later in his career—movies like the abysmal *Quintet,* for instance—*The Silver Chalice* was a masterpiece.

In any case, making *The Silver Chalice* was not a pleasant experience for Newman. "I was uncomfortable with what I was doing," he said later. "I couldn't handle the language I was supposed to speak." Used to working with seasoned film professionals, Saville lost patience with Newman's Method approach, the constant questions he asked and, worse, the suggestions he would have the gall to make to the director when he had never even been in a picture before.

A few years later Gore Vidal was working on an early

script for William Wyler's remake of *Ben-Hur* when Newman's name was mentioned as a possibility for the lead. Vidal told them to forget it. "Paul swore never to act in a cocktail dress again," he quipped.

Before the picture wrapped, Newman was on the phone to his agents, begging them to get him some work in New York. He was afraid each picture he'd be cast in as part of his contract would be worse than the one before. Now that his ambition had led him to Hollywood, he wasn't prepared for the price he had to pay. He would have to appear in whatever movies Warner Brothers told him to appear in.

When *The Silver Chalice* opened, Newman got mixed reviews. In 1933 Dorothy Parker said of Katharine Hepburn in the play *The Lake*, "She runs the gamut of emotions from A to B." The *New Yorker* critic opined similarly for Newman: "Paul Newman, a lad who resembles Marlon Brando, delivers his lines with the emotional fervor of a Putnam Division conductor announcing local stops." Newman was possibly more annoyed by the reference to Brando than he was to the infamous summation of his acting ability. He would eventually grow quite tired of people saying that he looked like Brando, swearing that the day would come when they'd say Brando looked like him.

Luckily, his contract—approximately two pictures a year for five years—allowed him occasional television work, so he could return to New York for awhile and clear his head. Television projects were lined up for him immediately. One of his favorites was Tad Mosel's "The Army Game," presented on the *Kaiser Aluminum Hour*, in which he played a soldier who pays a call on the family of a friend who has been killed. Newman's character feels responsible for his friend's death, and as the story proceeds, he tries to take the dead boy's place. "It was the first part I'd ever played that I found the character for," he said. He particularly enjoyed his scenes with the dead man's mother, played by Fay Bainter. Newman also retained fond memories of Stewart Stern's "Thundering Silence," which was presented on *Philco Television Playhouse*.

Jackie and the children were now back on Long Island. Their marriage had weathered, indeed possibly prospered, during the separation, and Jackie was encouraged by Paul's vows to somehow get out of his contract with Warner and stay in New York to do theater. Jackie assumed that his friendship or whatever it was with Joanne had died of neglect while Paul was in Hollywood. She didn't know that her nemesis was not about to give up so easily or that Paul still had very strong feelings for Joanne. Thinking a third child would certainly cement her relationship with Paul as well as his sense of responsibility, she got pregnant again. She was as determined to hang on to Paul as Joanne was to steal him away from her.

There were people during this period who wondered where Joanne's morality was and why she wouldn't respect Paul's marital vows or have any compassion for Jackie. "Joanne was very bright," someone in their circle at the time said years later. "But she had a habit of justifying everything she did. Paul was a decent guy and wanted to do the right thing, but she beat down all his defenses. There was an attraction on both sides after awhile, but Joanne did her best to stimulate his feelings for her. I think she saw that Jackie and Paul weren't that happy, she saw how *right* she and Paul were for each other—and their years together proved that she was right on that account.

"Also Joanne resented Jackie. Jackie was prettier, sexier, and she had the guy Joanne wanted. Joanne justified what she did because she thought that she was plain and Jackie was pretty and had all the luck because of that and why couldn't the plain girl get the guy for a change? She thought Jackie had only got Paul in the first place because of her looks. She had real contempt for the way Jackie kept getting pregnant, as if that was the answer to all the problems they had. But then, Joanne resorted to the same trick in the end. A lot of people who were in the know thought *that* was really funny."

But that particular "trick" was still in the future. One of Joanne's earlier ploys to snare Newman was to get engaged to other guys, hoping he would make his move when he thought he'd lose her forever. One of the first fiancés was playwright James Costigan, who later wrote a play that both Woodward and Newman would appear in. Still tied to Jackie, Newman didn't take her bluff. Costigan was soon out of the picture, romantically speaking at least. This was only the first of Joanne's flagrant attempts to catch herself a Hollywood hunk, 1950s style.

For the time being, Newman had other things on his mind besides Joanne and Jackie. He was cast in a new play, this time as the lead. In Joseph Hayes's *The Desperate Hours*, which Hayes based on his own novel, he would essay the role of a psychotic crook who invades a family's home with two other desperadoes. Newman didn't think Warner Brothers would give him any hassle about doing the play, and he was right. They'd be happy to let him do *The Desperate Hours*, but only if he renegotiated his contract. The five years of "servitude" went up to seven, and Warner could insist on his doing a third picture each year if they wanted.

Newman wanted to do the play badly, so he bit the bullet and signed. He'd get paid $700 a week, only $300 less than what Hollywood was paying him. This was not only the perfect way to show anyone who might see *The Silver Chalice* how butch he could be but also a chance to prove to Josh Logan that he could be as tough, gritty, and low-down as Ralph Meeker or anyone.

For her part, Jackie had mixed emotions. The lead in *The Desperate Hours* meant Paul would be home with her in New York for months if the play were a hit, but she wasn't at all thrilled with the new seven-year contract he'd signed. So much for his talk of quitting Hollywood for good and staying in New York with his family. Jackie knew instinctively that she and the kids would wind up in Wisconsin again, or alone on Long Island, when Paul filmed his next picture. He had already made it clear with *The Silver Chalice* that he needed to be alone in Los Angeles to concentrate on his screen role—or so he said. She and the kids would be a distraction he didn't need, what with all the other tension inherent in filming.

Newman proceeded with his usual combination of insecurity and cockiness. Robert Montgomery, who had been a leading man in Hollywood, was the director of *The Desperate Hours*, and he had his hands full. As he told me years later, "Paul was good, but he wanted to start out from his first appearance very *big*, and that left him nowhere to go. I tried to get him to tone it down a bit, but he was not easy to direct. He was really very young, just starting out practically, I mean in terms of all that came later. I was basically pleased with the results. A couple of the critics noticed the problems, that he started too high and had nothing to build on, but halfway through the play the tone of the piece, its tension matched his histrionics, so it wasn't a problem anymore. Most of the audience left impressed. I thought he'd have a successful career, but nowhere near as big as it became."

Montgomery was relatively tactful; he and Newman often argued bitterly over how Paul should play the role of Glenn Griffin.

Josh Logan saw *The Desperate Hours*, as Newman had hoped he would, but wasn't convinced. He basically thought Newman did a good job of faking it but that the part was all wrong for him in the first place. It was still too soon for Newman to take on parts that were so alien to him. Newman would disparage his own performance years later, but this was typical of him. At the time he undoubtedly thought he was the greatest thing since sliced bread.

His next picture, in which he gave one of his finest performances, would almost have everyone else thinking so too, which was nearly enough to salve the psychic wound inflicted on Paul when he learned that the great film director William Wyler, who had acquired the rights to *The Desperate Hours,* had cast Humphrey Bogart as Glenn Griffin. Though Bogart was many years too old for the part, he had the box-office clout Newman lacked.

6

ROCKY ROAD

In 1955 the birth of the Newman's third child, a girl named Stephanie, temporarily turned Paul into a family man again. He would spend his daylight hours at his wife's side, playing dutiful daddy, then would drive from Queens Village to Manhattan to perform in *The Desperate Hours*. In the meantime, Joanne Woodward wondered who she could become engaged to this time. Her plans for Newman were temporarily set aside while she went to Hollywood to make her first picture, a post–Civil War drama entitled *Count Three and Pray*.

As Paul waited to see what horror Warner Brothers might cast him in next, he kept busy with a variety of television roles. He played a high-school student named George in a musical adaptation of Thornton Wilder's *Our Town*, which also featured—more appropriately—Frank Sinatra. In *The Battler*, an adaptation of an Ernest Hemingway story scripted by Hemingway's biographer A. E. Hotchner, he gave a first-class portrayal of a punch-drunk old pug. Newman's rendition followed the pug's regression, via flashbacks, from cocky and unbeatable young champion of twenty to untamable prison tough of thirty to panhandler of forty and bum of fifty-five whose mind and body have deteriorated to the point where he is little more than a vegetable. It was a tour de force.

Paul had originally been cast in the other lead role of Nick Adams, Hemingway's narrator and stand-in. James Dean was supposed to have been the boxer. (Paul had no problem working with Dean as long as their relationship remained on the set.) When Dean was killed when his Porsche crashed, Newman was very upset and balked when the producer asked him to step into the role Dean was to have played. Paul told the producer he wanted nothing to do with the play anymore and wouldn't even portray Nick Adams. Finally the director, Arthur Penn, told him that there was no one else they could get, particularly at such short notice, and that the show would literally not go on if he didn't choose to participate. Dean would have wanted him to, Penn argued. Paul agreed to play the boxer.

Largely on the strength of this performance, he got to play Rocky Graziano in the film adaptation of the boxer's memoirs. Dean had already been cast in the film at the time of his death, and Newman figured if he did a good job in *The Battler*, he was a shoo-in for the role in the Graziano biopic. He'd prove that he could play it down and dirty if he had to, just like Dean.

Another television highlight for Newman was *Bang the Drum Slowly*, broadcast late in 1956. Forty years later *TV Guide* chose it as one of the hundred most memorable moments in television history. Newman played a baseball player who befriends a prickly catcher (Albert Salmi) who is dying of cancer. In this telecast Paul did something he had always feared—at one point in his climactic soliloquy, he badly, and noticeably, flubbed a line. However, "His stumbling speech somehow added even *more* pathos to the moment," *TV Guide* opined. Even when Paul screwed up, he couldn't lose, perhaps because, as *TV Guide* also noted, "He was at the peak of his blue-eyed beauty."

Just as Paul had hoped, he was tapped to step into Dean's shoes again and play Graziano in *Somebody Up There Likes Me*. Warner Brothers loaned him out to MGM Studios, getting considerably more in payment for his services than Newman would ($75,000 compared to the $8,000 or so Newman would get for approximately two months' service). The film's director, Robert Wise, was pleased. "I always had in my mind that maybe Dean was not physically a middleweight, somehow. And Paul did one of his best characterizations in it; he really caught that man."

Wise had started out as an editor on Orson Welles's formidable *Citizen Kane*, but his direction of a previous boxing film, *The Set Up* in 1949, got him the plum assignment of *Somebody Up There Likes Me*. *The Set Up* was notable not only because of Robert Ryan's excellent performance but also because the entire film took place in "real time." The film was seventy-two minutes long and took place during those same seventy-two minutes. There was no question that Wise was the perfect one to be at the helm of *Somebody*. (Years later Wise would gain fame as the director of such films as *The Sound of Music*, *West Side Story*, and *Star Trek: The Motion Picture*.)

Although some filming of indoor scenes took place at the studio, Wise insisted on at least ten days of shooting on the actual streets of the Lower East Side of Manhattan, as it had an atmosphere that could simply not be recreated on a back lot. He told the cast to play everything 10 percent faster than normal to get the right energy that he felt the film needed.

However, just as Newman had irritated Victor Saville with his suggestions and questions, he did the same thing to Wise, who was equally unamused. Some of the suggestions Newman had for a particular scene were okay, and Wise would incorporate them, but many of them were terrible. After awhile Wise developed a strategy for dealing with Paul: "I would talk him out of it. But after a few days I realized that an idea I had turned down was still lurking in his mind and bothered him I found the best way to handle it was to let Paul try the suggestion and find out it was no good himself. Then his mind was cleared of it and he'd go on with the scene."

Originally, the powers-that-be felt that the film should be a comedy, perhaps to make light of the fact that, despite his later fame, Rocky Graziano had had a pretty sleazy early life. Newman resisted the comedic approach, knowing it would minimize the importance of his performance and make Rocky—and Paul Newman—seem like a clown. Wise backed him up on this, although in some of the lighter scenes Newman does act cutesy, like a caricature of a dumb person.

Newman knew that he had as much at stake as Graziano had when he fought the match that made him a champion. To prepare for the role, he hung out with the boxer, studied his mannerisms, the way he walked and talked, the way he ate, grabbed a fork, swore, in short anything and everything that added up to Rocky, which he could use to evoke a convincing portrayal. He also went to the gym on a regular basis, got in shape, and learned how to really box from enthusiastic professionals. "Just don't hit the face, guys," he'd quip.

By and large, Newman learned his lessons well and succeeded in becoming an alternate, better looking version of the fighter. "I didn't try to imitate him in the part," he once said. "I tried to find a balance between him and me—him as the part, and the part in me. I tried to play *a* Graziano, not *the* Graziano." To make him look a little more like the rather homely man he was portraying, makeup artists gave him a thicker, flatter proboscis.

There was an unfortunate side effect of his studying Graziano so closely, however. Everyone started comparing him to Brando again. What no one knew at the time was that

Brando had studied Graziano himself while preparing for the role of Stanley Kowalski in *A Streetcar Named Desire*, which Brando later admitted to Newman and which Graziano confirmed in his autobiography. No wonder filmdom's Rocky and the stage's Stanley had so much in common.

Although it was the lead role, Rocky was essentially a character part, and Newman made the most of it. Despite an unconvincing low-class accent, he triumphs over his miscasting and offers one of the very best performances of his career. In many later roles Newman could be extremely self-conscious, but for the most part he seems completely lost in the role of Rocky. It is a perfect example of the energetic, stylized acting that passed for naturalism in the 1950s. A highlight of the picture is Rocky's confrontation with his failure of a father (played expertly by Harold J. Stone), who breaks down and cries. Newman is also wonderful doing a mock ballet with his sparring partner in the gym when the girl he's courting—who hates violence—shows up unexpectedly.

The picture doesn't gloss over the negative details of Graziano's early life, when he was a "nonconformist" in all the wrong ways. A hoodlum whose behavior gave his mother a nervous breakdown, Graziano got a dishonorable discharge from the army during World War II after going AWOL. "To listen to him, you'd think he was an innocent bystander!" his wife says of Rocky when he indulges in self-pity. On the one hand *Somebody Up There Likes Me* is a reminder that even forty years ago a lowlife could make good for all the wrong reasons—Rocky is not a great hero; he's simply good at punching people. On the other hand the film isn't really about boxing, but about courage and survival over human failings. Ernest Lehman's screenplay makes the most of the material and turns Graziano's sordid memoirs into a deeply human document. The picture is very swiftly and smoothly directed by Wise.

Eileen Heckart, who had been on stage with Newman in

Picnic, was cast as Rocky's mother. Pier Angeli, who had ably supported Newman in *The Silver Chalice*, was chosen to play his wife. Angeli had also been deeply upset by the accidental death of James Dean, who had courted her—and Newman—on the set of *Chalice*. After a failed marriage to Vic Damone, she would appear in forgettable European productions in an effort to revive her career, then die tragically young at thirty-nine from an overdose of sleeping pills.

On each set there were always a few women—and men—who found themselves attracted to Newman no matter how disinterested he may have been in them. On *Somebody Up There Likes Me*, the one who fell head over heels for Paul was Sal Mineo, who admitted this to me many years later after he had "come out" publicly and appeared in such gay-themed plays as *Fortune and Men's Eyes*. Sal had the supporting role of a neighborhood youngster who looks up to Rocky but can't escape his environment the way the boxer did. Mineo said that Paul was "not only manly, but kind and understanding. We used to talk about Jimmy Dean a lot [Mineo had worked with Dean in *Rebel without a Cause*]. He felt Jimmy would have grown and developed had he lived, that his death was a real loss."

Veteran character actor Everett Sloane was cast as Rocky's manager, Irving. In 1957 he spoke to me about Newman when in upstate New York working on location for *Marjorie Morningstar* (released the following year). He felt great respect for Newman as an actor. "He gave himself over completely to the Rocky Graziano he was depicting. He had spent much time with Rocky, had his mannerisms and walk down as pat as you could want. He really lost himself in the characterization." He remembered Paul telling him that acting was a serious business to him, that there might be actors out there with more natural talent than his own, but that you'd be hard pressed to find any who would work harder.

"He was very intently focused. You could see he was digging, digging, digging into himself while at the same time depicting an authentic Rocky Graziano."

Newman also made two other films before *Somebody Up There Likes Me* was released: *The Rack* and *Until They Sail.* Loaned out to MGM again for *The Rack*, Newman gave one of his most sensitive performances in a role originally meant for Glenn Ford, that of a young army captain on trial for treason whose will is broken by subtle Communist brainwashing that exposes his secret weaknesses. One of the most revealing scenes Newman ever enacted on-screen occurs in an automobile when he asks for, and finally receives as an adult, the nurturing love that his father, a stern martinet played by Walter Pidgeon, had always denied him, then winds up weeping in an abashed and contrite Pidgeon's arms.

Walter Pidgeon told me in 1972 that the scene in the car where he finally achieves an affectionate rapport with his son "highlighted Paul as an actor of real depth. And the miracle was that he never overplayed an extremely emotional scene; he never descended into pathos—kept it emotionally on target. I found myself 'losing it'—crying without control. Paul on the other hand was controlled and emotionally open at one and the same time."

Edmond O'Brien played his defense counsel in the picture. In 1958 he told me: "I was sure Paul was going to be a topflight star. He was really powerful in his interpretation. He kept me on my toes, challenged me; that's the kind of actor I like to work with."

The Rack was directed by Arnold Laven. Robert Wise was at the helm again for Newman's next film, *Until They Sail.* As *Somebody Up There Likes Me* had not come out yet and turned Newman into a star, he was given a supporting part in the film, which starred Jean Simmons, Joan Fontaine, Piper Laurie, and Sandra Dee as four New Zealand sisters involved with assorted soldiers in 1945. If nothing else, the picture proved that Newman—who doesn't show up for half an hour aside from a brief bit at the opening—could play a romantic, reasonably contemporary part with the best of them.

Joan Fontaine wasn't thrilled to be playing a repressed, middle-aged spinster, but there was good chemistry between Paul and his love interest, Jean Simmons. The highlight of the film is a sizzling love scene halfway through that is well played by both actors. Paul's character is an army investigator who looks into couples (comprised of American soldiers and young New Zealand ladies) who want to get married and makes sure everything is on the up-and-up as far as both parties are concerned.

Newman used his conflicted feelings over Joanne and Jackie to good advantage, convincingly etching a portrait of a man who is of two minds. Part of him desperately wants to love—and make love to—widowed Jean Simmons, but he's aware that he might be killed in action and the terrible psychological toll it would have on her. When he says, "I don't love you and I don't want to marry you," and puts his head on her lap so she can hold him instead of kissing her as she expected, he makes it clear that he is perhaps thinking just the opposite. In other scenes, however, he is merely perfunctory.

Until They Sail is not just another mindless soap opera, despite its reputation as such, but it has some serious flaws. The superficial characters are never allowed to react to or work through their grief as their menfolk die around them, and the courtroom finale, in which Newman successfully defends the husband who bludgeons unfaithful Piper Laurie to death, is ludicrous. The production code forced this offensive ending on the film, as it stated that adulterers (nevermind murderers) had to be punished for their sins.

Piper Laurie was impressed by the fact that Newman

read a newspaper while in the makeup chair—apparently most actors she knew would concentrate just on their parts or their mirrors. Charles Drake had a supporting role, as Fontaine's suitor, in the picture and watched and talked with Newman all through it. "The concentration of the guy—he made it all so real, yet he underplayed," Drake told me. "He had a real confidence in himself and what he was doing."

The year *Somebody Up There Likes Me* was released, 1956, was the same year Joanne appeared in her second film, an excellent thriller entitled *A Kiss Before Dying*. Like Newman with *The Silver Chalice*, Woodward would for years afterward yak about how bad the picture was when *A Kiss Before Dying* was actually a smoothly directed suspenser with fine performances and some chilling sequences, such as when Robert Wagner takes a pregnant Woodward, whom he has promised to marry, to the roof of city hall and, as she wistfully plans the honeymoon, pushes her off.

Woodward must have been struck by the irony, considering the trouble she was having getting the right man to leave his wife and propose to her. Certain, of course, that Paul would never resort to murder, she was eventually to borrow a trick from the dead heroine, but not before getting some other poor sap to ask her if she'd marry him. She said yes, made sure Newman knew, but when he didn't balk at the proposition, she dropped fiancé number two like a hot potato.

Paul and Joanne could not help running into each other when they were both in Hollywood shooting pictures. To be fair, Joanne's parents had divorced, and she knew what a trauma it might be for Alan Scott, Susan, and Stephanie if Paul and Jackie were to call it quits. But she had such a strong need for Paul that nothing else seemed to matter. Paul told her bluntly that he cared for her deeply—she was his best friend above all others—but there was no way he would ever leave his wife and kids for her. Joanne told him they would have to stop seeing each other. Even a platonic friendship would be too painful.

Paul now knew what James Dean had felt after Paul rejected him. Dean had still wanted his friendship even if Paul could offer nothing else, just as Paul badly needed Joanne in his life, even if he could give her nothing more. But Joanne would not settle for friendship when what she wanted was deep, enduring, passionate love. Paul had to agree not to bother her anymore. Joanne fooled herself into thinking she could forget about Paul and find someone new, perhaps a fiancé who would really become a husband. It wasn't long before they were seeing each other again. Put simply, they were in each other's blood and that was that. Still, Paul was torn in two directions and didn't know what to do about it.

There were reasons Joanne, no beauty she, had a tug on his heart. For one thing, she didn't personify the feeling of entrapment as did Jackie with her (understandable) demands on his time and income. Jackie had set aside her own ambitions to take care of their children, assuming this was what her husband had wanted, but as soon as she was domesticated, outside the theater, Paul could no longer relate to her. Joanne, on the other hand, had (at that time) the same interests and ambitions as he did. Many felt that Jackie had lost Paul by encouraging his ambitions, but perhaps it was truer that she actually lost him by stifling her own.

The whole awful situation began to take its toll on Paul, who was drinking heavily, which was how he would always react to a crisis or major stress throughout his life. Paul drank enough as it was—he always seemed to have a beer in his hand when the cameras stopped rolling—but now he was doing it at a self-destructive pace. Sensing what was wrong and knowing somehow that Joanne was involved in it, Jackie became belligerent—Paul responded in kind.

According to Josh Logan, who heard the story from someone close to the couple, Jackie made certain insinuations about his good friendships with the likes of William Inge and the late Jimmy Dean. Logan claimed that Newman belted Jackie. ("Any suggestion that he was a fag, even in jest, made Paul angry as hell, especially if he was drinking," Logan said.) Paul stormed out of the house in a drunken rage. Jackie nursed her black eye while the children screeched. This presumably occurred on the notorious evening of July 7, 1956, although other sources say that the insinuations and fight occurred when Newman and Jackie were out having dinner with friends in nearby Roslyn and no punches were thrown.

Late on the night of July 7, Newman was picked up by the Mineola, Long Island, police for passing a red light and leaving the scene of an accident in which he destroyed some shrubbery and a fire hydrant. Rowdy and hostile, he gave the police a hard time and was brought handcuffed to the station. *Somebody Up There Likes Me* had opened—to rave reviews—and as Newman was taken to a cell he yelled, "You can't do this to me—I'm Rocky!" The arresting officer, whose name happened to be Rocco Caggiano, shot back, "Yeah, well I'm Rocky, too, and you're under arrest for driving under the influence and leaving the scene of an accident!" An inebriated, sullen, highly agitated Newman was thrown into a cell, although he dopily protested that he was claustrophobic and wouldn't last the night if they didn't let him out immediately.

Newman got nervous when he saw a dozen or so reporters hanging around the jail house and was afraid they were there to report what had happened to him. One of the officers told him that the reporters were actually covering a kidnapping, and he had nothing to worry about. Unfortunately, some of the reporters did recognize the actor, and his humiliating arrest made the papers and some television stations. This was the beginning of his lifelong hatred of the press. He made up his mind to sharply limit his interviews and to keep mum about his personal life. He also realized that he needed professional help, not only to deal with the excruciating situation with his wife and Joanne but also to help him deal with the fact that he was now a public figure and everyone would be interested in things about him that he felt should remain private.

He made an appointment with an analyst—the first of many—and braced himself for whatever would come next.

7

THE END OF THE LONG HOT SUMMER

"I ALWAYS GET INVOLVED WITH MEN WHO ARE WRONG FOR me," Ann Blyth as Helen Morgan complains with classic understatement in *The Helen Morgan Story*. The character of Larry Maddox, played by Newman, was much worse for Morgan than Woodward may have felt Newman was for her. Joanne knew that Newman was the only guy in the world for her, but if he refused to divorce his wife, he was definitely wrong for Joanne. So she threw herself into her work, into pictures like *The Three Faces of Eve*, a multiple-personality drama that turned her into a minor star and won her an Oscar decades before her eventual husband won his.

Back on Long Island, Jackie seethed when she heard that her love rival, far from disappearing, was in the limelight for one movie after another, still busy working in the same town her husband periodically occupied. The marriage was one in name only by this time. Jackie and Paul were apart more than they were together, but Paul still felt he had to do the right thing and see through his responsibility to wife and children, no matter how painful the cost. Divorce was an alien thing to Paul. His parents had stayed together through thick and thin

for many years although theirs had not been a perfect marriage. Joanne's initial concern for his children and the effect
a divorce might have on them began to wither. They would
survive, as all children, ever resilient. She was back to justifying herself again: Was it good for the three kids if their mother and father were always fighting? It couldn't be good for
them, could it?

If *Somebody Up There Likes Me* had made Paul a star, *Until
They Sail* turned him into a matinee idol. His role as Larry
Maddox in *The Helen Morgan Story* was somewhere between
the two. Larry could love up the women as well as, if not better than, the army officer in *Until They Sail,* but he was an
unregenerate louse, a total heel, whose polished veneer only
concealed a much more common, Rocky-like, selfish inner
core. As one character says of Larry, "He'd shoot his own
grandmother in the back and bet on which way she'd fall."

Newman is quite good in the picture. Employing a kind
of Brooklyn accent that's a bit softer, and therefore more
convincing, than the one he used as Rocky. This was another
characterization he could get lost in, burying nice guy
Newman for the nonce. Ironically, he displays a light touch
in certain sequences that he was never able to display afterward in all his dismal attempts at out-and-out comedy.
Newman and Blyth play well together and have a particularly
good scene when Maddox confronts Helen when she comes
home drunk.

Newman must have felt certain frissons of recognition as
the story played out, as Helen drank at first to deal with sor-
row and disappointment, then became undeniably addicted
to alcohol. In spite of his arrest on Long Island, a onetime
freak thing as far as he was concerned (and which it essentially was), Newman was not ready to admit to himself that
there were times he relied on liquor for hope and happiness
a little too much to be healthy. Helen also drinks because she

can't be with Larry, the man she loves, who constantly betrays and disappoints her and refuses to marry her. Despite its glossy, often perfunctory surface, the picture works as a study of loneliness against which even money and success are no barrier.

Newman, who by now knew that often the worst kind of loneliness could afflict someone trapped in a bad marriage and separated from the one they truly loved, identified more with Helen than with Larry. At least he knew Joanne was too controlled a person to turn to drink the way he and Helen did.

When he wasn't busy coming up with techniques, such as the skewered angles of certain shots, to depict Helen's upset, alcoholism, and decline, director Michael Curtiz was working with Ann Blyth to help her craft her generally fine performance. He was never a man to praise actors unduly; while getting the best out of them, he could give them a hard time in the process. He remembered Newman as thoroughly professional and attentive: "But he wouldn't take any sass from me or anyone else." Curtiz recalled Newman saying something along the lines of "if criticism is honest, I'm all for it. But if it's done just out of meanness, I'll walk away from it."

Curtiz could be mean if he felt it was warranted, although to him it wasn't meanness at all. Actors, however, often felt his abrasive ways were quite gratuitous. Ann Blyth had a tough time making the picture and didn't take to Newman's cocky, Maddox-like manner, which he seemed to carry with him even when the cameras weren't rolling. When I interviewed co-star Richard Carlson (he played a "nice guy" who also courted Helen, but turned out, of course, to be married) on the set of a picture in 1969, his impression was that "Paul got so deep into himself that he was noncommunicado while doing his role. Some thought he was grumpy and remote, but I saw it as deep creativity, Newman-style."

Newman undoubtedly thought the ending of the picture was as stupid as everyone else did. Although Maddox does occasionally do something nice for Helen, at the film's conclusion he seems to undergo a complete character change, picking Helen up at the nuthouse, taking her to her old nightclub where he's assembled hundreds of her friends, and implying that he'll never leave her again. Earlier it's revealed that he even sent dozens of bouquets to her and signed other people's names to the cards so that she wouldn't feel forgotten. But if none of these people ever cared enough to actually send flowers or well-wishes to Helen, why would they bother showing up at the dilapidated nightclub? In any case, *The Helen Morgan Story* manages to get across the desperation of show biz and emerges a creditable tribute to a great singer and a time—before Elvis, rock, and rap—when songs actually had memorable melodies and lyrics.

For his next assignment Newman was supposed to join *Somebody* co-star Everett Sloane in *Marjorie Morningstar,* but he thought the script was treacle and refused to do it, risking suspension. Gene Kelly was put into the part. Luckily Twentieth Century Fox wanted Newman for one of their projects, and Warner was only too happy to lend him out and collect the big bucks, of which Paul would get only a fraction. The film was *The Long Hot Summer,* and Paul's co-star was to be— Joanne Woodward!

The two ladies in Paul's life had very different feelings about this unexpected development, but the initial reaction was the same on both sides: hysteria. Joanne was wild with joy about not only appearing with Paul in a picture but also spending weeks on location with him where she could further work her wiles. Jackie was wild also, with outrage. To her it was almost as if Paul and Joanne had moved in together. She knew there was no way they could avoid spending hours and hours in each other's company when they were on the same set, in the same picture.

She was livid, but by now she had no control over what her husband did or wanted to do. Paul told her that he was under contract and had to go where the studio sent him, but Jackie noticed he hadn't had such qualms when they'd wanted him to do *Marjorie Morningstar*. Paul argued that Warner easily filled that part with Kelly but that Twentieth Century-Fox had specifically asked for Newman and Warner would lose a considerable amount of money if they didn't loan him out. Jackie took the kids and went home to mother, convinced her marriage was over, as indeed it was.

Newman must have had mixed emotions about working with Joanne on *Long Hot Summer*. It promised to be a *very* hot summer, figuratively speaking, for everyone. As filming proceeded, Jackie nursed her wounds back in Wisconsin, so distraught and furious that at one point her parents were afraid she might have to be committed.

Although *The Long Hot Summer* was supposedly based on two short stories by William Faulkner, its true inspiration was Tennessee Williams's play *Cat on a Hot Tin Roof*, which had already opened on Broadway to much acclaim. When MGM acquired the film rights to the play, Twentieth Century-Fox figured they could come out with their own tale of twisted Southern passions and beat them at their own game. To be fair, the screenplay fashioned by Irving Ravetch and Harriet Frank, loosely inspired by the Faulkner stories, was a more than creditable one, and nearly forty years later, *Long Hot Summer* holds up as one of the best films Newman ever appeared in. Newman went down early to Clinton, Mississippi, where the film was shot, to soak up local color and absorb the accents, mannerisms, and speech patterns of the men in the area, for use in creating his characterization.

There was just as much drama going on offscreen as on. Orson Welles, already turning into the dissipated, bloated mess of his later years, was cast as Woodward's father, who prefers the rascally Newman as his daughter's suitor over the more gentlemanly man next door, played by Richard Anderson. Nearly unrecognizable as the same genius who directed and appeared in *Citizen Kane*, Welles was forty-three years old but able to play sixty-one without any makeup. Welles appeared in the film only because of his enormous tax debt of $150,000.

"I hated making *Long Hot Summer*," he said years later. "I've seldom been as unhappy in a picture. [Director] Martin Ritt said to me, 'I want you to relate to those windows,' and I said, 'Marty, you mean you want me to *look* at them?'" Welles had no patience with what he felt was Ritt's utterly pretentious directional approach, and the two would have nearly operatic quarrels. At one point Welles told Ritt that he had no intention of bothering to memorize his lines and that they could be dubbed in afterward, causing Ritt to wonder how Welles could memorize entire Shakespearean plays but not the few lines of dialogue for each scene of *Summer*. "I feel like I'm riding a bicycle in a barrel of molasses," Welles told Ritt, as Newman related years later.

In his memoirs, cowritten with Peter Bogdanovich, Welles commented that he enjoyed working with Joanne Woodward but made absolutely no mention of Newman. Years after making the film, he told me that Newman "was not a big guy, you know, physically, but he compensated with a lot of self-confident pizzazz. He was a striver, a pusher." He frowned and rolled his eyes as he added, "A lot of women, I suppose, found all that sexy," a contemptuous commentary, no doubt, on what he thought of Newman's acting ability. For his part, Newman called Welles "diabolical."

Newman worked well with Martin Ritt, however, as he caught on to his directorial "technique" rather early. "He would just make noises," Newman explained. "A growl, a grunt—and you'd know just what he meant." Newman must have liked this very basic form of communication because he worked with Ritt many times afterward.

Today Richard Anderson recalls that making the picture "was fun for [Paul] as the impression was he whistled to work every day. I liked playing scenes with Paul for that reason. He used everything he had to advantage—blue eyes included—and was easy and knowing. An engaging man, both on and off."

On the other hand, Lee Remick once told me that she thought Paul was "a rather self-centered grouch during the shooting. Boy, could he turn it off on you! Now I'm inclined to think he just needed to concentrate intensely—he wasn't a natural talent. He had to work hard to get what Marty Ritt was after."

Although Newman's instinct on a set was to be friendly with his associates—when he wasn't concentrating on his role—he had a lot on his mind during the *Long Hot Summer* shoot and could seem grumpy and preoccupied. Joanne Woodward was absolutely determined to get him to choose her over Jackie and was resorting to her old trick of trying to make him jealous. According to Shelley Winters, who had lost out on the part played by Lee Remick but traveled to the set anyway with her husband at the time, Tony Franciosa (cast as Welles's son), Woodward was "driving Paul crazy with her dates with young Timmy Everett, a gifted actor and director who was later to set Broadway on its ear in Inge's *Dark at the Top of the Stairs.*"

As jealous and exasperated as Paul may have been made by Everett, he apparently didn't see him as a serious threat, just as Joanne's relationship with Everett didn't prevent her from going out with Newman to local taverns in Clinton. Both of them knew how much Shelley had wanted to appear in the picture and, to cheer her up, took her one night to a weird Creole bar in New Orleans, where there were strippers of all varieties.

Meanwhile, work proceeded on *Long Hot Summer*. As Ben Quick, the drifter accused of being a barn burner, Newman radiates amused arrogance and insolence in equal measure, although when he puts on his white shirt and tie in one scene, he looks much too gentlemanly, still a problem for this nice college boy from Shaker Heights when portraying more common types. Occasionally Tony Franciosa, his rival for Welles's affections (Daddy Welles treats Newman more like a son than he does his real son), comes off better than the deliberately laid-back Newman because he has the more intense role. However, Paul manages to work up some intensity himself in scenes such as when he talks Franciosa out of shooting him and when he gives the climactic speech in which he tells how, as a boy of ten, he turned in his own father for barn burning.

Newman and Welles play quite well together; Newman never once seems intimidated by the giant (in every sense of the word) actor portraying his mentor. Oddly, Joanne Woodward, undeniably the better actor of the famous pair, does seem a little too mesmerized by the Great and Terrible Orson, with the result that her performance is good but not great. She also required but didn't always get careful lighting; in some shots her middle front teeth seem to disappear, turning her into a distaff Alfred E. Newman.

The Long Hot Summer was perhaps the first movie to betray the problem with much of Newman's film work: The techniques that worked so well for him on the stage did not play as effectively close up in the cinema. Years later Newman himself would observe that he seemed too busy *showing* the audience the thought processes of the character, instead of simply *being* the character and proceeding from there.

In spite of this, *Long Hot Summer* is not a picture he need take out any ads against. His performance is generally effective, and the movie quite memorable, even if it offers a very pat resolution of the conflict between father, son, and the drifter who comes between them.

However, there was still no resolution to the Jackie-Paul-Joanne triangle. When the filming of *Long Hot Summer* ended, Paul did not rush to Wisconsin to pick up Jackie, so at least Joanne had that major victory. But Paul and Jackie were still married, and it was driving Joanne crazy.

In Malibu Beach, Paul and Joanne moved into a house that they shared with writer Gore Vidal and his companion Howard Austen. Paul had already appeared in a teleplay written by Vidal, and Joanne had known him for awhile. Joanne and Gore were immediately attracted—to each other's minds. The brainy Woodward and Gore had stimulating discussions of a far more intellectual nature than Joanne and Paul. It was as if Paul satisfied the physical and Gore the mental.

Although Joanne was now living with Paul—if that was what it could be called when there were two other men living with them—Joanne was not satisfied. She knew Paul would never really be hers until the two of them were married. Jackie already had three children to hold over him; if they remained married, there was always the possibility that Paul would return to her. Joanne had waited long enough.

The next thing Paul knew he was greeted with the news that she and Gore Vidal were affianced! According to Vidal, it "was at her insistence and based entirely on her passion not for me but Paul Newman. Paul was taking his time about divorcing his first wife, and Joanne calculated, shrewdly as it proved, that the possibility of our marriage would give him the needed push. It did." But even this took time. For awhile the two men and Joanne, all sharing a roof with the nonplussed Howard, carried on a kind of weird, asexual ménage à quatre.

There was another factor. Joanne was pregnant. Like the poor sap that Bob Wagner throws off the roof in *A Kiss Before Dying*, Joanne had hit the tried-and-true way to get the right man to marry her. Now she had a hold over him, too. To Paul the pregnancy must have seemed like fate, the final sign that he was holding onto a dead marriage and a woman he no longer loved against all reason. He made up his mind to ask Jackie for a divorce.

It turned out that Jackie had already made up her mind to divorce him. She knew there was no sense in remaining Mrs. Movie Star Paul Newman when the whole world seemed to know who he was really in love with. She couldn't—and wouldn't—compete with Joanne. Her demands were entirely understandable; she would get custody of the children, as well as an extremely generous settlement. If there was any hassle, she'd go to the papers (a threat she might never have carried out for the children's sake).

Jackie was bitter and heartbroken and thoroughly disgusted. Years later some of this bitterness would recede—but never completely subside—and she would have a small part in one of her husband's films. They would keep in touch only because of the three children. Newman's oft quoted summation of the divorce: "I felt guilty as hell about it and will carry that guilt for the rest of my life."

In early 1958 Paul and Joanne appeared together—for the first time on live television—in a *Playhouse 90* drama entitled "The Eighty-Yard Run." In this they were reunited with *Long Hot Summer* co-star Richard Anderson. Based on an Irwin Shaw short story, the teleplay dealt with an unhappy man who is obsessed with what he considered the greatest moment of his life—his eighty-yard run in a college football game. Both actors, freed from the pressures they had been operating under for so many years, were excellent. In some ways the part prefigured Paul's performance as Brick in the film adaptation of *Cat on a Hot Tin Roof*, which was then a couple of months in his future.

Two weeks after the broadcast, in January 1958, Paul and Joanne were married in Las Vegas. They then went to London for their honeymoon, which they spent with, peculiarly enough, Gore Vidal and the ubiquitous Howard. While in London, Joanne had a miscarriage, which had to be covered up for the sake of her career. Studios had clauses about being pregnant on your honeymoon.

Whatever trauma the miscarriage engendered, Joanne still had one thing to which she could cling.

She was *finally* Mrs. Paul Newman.

8

LEFT-HANDED

HONEYMOONING IN LONDON, PAUL AND JOANNE BASKED IN each other's company—when they could get rid of Gore and Howard—and spent time sightseeing, sitting in friendly pubs, traveling into the countryside by car, and sleeping overnight in charming inns. They were happy to be away from Hollywood and work and Jackie and all the hustle and bustle and stresses of their lives.

Returning to the United States, the couple rented several dwellings, one of which was an apartment in the east eighties in Manhattan, a large affair with its own study, library, and maid's quarters, as well as plenty of extra bedrooms for Paul and Jackie's children when they visited. Eventually a maid named Tressie and two Chihuahuas were added to the household.

At that time Paul said, "There are a million things I like about the city, and I walk around it a lot, from one end of Lexington Avenue to the other; and up and down Fifth; up and down Second. Joanne and I are pretty self-sufficient. We enjoy being alone together." They were not to be alone for long, however, once Joanne got pregnant again.

Bi-coastal, they also rented a house in Laurel Canyon in Hollywood but lived comparatively simply for movie stars. Filmland gossip maven Hedda Hopper, for one, was scandalized, noting in her column that the Newmans dared to live on a simple lot, rented by the month and sans swimming pool, and they used tacky rental cars instead of their own limo and chauffeur. How déclassé!

Meanwhile poor Jackie and the kids weathered things as best they could. The problem was more emotional than anything else. Jackie, Alan Scott, Susan, and Stephanie had been well provided for, and the children would not really want for anything, comparatively speaking, through their formative years. They had become so used to their father's absences while he was in Hollywood, or even while working relatively nearby in a Broadway play or television studio, that the divorce wasn't as much of a shock to them as might have been expected. In fact, visiting their father and "Auntie Joanne" in California or Manhattan was to become a thrill to them.

In any case, they had little idea of what had really happened to the family. Years later Susan admitted that she was surprised to learn when she was older what a scandal the whole business had been at the time. Apparently Jackie did not spend her hours regaling the kids with sordid stories but rather bottled up much of the pain inside her. Eight-year-old Alan Scott, however, had become more of a terror than ever, undoubtedly reacting, if only on a subconscious level, to the stress his parents had been under and their occasional noisy quarrels. Hoping that her ex-husband would at the very least help her in her renewed efforts to revive her own acting career, Jackie would soon take the kids and move to the San Fernando Valley.

As previously noted, Joanne had appeared the year

before her marriage to Paul in *The Three Faces of Eve,* in a role originally intended for Judy Garland. When she found out that she had been nominated for Best Actress by the Academy of Arts and Sciences, she was—at least publicly—unimpressed, telling interviewers that she had no respect for the Academy because so many other factors besides who they really believed gave the best performance went into their decision on who or who not to nominate. Many Hollywood figures thought her ungracious and didn't mind saying so.

At the Oscar ceremony, Paul and Joanne presented the Oscar for Best Editing to Peter Taylor for *The Bridge on the River Kwai.* A little later the best actress winner was announced, and Joanne heard her name called. Clearly forgetting all her harsh earlier statements, she clutched her statue, cried copious tears, and told the audience, "I've been waiting for this moment since I was nine years old." She was all of twenty-eight at the time.

Representing old-guard Hollywood, Joan Crawford thought little of Joanne's wimpy dress and the utter lack of glamour and taste she represented. Her public statement: "Joanne Woodward is setting the cause of Hollywood glamour back twenty years by making her own clothes." Few of the friends and associates in Woodward's New York theatrical circle ever imagined that she, talented as she was, would wind up becoming a movie star.

Years later Woodward would state that winning the Academy Award was "exciting for five or ten minutes." She would proclaim that had she her life to do over, she would just as soon have settled for being a wife and mother. This was a complete turnaround from her attitude in 1958, when she planned on going full steam ahead with her career. Instead she wound up appearing in occasional movies, on her own and with Paul, including three films that he directed.

Frankly, for years people have clucked over what seems

to be Woodward's unselfish abnegation of her own career in favor of Newman's, with many assuming that it was her (wise?) way of catering to her husband's male insecurities. She might have initially had contempt for Jackie's attempts to hold her man with the routine of wife and mother who has no career of her own, but apparently at some point she came to the conclusion that that's just what Newman wanted in a woman. Someone to support him, to listen to his dreams, to take part in his schemes (such as the films he directed her in) when it suited him, when he needed her. Joanne had gone through so much, to her way of thinking, to get her guy that she was not about to lose him by making stupid mistakes. The feminist movement came too late to do Joanne much good. Besides, she had already won her Oscar, had reached the pinnacle so to speak, before the age of thirty. Perhaps she felt she didn't need the career anymore and thought dipping her toes in the water now and then was more than enough.

The basic truth about the Newman-Woodward marriage is that it is not one of the all-time great love stories but rather a deep, enduring friendship based on shared needs and similar experiences. It has persisted through the years primarily because Paul and Joanne give each other space to go their separate ways. Each admits that, aside from acting, they have little in common, which is ironic when one considers that Newman hasn't much interest in acting anymore and Joanne essentially gave up her career years ago. Newman calls his wife "the Last of the Great Broads." When asked if he was ever tempted to stray, he wisecracked, "Why go looking for hamburger when you've got steak at home?" but never really answered the question.

Not long after the marriage and all the resulting publicity, Newman took to refusing to sign autographs. He said that only people with a pretentious "star attitude" would do it, unaware that refusing to sign autographs could be interpret-

ed as a "star attitude" in and of itself. He would scoot around
Manhattan on a motorbike, disguised in dark glasses and hat,
hoping to avoid the nubile ladies who seemed to screech at
him from every street corner.

Like all things, the honeymoon was over, and it was time
to go back to work. Gore Vidal was hoping to make a film version of a teleplay he had written entitled *The Death of Billy the
Kid*, which Newman had starred in. Vidal wanted this to be *his*
picture, one that he had control over that no one else, not a
director, producer, or actor, could screw up. He and Newman
approached Warner Brothers together and got the green
light. They were kind enough to turn over the job of producing the movie to an out-of-work television person. Acting with
the typical gratitude of many entertainment types, this producer promptly fired the director Vidal had chosen for the
film and brought in another one of his television associates,
Arthur Penn. (This was the first film for Penn, who later when
on to direct *Bonnie and Clyde* with Warren Beatty.) Even worse,
he brought in another writer to "punch up" Vidal's script, all
of this without Vidal's knowledge. Gore was appalled that
Newman had just stood by and let all this happen. As he put
it, "Paul, no tower of strength in these matters, allowed the
hijacking to take place."

Years later Newman would complain about the screenplay and how its original concept had gotten lost, without
ever acknowledging that Vidal's script had been "punched
up" by another writer and that this might have accounted for
the bad results. (The screenplay is attributed to Leslie
Stevens, based on Vidal's teleplay.) In addition, Newman's
friendship on the set with Arthur Penn—Paul would play
practical jokes on him like putting pebbles in his hubcaps to
make his car sound like it was falling to pieces—might have
blinded him to what was going on.

Although Vidal has been friends with the Newmans for

decades, sources concur that Vidal is more friends with Joanne than with Paul, whom he reportedly considers a bit of a "lunkhead." Incidents like the one with *The Death of Billy the Kid*—whose title was changed to *The Left-Handed Gun*—couldn't have helped any. Vidal's bitchy comments about anyone and everyone have occasionally included Mr. Movie Star Newman.

In any case, Newman is every inch the movie star in *The Left-Handed Gun*, giving a confident and assured performance—if not a truly great one—as Billy the Kid, even if he seems mildly retarded in the opening scenes. His performance lacks greatness because Newman is not really an artist who's able to convincingly detail Billy's pathology. Instead he makes the most of the alternately sullen and swaggering aspects of the character, such as when he confronts one of the men who killed an associate at a party and swears that eventually he'll kill him, too.

"Left-handed" being an old-fashioned euphemism for homosexual, one can expect to find such references in the picture (the Kid is too shy to talk to a girl at a party, even after being encouraged to do so, and his later attempts at lovemaking seem almost desperate). Still, there're far fewer homosexual references than in Howard Hughes's notorious *The Outlaw*, which said all the psychological stuff there was to say about Billy the Kid fourteen years before *Left-Handed Gun* and said it better. Billed as an adult Western, *Left-Handed Gun* is certainly more adult than, say, a Roy Rogers movie, but its psychology is strictly of the pretentious, dime-store variety. Confused, meandering, anti-climactic, and tedious, *Left-Handed Gun* proved that Newman could star in much worse movies than *The Silver Chalice*. At least the picture doesn't glamorize Billy; Penn would wait until *Bonnie and Clyde* to make outlaws look sexy.

Gore Vidal, whose movie had been essentially stolen

away from him, had the last word. He recorded in his memoirs: "[*The Left-Handed Gun*] is a film only someone French could like." Vidal had learned that in Hollywood, the writer, even if he originated the project or thought he was in control, was at the bottom of the totem pole.

The great Tennessee Williams wasn't to have much luck, either, when his plays were transferred to the screen, although the results would be a little more felicitous. Although Ben Gazarra and Barbara Bel Geddes had played the lead roles in the stage version of *Cat on a Hot Tin Roof,* they weren't considered bankable enough by tinsel town standards, and Paul and Elizabeth Taylor were tapped to replace them on celluloid.

Given his earlier bouts of homosexual panic, it is ironic that Newman became a major interpreter of the works of flamboyantly gay Southern playwright Williams in the fifties and sixties. Williams himself was very amused by this and for years after would often call Newman's sexuality into question (more in an affectionate than nasty manner) whenever the latter's name came up in conversation. Observers noted, however, that this may have been mere wish fulfillment on the playwright's part, as Newman's good looks and manly charms had certainly not been lost on Williams.

Williams always defended Paul's acting ability, even going so far as to say in his autobiography, "Paul Newman . . . is terribly good. He works up to a part slowly, but when he finally gets to it, he's marvelous." While he may have overrated Newman for the same reason William Inge did—he was smitten—he may also have simply noticed how hard Paul prepared for roles and tried his damnedest to stretch his talent. Newman may not have been a brilliant or naturally gifted actor, but to his credit, he always tried to give a good performance.

As Brick (perhaps the most sexual name until Pussy

Galore in *Goldfinger*), Newman played a man who is unable to function sexually with his highly sexed wife because he's still under the spell of his crush on his dead buddy Skipper. At least that was what Newman was supposed to play until the production code reared its ugly head and insisted all homosexual references be excised. Instead, Brick would suffer from "emotional immaturity".

The director of the film, Richard Brooks, had been this route before. He was an ex-marine who had written a controversial novel, entitled *The Brick Foxhole*, about a gay man who is murdered by another man who hates homosexuals. Brooks was nearly court-martialed because he didn't submit the manuscript for review by Marine Corps officials. The novel elicited considerable acclaim, but when the film rights were bought, the gay stuff had to go. The victim was turned into a Jew, and the killer an anti-Semite. (The film was retitled *Crossfire*.) Brooks married Newman's co-star from *Until They Sail*, Jean Simmons, and turned into a card-carrying bleeding heart whose screen adaptation of Truman Capote's *In Cold Blood* was exasperatingly sympathetic to the cretinous killers.

The first screenplay, written by James Poe, not only had the gay elements intact but even dramatized some of the flashbacks between Brick and Skipper (who is only referred to in the play). These included a drinking bout between the buddies when Skipper admits that he's really not much of a ladies' man, for all his macho pretenses, and that it scares the hell out of him. There was also a fatal phone call when Skipper threatens to kill himself (which he does) after learning from Brick that the latter has slept with Maggie. The major change from the play was that in Poe's version Brick pleads with Skipper not to take his own life, whereas in Williams's version, he angrily ignores Skipper's outcries. Poe's adaptation also has a happier Hollywood ending and a much more conventional hero.

George Cukor was the first choice—and a wise one—to direct the picture, but he backed out when the censors got through blue-penciling. He was certain the excision of the gay material would totally destroy the movie and was surprised when—because of the strong characters—it turned out that it didn't. In fact, the homosexual aspects, despite being downplayed, still come across to more perceptive viewers. *Cat on a Hot Tin Roof* is actually one of the best motion pictures to come out of Hollywood, a showcase of trenchant dialogue, absorbing situations, and some powerhouse performances.

Grace Kelly was supposed to play Maggie the Cat, but her marriage to the Prince of Monaco ended her career. Brooks wanted Newman for Brick all along because he recognized that the character was passive and quiet for long stretches and required an actor who, like Newman, could convincingly listen and react. Whatever his flaws as an actor, Newman has always been a good listener.

As rehearsals began, Newman got rather nervous about Elizabeth Taylor. She seemed completely unenthused with what she was doing; there was no give and take when they were performing. It was as if he were all alone in the room as she stood by just going through the motions. He went to Brooks and told him his concerns. Brooks assured him that Liz was a real movie gal and once the cameras were rolling it would be a different story. Newman wasn't convinced, but he told Brooks he would wait and see.

Rehearsals were over, and it was time to start filming. Personally, Newman didn't see a hell of a lot of change in Elizabeth, but he felt better after he took a look at the rushes. The camera captured *something* that made her come alive; she knew, as perhaps he knew without even realizing it, how to make her limited talent work and play for the camera. Never the greatest of actresses, Taylor gave one of her better performances in *Cat.* A few years later, Newman would say of

Elizabeth that she was a "real pro" and that she "took chances" and "had a lot of guts. She'd go ahead and explore and risk falling on her face."

Newman and Taylor did not hit it off especially well at first. With the exception of Judith Anderson, who took a liking to Taylor, most of the cast and crew found her a bit bratty. There were even crew members who thought she and Newman radiated zero chemistry together as the film was shot, although this was not the case in the finished product.

Richard Brooks had been told by the front office that *Cat* was to be a black-and-white film to keep costs down. He argued that it was a story about a millionaire with a beautiful mansion and plantation, not a gritty study of life in the slums. When Taylor's husband at the time, showman Mike Todd, came to the set, Brooks told him what a bad decision it was to film in black and white but there was nothing he could do about it. Todd said, "Let me see what I can do."

An hour later Brooks was visited by some men from the front office. "Why do you want to film this in black and white?" they asked him. "You've got a millionaire, a beautiful girl, a plantation—this isn't a story about the slums." Rather than remind them that it had been *their* idea, not his, to make a black-and-white movie, he simply agreed with them that *Cat on a Hot Tin Roof* must be filmed in color.

Ever mindful of his wife's career and image, Todd asked to see the dailies one afternoon and told Brooks he was pleased. He then asked Brooks if he wanted to go with him and a few others for a ride in his private plane for a weekend vacation. Brooks was too busy with rewrites and had to beg off. There was a terrible storm that weekend, and on March 22, 1958, Todd's plane crashed somewhere in Arizona, killing all aboard.

Liz was hysterical, as to be expected, when she got the news. When Brooks went to see her, she screeched at him,

"You know what they asked me? How long will I be out for the funeral! Sure, they bought a lot of lousy flowers—so what!" Brooks assured her that he was more concerned with her than with *Cat on a Hot Tin Roof* (or so he claimed) and that she could come back to work whenever she felt like it—or not. "It's only a movie, Liz. You don't want to come back, don't come back. It's only a movie." Friends of Taylor's were afraid she'd go so far as to attempt suicide.

Brooks shot around Liz for a month before she came by in her limo one afternoon and asked if she could come back to work. She *needed* to come back to work. In a small voice she said, "Mike liked the dailies." (Elizabeth had wanted to retire, in spite of her MGM contract. Todd got her to start work on *Cat* and, indeed, made most of the decisions in her life while they were married.)

Liz shot one hour the first day, then eventually got back into the spirit of things and put in as many hours as anyone. Part of the reason for this was her co-star. "Paul Newman is one of the sweetest men I know," she said years later. "He was so unbelievably supportive [after Mike's death] with his kind words and just by being there for me. He helped me through an enormously difficult time in my life and I will always be grateful." There were still some very difficult moments, such as when Judith Anderson (as Brick's mother) gave a speech in which she said, "I guess things never turn out the way you want them to."

Taylor's sad mood and the sad undertones of the movie probably combined to help her give a performance of understated desperation and despair. Newman understood Brick's "panic" and embarrassment, and it shows in his performance, which is one of the best of this early period. The two are, of course, out-acted by such heavyweights as Judith Anderson and Burl Ives (as Brick's father Big Daddy), but that is to be expected.

In 1960 Burl Ives told me: "Paul is a better actor than he thinks he is. Some people think his range is limited and I think Paul does, too. Strange thing, though, is that when he cuts loose he acts like he *knows* he's good—he did some really wonderful things in *Cat*, things that stay in your memory."

As previously stated, Newman doesn't always take his coworkers' feelings into account, which was certainly the case when he gave an interview to Lillian Ross in 1962 and came out with this amazing statement about *Cat on a Hot Tin Roof*: "That was the first of my pictures, except for the one I made with Joanne, that I didn't have to carry pretty much on my own. Before that, it had just worked out, somehow, that I'd never played with a star."

True, Liz Taylor was and is a superstar, but it's also true that Virginia Mayo, Walter Pidgeon, Joan Fontaine, and Ann Blyth, all of whom he'd worked with previously, were not exactly lightweights. It's also hard to believe that anyone with a smaller ego would think of themselves as "carrying" *The Helen Morgan Story* or *Until They Sail*, in which Newman was mere co-star and even supporting player.

Still, Newman's good performance in *Cat* did not go unnoticed. He received his first Academy Award nomination for the role of Brick.

9

RALLYING

AFTER THE STRESSES AND DIFFICULTIES OF *CAT ON A HOT TIN Roof*, Newman's next assignment must have seemed like child's play. In *Rally 'Round the Flag, Boys*, he was teamed not only with Joanne for the second time but also with the poor man's Liz Taylor, Joan Collins. It was his first attempt at comedy. Unfortunately, it wouldn't be his last.

Joanne had reservations about the script, but as long as Paul had to do the picture on loan to Fox, she would do it with him. Maybe it would be fun. Exhibiting some of the poor judgment that was to plague him throughout his career, Newman figured a comedy would be a lot easier to play than a powerful Tennessee Williams drama. He was wrong.

Newman and Woodward were both badly miscast in this labored farce about a husband and wife taking different sides when the army wants to build a secret base in a suburban community. Collins tries to spice things up as a sexy next-door neighbor, to no avail. Newman is not Jack Lemmon—who would have been perfect in the part—and even Woodward is lackluster. (Years later she would admit that she hated herself in it.) The basic material was decent enough, but it needed gifted comic actors to pull it off. Producer-director Leo McCarey, who had helmed many screen comedies over the years, was at his wit's end trying to get these "serious" actors to play it straight instead of constantly mugging and trying to be funny.

Jack Carson, who had also appeared in *Cat on a Hot Tin Roof* with Newman, was much better in *Rally*—it was more his forte—and never thought much of Newman, describing him as "arrogant" in 1960. "He likes to strut around and show off all the time. He overdoes it." Possibly Carson, who had appeared in such films as *Mildred Pierce* with Joan Crawford, resented Newman's star billing, especially when Newman was so bad in a part Carson could have played with little effort.

Newman's next assignment for Warner Brothers was much more on the mark. *The Young Philadelphians* featured Newman at his best, as a young guy on an upwardly mobile course who sets values and morals aside until he recognizes what really matters in life at the film's conclusion. Newman plays Tony Lawrence with a lot of charm and insouciance and is consistently natural, spontaneous, and un-self-conscious. Part of the reason for this was that Newman was playing a man from a relatively similar background, someone he could understand.

Although Tony Lawrence is illegitimate, he has been raised as the son of a deceased, top-drawer Philadelphian aristocrat. He hasn't much money of his own but has plenty of social contacts, as well as the sex appeal to make use of them. How could Newman not relate?

Newman has some splendid scenes in the picture, such as when he learns his fiancée (Barbara Rush) has gone off and married someone else in Europe and when he confronts this same woman sometime later. He nicely underplays the scene when he learns that his mother's friend and frustrated suitor of many years (Brian Keith) is his real father. A high-light of the picture is the bedroom sequence between Paul and Alexis Smith, who plays the wife of Tony's mentor. Smith gets across perfectly the desperation of a woman who has put up with a lack of passion for too long and has to have Tony or else. In a clever bit, Tony tells her that he is in love with her and she will have to divorce her husband. Since the sex-starved Smith is perfectly aware which side her bread is buttered on, she backs off without being rejected and possibly causing trouble for Tony along "hell hath no fury" lines. Wise man, Tony.

The Young Philadelphians also features a standout performance by Robert Vaughn as a wounded veteran who becomes alcoholic and is framed for murder so he can be cheated out of his inheritance. Newman successfully defends his old friend at the film's conclusion. Vaughn was nominated for a 1959 Oscar. In 1966 Vaughn told me, "Paul helped me shape up my performance in *The Young Philadelphians* by playing back to me perfectly. He was very unselfish. If he saw that a particular scene belonged to another actor in the cast, he played himself down and lent solid support."

Vincent Sherman, a veteran Hollywood director, was behind the helm of the picture and kept it playing at a smooth, rapid pace. Undoubtedly he had much to do with helping shape the superlative performances, although Newman deserves credit for coming through in virtually every scene. His performance is the glue that holds the whole thing together, proving that films can often be as much an actor's medium as a director's.

Of all his films, Paul's mother always liked him best in *The Young Philadelphians*, perhaps because he played the role of a strong, handsome, ambitious—but basically decent—young man, who was in some ways much like Newman himself.

The irony of *Young Philadelphians*, made after *Cat on a*

Hot Tin Roof, was that it was franker on the subject of homosexuality in some ways. In an early scene, Tony's mother is
spurned by her new husband (Adam West, who later became
famous as the campy television Batman) on their wedding
night when he tells her that he can't love her or any woman.
The reason for this is never given—impotency? an injury?—
but the audience can't help but figure the character might be
gay, especially when the bride blackmails her mother-in-law
(she wants her illegitimate son to have her husband's name)
by threatening to reveal all the details.

Newman later claimed that he did the picture only so
Warner Brothers would let him have time off to appear on
stage in Tennessee Williams's new play, *Sweet Bird of Youth*
(see chapter 10), but surely he must have realized what a
terrific part the film provided for him and how much it
would showcase him to fine advantage. But then Newman
was not always the best arbiter of what was good for him and
what wasn't.

In any case, he was able to appear in the play, but while
it was running, he had to spend his days filming another
Twentieth Century-Fox loan-out, *From the Terrace.* Newman
had to battle to get Fox to cast Joanne as his wife, just as he'd
had to battle to get her the spousal assignment in *Rally
'Round the Flag, Boys,* but at least this was a more dramatic,
juicier part. In fact, Woodward as the bitchy wife made Jackie
at her worst seem sylphlike by comparison. She told reporters that she and Paul could get out all their own frustrations with each other by screaming at each other in character
on the set. Once that was done, they could go home and
make like turtledoves.

Director Mark Robson, who had helmed *Peyton Place*
three years earlier, was working from a more vaunted literary
source this time, a novel by John O'Hara, but the results
would hardly make it matter. Again Newman was a man on

the rise, a veteran embroiled in a miserable marriage and an all-consuming affair as well as ruthless business strategies. Somehow the whole formula just didn't click this time, and the pacing was off. At 144 minutes, *From the Terrace* seemed plodding and interminable. It did not get very good reviews and neither did Newman. Preoccupied by his role on Broadway, and perhaps a sense of déjà vu after just filming *Philadelphians*, he seemed to sleepwalk through the role.

One of his co-stars was impressed with him, however. Myrna Loy was appearing in a supporting role as Newman's mother. She recalled returning to Twentieth Century-Fox, where she had made some earlier films, and discovering that her dressing room was bare. "Noticing the tributes stacked in Paul Newman's dressing room, I realized that I was yesterday and he was today." But when she walked out on the set, the crew all gave her a standing ovation. They then proceeded to subject Paul to merciless teasing, asking Myrna who that "kid" she was working with was and if she was giving acting lessons on the side now. Paul took all the teasing good-naturedly.

Loy told her biographer, James Kotsilibas-Davis, that Paul "was very sweet about it, displaying none of the cockiness of so many young stars. He gave me a lot to work from as his dissolute mother, a real departure for me. One scene—I'm sitting in front of a mirror telling him to go for his own good—is a stunner. Paul was already a pro."

Joanne kept reasonably busy during this period herself, not only appearing with Paul in *Terrace* but also doing such films as *The Sound and the Fury*—another Faulkner story or approximation thereof—and *The Fugitive Kind*, in which she was teamed with Paul's old nemesis, Marlon Brando. Although some people still said Paul was a Brando knockoff, it happened much less frequently. *The Fugitive Kind* was based on Tennessee Williams's *Orpheus Descending*, itself derived from the playwright's earlier *Battle of Angels*, which

Paul had inadvertently used to successfully audition for the Actors Studio before he'd met Joanne. Before *Terrace* and Paul's run in the Broadway production of *Sweet Bird of Youth,* Joanne discovered she was pregnant and took some time off to await the baby, what might be called Paul and Joanne's first *real* coproduction.

The child was born on April 8, 1959, and named Elinor Teresa after Joanne's two grandmothers; her nickname would be Nell. Years later she would appear in some Newman films under the stage name Nell Potts. Jackie was not thrilled when she heard about the baby. She knew this new arrival would make a deserved claim on, and deprive her own children of that much more of, Paul's attention.

Meanwhile Newman was completely disgusted with Warner Brothers. The only films he'd really liked making while under contract to them were loan-outs. The studio was getting $75,000 from Fox for *From the Terrace,* but he was getting less than $20,000 for both Warner films and loan-outs. Warners would make three or four times as much as he would just for lending his services to another studio. To make matters worse, they had promised he could work on a picture he wanted to do—another loan-out, which meant easy money for them—and then changed their minds and told him he couldn't do it.

Furious, Newman began issuing public statements about how Warner was determined to keep him "poor" and how they had so little confidence in him they kept loaning him out to other studios. He was bitter about the fact that, although he was always free to go talk to Jack Warner, nothing he said ever made much of an impression on the studio head. He also resented the fact that the films Warner gave him to choose from were always the runts of the litter, terrible scripts he wanted no part of.

Finally Newman went once more to talk to Jack Warner,

who had heard all about Newman's outrageous verbal carryings-on and was not at all happy about it. (He tended to think stars who complained, like Newman or an earlier Bette Davis, were utter ingrates.) Smiling—Warner always smiled when he was dealing with "difficult" talent—Warner said he was sorry Newman was so unhappy. "You can buy out your contract if you'd like." There were still three years left on the contract.

"How much?" asked Newman.

Jack smiled. "Only half a million," he said.

Warner was still smiling when Newman dashed angrily out of his office.

Newman spoke to his new agent and adviser, Lew Wasserman, who told him that he could *probably* get him a quarter of a million for each picture if he struck out on his own. That way he wouldn't be in debt for long if he paid Jack Warner the half million he wanted.

Newman was in a good position at this time. *Cat on a Hot Tin Roof* had been the highest grossing picture of the year, and several other Newman films had done boffo box office. If that hadn't been the case, he probably would have sunk his career right then and there. Years later Newman would shiver a bit recalling how he had taken on Jack Warner when he was still relatively new at the film game and things could have gone either way for him. Luckily, his move to become an independent movie star, selling his services to the highest bidder, was the right one.

However, when he wound up in *Exodus* (1960), his first film as an independent, it didn't seem that way. The project had seemed worthwhile; the film was based on a best-selling novel by Leon Uris and was to be directed by Hollywood veteran Otto Preminger, who wanted Newman for the part of Ari Ben Canaan. The story concerned the 1947 Israeli fight for independence.

According to Preminger, Lew Wasserman came to his office to negotiate and told him that Newman had to have $200,000 or else. "That's too high," Preminger said. "I'll give him half."

"Fine," Wasserman said. "It's a deal." As Preminger put it, "The part was good for Newman and he wanted him to do it and that was that." Apparently Wasserman then went back and told Newman what a struggle it was just to get $100,000.

Preminger's brother was Leon Uris's literary agent and had sold the film rights for *Exodus* to MGM for $75,000. Since Otto decided he wanted to make the film, he developed a strategy for getting MGM to give up the rights. He went to the studio and asked them, "Aren't you afraid the Arabs will boycott all of your movies? I don't have to worry about it, since I'm an independent producer." Thinking it over, MGM decided he was right and sold him the rights to *Exodus*.

There were more problems. Preminger didn't like Uris's screenplay and fired him, prompting Uris to later declare that Preminger had "ruined" his book. And Preminger, never a particularly pleasant person to begin with, did not get along with his star, who frankly hated the director. As he had done with Saville and Wise and others before, Newman alienated Otto by coming up with suggestions, not only for his performance but also for improving the script and even blocking a scene. "*I* am the director," Preminger told him, and that was that. Now it was Newman who was alienated. Used to give-and-take with directors who respected his right to have an opinion, even if they might not agree with what he had to say, Newman was livid and, for the rest of the working experience, just went through the motions. For his part, Preminger was glad that he had headed off the tiresome possibility of Newman coming by with suggestions day after day.

Publicly, Preminger tried to be diplomatic—for him. He told me, "Newman was a son of a bitch personally at times, but I admit he was effective enough in the picture. Of course, I had to help him a lot. The man needed guidance, he went overboard too much—all this Method stuff, you know. I had to plane him down, discipline him." According to Peter Lawford, who was also in the picture, "Paul took no shit from Preminger. He could really be a bastard to work with, but Paul could cut him down to size." Peter always thought that Paul's performance in *Exodus* had been under-rated. "He worked hard and he had real humility. If he thought something was wrong the first time, he'd rework it until it was right."

The trouble with Otto the Terrible was unfortunate because Paul had looked forward to making *Exodus* as a trib-ute, of sorts, to his late Jewish father. He took Joanne and baby Nell with him to Israel, where they resided for over three months. Even overseas, they were occasionally treated as movie star curiosities, such as during a dinner in a restaurant when hundreds of people stared at them—or rather at Newman—as they ate. Joanne felt as if they were in a cage at the zoo.

Once released, *Exodus* wound up a major disappoint-ment for all concerned, with Ernest Gold's powerful theme music taking top honors.

Newman, at least, would go on to better things.

10

HOW SWEET IT IS

AFTER THE CREATIVELY AND ARTISTICALLY BANKRUPT EXPER-
ience of *Exodus*, Newman was ready for the stimulating challenge of *The Hustler*. Eddie Felson, the pool hustler, was one
of his most memorable roles. The picture was filmed mostly
on location in New York City, to good advantage. The director, Robert Rossen, had a terminal illness and knew that *The
Hustler* would be his swan song. "We had three weeks of
rehearsals, using television technique," Newman said, "where
you lay out tape on the floor to mark the sets."

The Hustler emerged as a very good picture, though pool
is not exactly the most cinematic of subjects. The atmospher-
ic, moody photography of the film illuminates the bleak,
depressing vistas of poolrooms, gin joints, crummy hotel
rooms, and seedy bus terminals with startling clarity.

Newman is completely convincing as Eddie Felson,
a character nothing like Tony Lawrence of *The Young
Philadelphians* or Paul Newman himself. Newman was a winner, and Felson, despite some minor victories at pool and a
major moral victory at the film's conclusion, is pretty much a

loser all of the way. In an early scene, after he beats the great Minnesota Fats (Jackie Gleason), he's so afraid people will think it was a fluke that he self-destructively plays Fats again and again until he's sick from fatigue and has lost all of the $10,000 he'd won. When he meets a pretty girl at the bus terminal, he doesn't exactly reveal himself to be a charm boy. "You don't look like a college girl," he tells her. "You just don't look young enough."

Newman's acting hides clues to Felson's character instead of laying it all out on the line as other actors might do. That's why the picture is nearly over before we're sure if Felson is a good guy or a bad guy or something in between; Newman keeps us guessing about him, never playing it heroically or like Eddie was nothing more than a sleaze. Paul is very convincing when he takes the girl (Piper Laurie) to a fancy restaurant for dinner and looks awkward as hell and a little intimidated—as someone like Eddie Felson would be but someone like Newman definitely wouldn't.

The highlights of the film—and of Newman's performance—are the strong emotional moments, such as when Eddie confronts his old partner Charlie (superbly played by Myron McCormick), who nearly begs Felson to come out on the road with him again; he can't make any money on his own. But Felson sees a better opportunity in traveling with his new associate, Bert Gordon (a marvelous George C. Scott) and bids Charlie good-bye. Newman's climactic speech after the girl's suicide, when in disgust he parts company with Gordon, is very strong and well played. Newman is also excellent as he hovers over Laurie's corpse in the bathroom, revolving his head up in the air with an anguished grimace. (He would, however, use this particular technique a little too often in the ensuing years.) The suicide doesn't really have as much impact as intended, because in some ways the girl is a rather unsympathetic person. Although Laurie's performance is very good, she never makes it clear that her character is supposed to be a cripple.

Actor Don Koll worked on *The Hustler* and recalled that if Newman needed a fourth for a card game when they were on location in New York, Koll was drafted. "There's a kind of caste system in Hollywood, where stars don't mingle with bit players," Koll said. "It just isn't done. But when we were on location Newman told me that it was a relief to be free of the caste system, that he could mingle with everyone and be his friendly self, because basically he's a very down-to-earth guy."

World champion pool player Willie Mosconi was brought in to teach the actors how to play so it would look convincing on camera. He had known Paul's father back in Cleveland. He took Paul down to the basement of the Finch Finishing School for Girls and taught him some moves. "I thought he looked pretty good in the movie," he said years later, "but Gleason was a much better player."

In spite of this, Newman got a little cocky, according to Gleason, and challenged him to a game for fifty bucks. "I ran fifty balls straight," Gleason said. "The next day Paul came to me with fifty bucks in pennies—five thousand of them!"

Gleason told me he thought Newman was a "real trouper" in *The Hustler*. "I didn't agree with everything he wanted to do, but he knew what he was doin' most of the time." Although Gleason was one of the stars of the picture, his role as Minnesota Fats was actually rather small, and he knew it was Paul's picture, even if he'd never admit it. Newman had no real problem with Ralph Kramden, but George C. Scott could have done without "the Great One": Gleason kept inviting him out for a few rounds, never realizing that Scott had a drinking problem.

Newman received an Academy Award nomination for his work in *The Hustler*. When Maximilian Schell won for *Judgment at Nuremburg*, Joanne's behavior backstage was shockingly gauche and childish. She refused to congratulate or even speak to Schell and, in her own words, "made a spectacle of [herself]," crying and cursing and rudely denouncing the Academy and the voters. Many of the other winners thought her behavior unbelievably tacky.

When Joan Crawford heard about it, she thought the woman who had been named after her had more serious problems than just bad fashion sense. "Does she think anyone in Hollywood is going to hire her?" she asked me. "She's *ugly* on top of everything else." Woodward only succeeded in cementing her image as Miss Bitch to those who didn't like her already and caused people to speculate even more about her marriage to Newman.

Many in Hollywood felt sorry for Newman, and not because he had lost another Oscar. "The impression was that Paul was a basically nice guy who was run around by the nose by his bitch of a wife," one observer commented. "Did Paul ever really ask or demand that she sublimate her career or needs in favor of his? Paul was just as disappointed, more so, when he lost the award to Schell, but he was *gracious*, he didn't carry on. I think Joanne embarrassed him terribly that night." Some sources say that the couple had a very bad fight when it was all over.

Jack Garfein, a television director that Newman had met at the Actors Studio, kept plying Paul with scripts until one piqued Newman's interest, a film adaptation of John Hershey's *The Wall*, a powerful book on the Warsaw ghetto. David O. Selznick had wanted to do it but thought a miscast Jennifer Jones would be perfect as the heroine. Garfein and Newman tried producer after producer and were shocked at how many of them, Jews themselves, wanted absolutely nothing to do with what would have been a powerful and important project, the *Schindler's List* of its day, perhaps. *The Wall* was never made.

Newman's next 1961 film project was *Paris Blues*, in which he was again teamed with wife Joanne. Newman and Sidney Poitier played expatriate jazz musicians in Paris who become involved with tourists Woodward and Diahann Carroll. In Harold Flender's novel, there was only the black couple, but Hollywood had to add a couple of whites or it was no sailing. The Newmans were attracted by the social consciousness of the piece, although the film has dated badly. It might have held up more if Newman had been teamed with Carroll and Woodward with Poitier, but that would have been too much for audiences in 1961.

The Newmans were happy to be working with Martin Ritt, who had helmed *The Long Hot Summer* and *No Down Payment* (in which Woodward appeared sans Newman). Ritt was to work with Paul many more times over the years. Woodward and Newman took a little place in Montmartre and, when they weren't working, explored all the jazz clubs and little hidey-holes of the city, enjoying the experience a lot more than they had the last time they'd gone on a location vacation.

Carroll and Poitier were having an affair at the time and were often preoccupied. Newman and Woodward, though only married for a couple of years, couldn't possibly generate the other couple's passionate heat, but Joanne undoubtedly took every possible advantage of romantic Paris to get hubby alone and in the mood.

Everyone was having such a good time that no one noticed the characters and story of *Paris Blues* were perhaps lacking all their dimensions, despite three screenwriters. Another script doctor was flown in, but once he got to Paris, he got into the spirit of things and spent most of his time touring the bars and getting polluted, swearing the script was a mess, that they should scratch it entirely and start over.

In the story of *Paris Blues*, Carroll tries to get Poitier to fight for black and white rights and integration, but he's too bitter to hear her. Actually, the most intriguing scene occurs at a party when an addict Newman's character has helped throws a tantrum about Newman "and your woman," as if he has "special feelings" for Paul's character, but this bit goes completely unexplored. *Paris Blues* is not a great picture by any means, but it is moody and interesting and has a surprisingly unromantic and unhappy windup. Jazz fans were undoubtedly happy with the musical score.

The whole thing was under the auspices of a production company, Pennebaker, set up by the one and only Marlon Brando, who was too occupied with other matters to push his—at that time, not *too* considerable—weight around.

Paul began filming the adaptation of *Sweet Bird of Youth* a short while afterward. His involvement with the project had begun back in 1959 when he starred in the stage play at Williams's request. (The play was sold to the movies even before it opened on Broadway; Newman's participation was undoubtedly a factor.)

His co-star in the theater production was Geraldine Page. She didn't want to play fading film star Alexandra Del Lago because she was afraid she'd overact and come off as grotesque. For another thing, she felt there were probably too many Alexandra Del Lago's around as it was, and she wasn't crazy about the idea of playing a has-been.

Nevertheless Williams and stage director Elia Kazan convinced her she'd be perfect. All was settled. The night of the first rehearsal at the Martin Beck Theater, things were going smoothly when halfway through Williams jumped out of his seat screaming, "Stop! Stop! It can't go on! It's too awful!" He ran out of the theater and into Times Square.

Newman, Page, and the other actors were stunned. Surely they hadn't been that bad. But Kazan assured them that he would get to the bottom of it, that Tennessee was often insecure about his own work and had probably been referring to the play itself, not to their performances. This was the case, as it turned out.

Williams needn't have worried: *Sweet Bird of Youth* was one of his finest plays. Newman played the role of Chance Wayne, a young hustler who yearns desperately to succeed at something but realizes his time is running out; he's getting older and going nowhere. He's hooked up with Alexandra Del Lago, who has been on the run ever since she saw what she thought was a disastrous preview of her latest picture. The two have driven to the Southern town Chance comes from. Del Lago checks into the hotel with Chance under the nom de plume of the Princess Kosmonopolis. Chance hopes to have a reunion with the pretty gal he left behind, who he infected with venereal disease, but her brother and father make it clear that if he doesn't get out of town, he'll be castrated. At the chilling end of the play, he is, right after his climactic line: "I don't ask for your pity, but just for your understanding—not even that—no. Just for your recognition of me in you, and the enemy, time, in us all."

Kazan did have one problem with the play: the main characters, Chance and Alexandra, didn't have enough to do in the second act; in fact, the princess was never even seen. Boss Finley, the father of the girl Chance infected, seems to take over the play even though he's only referred to in act one. Kazan's solution was to make Finley's presence felt more strongly and make it clear how much power he has over his family, the community, and Newman, by projecting his image on a big television screen in the background even as the actor playing Boss Finley addressed the audience in the foreground.

Newman's Oscar nomination for *Cat* was announced during rehearsals, and Kazan knew he had a problem. Newman was a major Hollywood star, someone whose path to the top

had been relatively fast and painless, but he was playing someone completely on the other end of the spectrum, a Paul
Newman who might have existed had he not had contacts,
lucky breaks, money, and the other things that helped him
along the way. Chance Wayne was only one of thousands of
good-looking guys who thought he could make it in
Hollywood just like Paul Newman, if he only got the chance.
How could Kazan subdue the winner, movie star Paul
Newman, and bring out the Newman that might have been?

As rehearsals proceeded, Kazan kept telling Newman to
try a line or a scene again. He was never satisfied, never gave
him a compliment. No matter what Geraldine Page did, even
if she was a little off, Kazan would tell her she was great. After
nearly three weeks of this, Newman was feeling a little more
like Chance Wayne. But there's more to it than that. Kazan
knew Newman needed more direction than the more gifted
Page did; she would work through whatever initial mistakes
she made by herself. Newman later admitted that he relied
on Kazan to guide him and to essentially shape his whole
performance. "Kazan did his best to keep me off balance,
because the character was off balance," Newman said many
decades later.

Kazan's stripping away of Newman's confidence worked
better than he realized. At the time Newman said in an interview, "There's always that terrible fear that one day your fraud
will be discovered and you'll be back in the dog kennel business." Or washing balls at the golf range. Newman knew deep
down that if life had been a little different for him, he might
well have ended up like Chance Wayne, albeit with his man-
hood hopefully intact. He added, "You know you'll get the
hell knocked out of you once in awhile here, but if you don't
you'll fall back on a lot of successful mannerisms." Kazan did
his best to rid Newman of those mannerisms that were inappropriate to the character.

When I interviewed Newman in his dressing room during the run of the play in 1959, he complained about autograph hounds and celebrity chasers and the nosy press. I made so bold as to remind him all that went with being a public person, that if he hadn't accepted that fact he should have chosen a profession out of the public eye. What about all of the Chance Waynes of the world who were never lucky enough to make it? Would Newman have preferred failure and poverty, and wasn't some autograph signing and all the rest a small price to pay for such major success? This seemed to give him pause for awhile, but he abruptly changed the subject.

Newman admitted he never got some areas of Chance Wayne, such as, as he put it, "the aspect of the male whore." Chance Wayne was essentially a male prostitute, his characterization culled from many that Williams had met and even hired over the years. The irony was that Newman, like most ambitious actors, was not above using his charm and looks to get something out of contacts and should have understood that this was a form of hustling, something he had in common with Chance, even if he'd never gone to bed with anyone for money.

Richard Anderson, who'd appeared with Paul in *Long Hot Summer,* was appearing in *The Highest Tree* on Broadway at the same time and compared notes with Newman on occasion. "He revealed acting wasn't his first choice," Anderson said. "He was really an organization man. Explaining further, he wanted to be attached to the nuts and bolts of the game. Surprised me . . . most actors have other plans." Apparently even as early as 1959, Newman was thinking of branching out into directing and even other non-acting business pursuits, although it would be some time before any of his vague plans came to fruition.

For the time being, he was doing all right as an actor.

Sweet Bird of Youth got wonderful reviews, as did his performance for the most part.

When work began on the film adaptation of the play, it was no surprise that Richard Brooks, who'd helmed *Cat on a Hot Tin Roof*, was behind the camera. He quickly realized that there was more censurable material in *Sweet Bird* than there had been in *Cat*. The main problem was the ending. Although Chance's castration was never actually shown on stage, and needn't be on camera, even the suggestion of it was much too raw. Furthermore, Heavenly Finley, Chance's old girlfriend, could be knocked up by him but definitely *not* infected with venereal disease.

Brooks, who wrote the screenplay, came up with a new ending, in which Chance has his face smashed by his enemies but gets to go off with Heavenly as her Aunt Nonnie (Mildred Natwick) tells Boss Finley (Ed Begley) to "go straight to hell." It's decidedly a cop-out but effective enough as it plays in the movie. Brooks also had an alternate idea, which he felt was closer to the spirit of the play and wanted to film, only to have the studio shut down production before he could. In this ending, Alexandra Del Lago and Boss Finley's ex-mistress would be riding a ferry out of town when they pass by a garbage scow where Chance has been dumped after being beaten by Finley's son and his buddies.

Although Williams and many others felt Brooks had emasculated the play, he did the best he could working within the confines of the production code. Williams himself had changed the ending for a revised acting edition of the play for nonprofessionals in which Chance, his bodily organs intact, leaves town with Alexandra, so the criticism heaped upon Brooks at the time may have been a bit unfair.

In the film, which of course was a quite different experience from the stage play even without the censor-mandated changes, Newman comes off as too theatrical and, at thirty-six, too old for the part (even considering that Chance is not in the first bloom of youth). Although he does have his moments, Newman clung for dear life to the performance Kazan got out of him and was too afraid to let go and lighten up, so to speak, for the camera and the close-up. As also noted, certain of his effects play better on stage at a distance than they do on film. To be fair, Brooks wasn't able to get much more than surface emotion from a lot of the other performers, either, good as they are. Geraldine Page comes off best, at times reaching below the surface histrionics to expand upon her undeniably grotesque characterization. But too many scenes in the picture don't ring true, although Williams's dialogue is still incisive and brilliant and the relationships between Chance and the princess is interestingly dissected. In any case, Brooks's version is miles ahead of a dreadful 1989 remake starring Liz Taylor as Del Lago and the less-than-impressive Mark Harmon as Chance.

Geraldine Page told me that Newman "kept me on my toes, all right. We worked together on both stage and film versions and I got to know every trick he had—and he knew every trick in the book. He upstaged me at times, but later I realized he had enhanced my performance as well as his own."

Newman received $350,000 to appear in the film version of *Sweet Bird of Youth,* a far cry indeed from his days at Warner.

11

THE FURTHER ADVENTURES OF A YOUNG MAN

DETERMINED TO GIVE PAUL AS MANY CHILDREN AS JACKIE had, Joanne was pregnant again. While Paul filmed *Sweet Bird of Youth*, she stayed in their rented Hollywood mansion and took care of little Nell, who was now two, and desperately hoped that this second child would be a boy. Instead she had a second daughter, Melissa, who was born on September 17, 1961.

After filming for *Sweet Bird of Youth* wrapped up, the Newmans thought of taking their brood—which now included two cats in addition to the two Chihuahuas—back East, but not to an apartment. Paul wanted his children, from both marriages, to be out of the crazy spotlight of Hollywood, and he and Joanne—not to mention Jackie—made every effort to shield them from public and journalistic curiosity. Newman may have been a movie star but his kids were not, and he saw no reason why they should be subjected to glaring invasions of privacy.

They bought a house in Connecticut not far from A. E. Hotchner and his wife; Newman had become professional friends with Hotchner after he'd appeared on television in *The Battler*, for which Hotchner wrote the script. Hotchner did not waste time using the proximity to bring further ideas to his famous neighbor. The two men bought a boat and went fishing together, although they drank more beer than they caught fish.

"Paul's friendship with A. E. brought out his worst instincts," claimed one who knew them both. "Hotchner is pathetically locked into this tiresome macho Hemingway shtick and pliable Paul just goes along with it. The two of them together are laughable, two old farts who think that writing and acting are for sissies and they have to act like big *men* to make up for it. They're ridiculous."

Ridiculous or not, Newman's friendship with Hotchner did get him to appear in a small role in a film Hotchner scripted, *Hemingway's Adventures of a Young Man*. Hotchner strung together ten of Hemingway's autobiographical Nick Adams stories, added a bit of the Italian scenes from *A Farewell to Arms*, and got Newman to reprise his role as "the battler" from the teleplay broadcast in the fifties. When Martin Ritt of *Long Hot Summer* and *Paris Blues* was brought in to direct, Newman was sold on it.

Newman's advisers, however, told him he was making a mistake. Acknowledged Hollywood stars simply did not do bit parts. (This was before it became common for stars to appear in small roles sans billing, as Bruce Willis did many years later in Newman's *Nobody's Fool*.) But Newman wanted to do something that didn't trade on his glamorous image after a variety of pretty boy roles like Chance Wayne.

If there was one thing Newman regretted, it was tackling the part of the dissipated middle-aged boxer the same way he had for television, but Newman's insecurity over his acting ensured that he would always repeat what had worked before; it was simply too risky to try a radical approach. In spite of this, he got generally good reviews. One critic noted that "grotesque" parts were, contrary to popular opinion, always easier to do than more subtle characterizations but that Newman went beyond "having a holiday" in the makeup and gave a sincere, genuine performance.

The actual star of the film was Richard Beymer, pre–*West Side Story* and *Twin Peaks*. He had just come off a picture with Joanne Woodward, *The Stripper*, based on William Inge's play *A Loss of Roses*. Beymer got a terrible drubbing for his performance in *Adventures* when it was actually his miscasting that was the problem and not his ability; he was more the sensitive than the macho Hemingway type. Beymer talked in 1962 about his encounters with the Newmans: "Paul was supportive and helpful, and took a kind of older brother interest in my work. Joanne was swell, too. As actors, they're very giving people."

With some time on his hands due to the reduced role he was playing, Newman started getting ideas about politics. In the sixties he spent a lot of time speaking out against nuclear weapons, atomic testing, and the like. Newman felt that because people had made him a movie star, they were therefore interested in what he thought and had to say. It would be irresponsible of him not to speak out on important issues. Unfortunately, Newman and the antibombers of the sixties and later were much more idealistic than realistic about disarmament.

When it came to politicians, Newman had not only gotten involved in JFK's campaign but also supported Lyndon Johnson because he thought Johnson would de-escalate the war in Vietnam. He made many public appearances on Johnson's behalf. One can only imagine how Newman felt when the promised de-escalation failed to materialize.

On one cause his thinking was at least a little more clear, perhaps because it was something closer to him as both a par-

ent and an actor. He argued that it made no sense for the
government to classify movies according to levels of obscenity
because parents who didn't care what their children looked
at, who didn't bother investigating a movie or television show
beforehand, would most likely ignore the classifications anyway. Eventually the movie industry would itself give ratings to
each picture.

Like other guilt-ridden, white, limousine liberals, Paul
and Joanne found themselves caught up in radical chic, when
high-living citizens and members of the social register, who
normally wouldn't have gone within two feet of a picket line,
entertained the likes of the Black Panthers, lesbian feminist
Liberationists, and anti-nukers in their apartments and
salons. Before long, it became a one-upmanship game in
which each hostess would try to have the most outré guest of
the season. Naturally the Newmans had no trouble getting
whichever guests they wanted. They were movie stars, after all.

In the early sixties Newman and a few other actors got
involved in a bit of silliness in Alabama that had real activists
doubled over with laughter. One afternoon Paul got a call
from Marlon Brando, who told him that apparently Martin
Luther King Jr. had been trying to get in touch with him.
According to Brando, King wanted Newman and other movie
stars to come to Alabama to try to somehow calm the racial
unrest. This was, of course, on the same level as having suburban housewives come into Manhattan with buckets and mops
to scrub the dirty floors and walls of Lower East Side tene-
ments—an empty cosmetic treatment that left completely
untouched the very real problems beneath the surface.

So Newman, accompanied by Brando, Tony Franciosa
(his *Long Hot Summer* co-star), and a few others, marched in
Alabama—and were completely ignored. Then as now, real
people may want movie stars' autographs, they may want to
know who they're sleeping with or even sleep with them
themselves, but that doesn't mean people actually think stars

have some magical power or the infinite wisdom to heal centuries of misunderstandings. Why should the poor blacks and whites of Alabama have listened to multimillionaires like Newman and Brando? They flew out of Alabama with egg on their faces. One can imagine Newman turning to Brando and intoning, "This is another fine mess you've gotten me into."

Admirably, Newman later participated in sit-ins and took part in the famous march on Washington for civil rights. Would he have refused Martin Luther King Jr. an autograph?

Newman was more at home on the movie set than in occupying government buildings, so soon he was caught up in making *Hud* with Patricia Neal and Melvyn Douglas. Since Newman liked the director—again it was Martin Ritt—and since he had always enjoyed working with Ritt, he decided Ritt would make a perfect partner in a production company. They took the second syllable of Ritt's wife's name and the first syllable of Joanne's and came up with Jodell Productions. They made a deal with the studios in which Ritt would have to direct two out of three films, Newman would star in two out of the three and both must produce the third without necessarily being creatively involved, which was how it worked.

The scriptwriters for *Hud* were the same team that had concocted *The Long Hot Summer*, Harriet Frank and Irving Ravetch. This time they were working from the literary source of Larry McMurtry's novel *Horseman, Pass By*. Ritt had noted that in many movies of the golden era, the hero could be a complete louse throughout most of the movie as long as he somehow demonstrated his essential decency before the fade out. Even Eddie Felson of *The Hustler*, although not a louse per se, showed his basic humanity in his reaction to his girlfriend's suicide. But Ritt wanted to make a more realistic film in which the no-goodnik remains a stinker to the end. Hud was actually a minor character in the novel, but he became the antihero of the film adaptation.

Hud, the no-good bastard son of rancher Melvyn

Douglas, alienates everyone who cares for him including his nephew (Brandon de Wilde), who looks up to him; his father, who is appalled that Hud wants to go ahead and sell cattle that he knows are infected; and the attractive housekeeper (Patricia Neal), whom he tries to assault. Hud thinks of no one but himself, and the film points out—ahead of its time— the danger in blindly idolizing the callous and cold-blooded antiheroes who would pop up in more and more films as the sixties gave way to the seventies.

However, with some audiences *Hud* ran into a variation of the same trouble that *Picnic* did; that is, people had thought that the protagonist of *Picnic* was being presented to them as a completely admirable character. With *Hud*, some viewers also thought Hud was supposed to be admirable and reacted to positively. Years later, Newman would blame himself and Ritt and the writers for "screwing up." Countering, Ritt would point out that it wasn't their fault if the cynicism that would eventually lead to the emergence of the drug culture in this country had changed values so completely that kids wrongly saw Hud as a hero.

The trouble is that Hud is not just a sexy rascal or a guy kicked out of the Boy Scouts or a winking-eyed reprobate who scandalizes the prudish while delighting everyone else; rather, he is the kind of person who will sell diseased cattle to another rancher without telling him. Not only is he unconcerned with the loss the unsuspecting sucker will take, he's not even bothered by the possibility that the disease will spread, causing major problems for everyone. Only an immature or criminal mind would ever find Hud admirable.

Newman did his usual preparation for the role, going down to a ranch in Texas and working as a cowhand for a few days until he was practically bowlegged. He felt the picture illustrated Tennessee Williams's famous quote about "the beautiful making their own laws" and showed just how much the American public would forgive if someone was young and good looking. Deep down, Newman must have suspected that if that was not the case, he would probably never have had a career in pictures. Newman was not a Hud, but he got parts because of his looks that other, less attractive actors could have played the pants off. The poster for *Hud* had Newman posing provocatively in blue jeans and smug attitude.

While filming took place down in Texas, Newman had his hands full with lady fans. There was a junior college near-by, and members of the crew often made dates with the girls and brought them back to the motel for some beer and what-ever else might develop. As soon as the girls found out dreamy Paul Newman was staying at the same motel, the crew members found themselves dateless. Newman would step out of the shower wrapped in nothing but a towel, if that much, and look up to see girls trying to squeeze in through the transom over his door. Love notes written in lipstick were scrawled all over the walls outside, along with lip prints, and some girls even left their panties or sanitary napkins for him to autograph if he felt like it. Newman was afraid to walk out his door without an armed escort. Crew members fumed that he could have had all the women he wanted and he wasn't even interested.

One night Newman was in the middle of a sound sleep when he heard a frantic banging on his door. The first thing that went through his mind was that something terrible might have happened to his wife and family. The banging continued as he pulled up his pants and went to the door, suspecting now that some emergency elsewhere in the motel required his attention. He opened the door to be confronted by a drunken coed who, squealing, tried to throw her arms around him before he slammed the door in her face and started hollering in exasperation. As he tried to go back to sleep, she continued knocking on the door for another ten minutes before leaving, passing out, or returning to the crew members who'd brought her. This sort of thing repeated itself throughout the shoot.

When reports of this activity got back to Joanne, she was not happy about it and threatened to fly down to Texas and slap some sense into those college girls if it was necessary. Thoughts of Paul surrounded by nubile, adoring beauties did not exactly give her pleasant dreams. She tried to put it out of her mind and concentrate on the children, but it wasn't easy, the price one had to pay for marrying a hunk.

Patricia Neal, who played Alma, the housekeeper, re-called a disturbing incident that happened one Sunday after-noon early in the shoot. She and Newman had not yet had any big scenes together and were possibly discussing the work they'd be doing the following day as they sat by the motel's swimming pool. Shortly before filming had begun, Neal's daughter Olivia had died from measles at age seven. Neal started telling Paul all about her daughter and how much she had meant to her. Neal wondered why her sisters-in-law hadn't let her see her daughter right after she died, and if she shouldn't have taken more of a stand on the mat-ter. She asked Paul what he thought, but he didn't answer. He just stared at her a moment before saying "tough" and striding away.

Neal was stunned. She couldn't believe she could pour out her heart to someone and have him show such utter dis-regard for her feelings. She made up her mind never to talk so intimately to Newman again, and the filming proceeded.

Thereafter she found Newman completely professional and enjoyed working with him but noted that he was in char-acter all the time: "I began to realize that although I had poured out my heart to Paul Newman, it was Hud Bannon who had responded." Newman was always courteous and kindhearted to her in their later dealings.

Nevertheless, Newman was carrying Method acting a little too far when he responded to Neal as Hud Bannon would. In all likelihood, Newman was embarrassed by her outcries of grief and emotion.

Newman has always had trouble expressing feelings, except in character, which was part of the problem in his relationship with his only son, who died tragically many years later. Neal knew just what Newman was going through when Scott Newman died, but she wouldn't have been human had a little part of her not thought "now you know what it's like."

Some feel Newman gets along with Joanne better than he did with Jackie because his second wife is as cool and unemotional as he is, though the few times Joanne breaks out of this reserve—such as backstage at the Oscars—Paul is at a loss as to how to react to her in addition to being mortified. Newman has personality to spare; he loves practical jokes, having good times with his buddies, and lots of beer, but this does not mean he is *emotional* or in touch with his feelings.

On location for *Hud* Newman made friends with young Brandon de Wilde, a handsome kid of sixteen at the time. The two would go off at night and, as Pat Neal put it, "tear around the small Texas town, much the way their characters did." Newman knew Joanne could hardly object if he spent time with de Wilde, but Neal was a little too sexy.

One afternoon Neal and Newman were shooting a scene when Hud starts fondling Alma and nuzzling her neck as she's trying to get some work done. Neal was distracted by a humongous horsefly creeping up the screen on the porch and, without thinking about it, grabbed a dish towel to snap the fly into the next world while delivering her withering line about what "a cold-blooded bastard" Hud was. "Terrific!" Martin Ritt shouted. "The bit with the fly was great!" The take—and fly—didn't make it into the finished film, however.

Melvyn Douglas also enjoyed working with Newman. As

he told me, "He's a more gifted actor than he admits even to himself. Everyone says Joanne is better, but Paul makes the absolute most of what he has, believe me. Playing with him was a pretty lively experience."

Newman was nominated for another Oscar for Best Actor in *Hud*. Once again he lost, although Pat Neal and Douglas picked up Best Supporting Oscar statuettes. Since Sidney Poitier, co-star from *Paris Blues*, won the Best Actor award for his performance in *Lilies of the Field*, Woodward kept her mouth shut. At the time people thought Newman had lost out because he dared to take on Jack Warner, the Hollywood hierarchy, and the whole studio system, and go it alone, but time had not been kind to his performance. To be frank, he didn't deserve an Oscar for *Hud*.

The movie has serious problems. In spite of some good scenes, the film never really develops into anything deep or profoundly moving; a lot of it seems phony and contrived. As usual, Martin Ritt's direction is adroit, better than usual in fact, but it never even aspires to the poetic. Newman has his moments, but he doesn't really have the range to make his portrayal work and is easily out-acted by virtually every other performer, including Yvette *"Attack of the Fifty-Foot Woman"* Vickers, who has a small part as a married woman Hud dates and who appears in a brief scene in a soda shop.

After *Hud*, Joanne felt like working again and wanted to do another picture with Paul. Out of the piles of scripts they received, she settled on one called *A New Kind of Love*, another comedy. Obviously at this point she had not yet come to despise her performance in their last comedic outing, *Rally 'Round the Flag, Boys*, or she might have shown better judgment. In the 1963 *A New Kind of Love*, she plays a dowdy fashion buyer who transforms herself into an exciting blonde after hitting a Parisian beauty parlor. At one point she is mistaken for a prostitute by Newman's character, a columnist, who knows the dowdy version of her character but doesn't recognize the made-over gal.

Just as Newman wanted to ditch his glamorous image, Woodward wanted to create one for herself. Although she didn't really look that much better after the big transformation, she could imagine she was sexy. Paul didn't want to do the picture. He knew it would be fun for her, but all he did was react to her silly antics and occasionally throw out a gag line.

Joanne went into a snit when he informed her he wanted no part of *A New Kind of Love.* She told him that she spent most of her time watching the children—this included Jackie's kids, who often came to visit—trailing after him when he went on location overseas no matter what her own plans might have been. She wanted to have a good time and make a decision in their lives for a change, and he had damn well better do the picture *or else.* Afterward, she would come to regret Paul's hasty compliance, but at the time she was glad to see that she had won her point.

At the helm was a triple-threat Melville Shavelson, who produced, directed, and even wrote the thing, but no matter what trick he tried, *A New Kind of Love* was an instant dog. Frank Sinatra was hired to sing the title tune, there were camera tricks and sight gags to spare, but the plot and the parties involved made it all wasted effort.

The story has Newman sent to his newspaper's Paris bureau because the publisher has caught Newman with his wife. Newman and Woodward meet on the plane and immediately take a dislike to each other. Then comes the miracle transformation, and Woodward lets Newman think she's a high-class hooker so that he can write about her and beef up his circulation. Eventually the masquerade is ended, and the two fall in love.

As was the case with the earlier *Rally,* the Newmans are

not suited for the picture at all. Supporting players Thelma Ritter, George Tobias, and even Eva Gabor have to supply the laughs. Reportedly a slight contretemps between sexy Eva and the not-so-sexy Woodward occurred.

"You have such a *handsome* husband," Eva said to Joanne.

"Yes, I do have a handsome *husband*," Joanne replied. "Please remember that."

When asked by someone what she thought of the film and the Newmans, Eva reportedly replied: "He's a doll. She's a bitch." Other women would essentially make the same statement over the years.

Ernest Lehman, who had written the fine script for *Somebody Up There Likes Me* (and the lesser one for *From the Terrace*), had a new story he thought Paul would be interested in, a comedy-thriller entitled *The Prize*. With this script, Lehman was hoping to create another *North by Northwest*, the brilliant thriller he had penned for Hitchcock. He even fashioned a scene that was to go one better than the sequence in *Northwest* in which Cary Grant evades pursuers by causing a scene at a fancy auction house. In the new scene, Newman, clad only in a towel, would heckle a speaker at a nudist colony. The plot had him embroiled in intrigue during the ceremonies in Stockholm. Unfortunately, director Mark Robson, also of *From the Terrace*, was no Hitchcock.

Newman wanted to wear a beard for the picture—he'd look less pretty and more masculine, not to mention more like a Nobel prize winning author—but producer Pandro Berman, who always kept actors in line, would have none of it. He had hired Paul Newman, and he wanted Paul Newman, the one the public knew and without any facial hair, and that was that. Unlike his stance with Jack Warner, Newman figured this really wasn't worth the battle and shaved the beard.

The Swedes thought the whole production cheapened the Nobel prizes, but worse, it was simply a bad picture.

Robson couldn't fashion convincing action sequences, and—unlike *North by Northwest*—the comedy of *The Prize* dissipated the suspense.

The most memorable thing about the movie is a line from pert Elke Sommer that is sort of an answer to Newman's "why go out for hamburger when I've got steak at home" quote. Looking Newman up and down as if he were a meatball, Elke says, "Why settle for one dish, when there's smorgasbord?"

Paul did get to wear a beard, albeit a costume one, in his next film, *What a Way to Go*, in which he was one of several male guest stars teamed with Shirley MacLaine. Newman is her second husband (out of five), a taxi driver in Paris who wants to become an artist and succeeds when he invents a machine that turns sound waves into paintings. Feeding classical music into the machine creates a masterpiece that makes Newman wealthy and famous, but he gets caught in the complicated works of the gizmo and dies.

The other husbands were played by Dick Van Dyke, Robert Mitchum, and Gene Kelly, with Dean Martin along for the ride as an early beau and final husband. With each husband, who survives poverty but not wealth, the widow MacLaine gets richer.

Newman is better in this film than expected, although still hardly a great comic actor. His performance seems to match the broad conception of the character in the farcical screenplay by Betty Comden and Adolph Green. A light touch—which he could rarely manage—wasn't required. A lot of the critics were charmed by him in this. But, despite a lot of songs and brilliant cinemascope, the picture itself did not do that well with reviewers or the public.

According to MacLaine, Newman "is a pleasant but reticent friend. In real life, I always had the feeling he wished he were somewhere else—probably racing cars." Shirley was amused by his Method acting approach. One day he said, "I need to know whether my character makes love with his boots on or not." Shirley told him he probably made love *to* his boots. After that, "we got the scene." MacLaine deemed Newman "a man who has survived all the pitfalls of Hollywood."

Next Martin Ritt came up with the idea of doing an Americanized version of Akira Kurosawa's *Rashomon*, which had been made into an English-language play with its original Japanese setting in 1959. Michael Kanin, who had written the play with his wife, Fay, changed the setting to Mexico for the screen version. The producer, A. Ronald Lubin, sent the script to Newman, who rejected it. "Maybe Brando would be interested in it," he told Lubin. "It's not right for me."

Lubin went after Brando, who loved the script and wanted to do the picture but was unable to make a commitment. The starting date for the picture was rapidly approaching, and Lubin happened to mention his problem to Newman. Suddenly, when Paul heard how much Brando admired Kanin's screenplay, he decided he would do the picture after all. Apparently Newman had never forgotten all the times he'd been compared to Brando and gotten the short end of the stick. He would prove he could do Brando as well as Marlon himself, if not better. Unfortunately, it didn't quite work out that way.

The story of *Rashomon* and *The Outrage* has to do with a husband and wife who are beset by a bandit who rapes the wife and murders the husband. Or is that really what happened? Each witness, including the wife herself, has a different story to tell. *Rashomon* has a rather open-ended conclusion while *The Outrage* makes the solution clearer.

Rod Steiger had played the part of the bandit on the stage, but now it was Newman's turn. As usual, he went on the road to Mexico to "do research," to listen to and try to recreate the right accent, and so on, but whether this field trip was really any more than an excuse to soak up lots of spirits in local cantinas is debatable. In any case, Newman decked himself out in a mustache, wig, neatly trimmed beard, and plenty of dark brown skin toner, and laid on an accent as thick as molasses and peanut butter on sourdough bread.

Newman is rather vivid—if not exactly great—in the picture, but the critics for the most part were merciless, crying "caricature" more often than not. Newman had tried hard to break out of himself and evoke someone who was so far from Paul Newman that Rocky and Eddie Felson would have seemed like clones in comparison, but it didn't quite work. He was not a character actor, at least not yet. Whether the overrated Marlon Brando would have been any better in the part is debatable, however. Edward G. Robinson, who'd had supporting parts in both *The Prize* and *The Outrage*, did think Newman was "a real scene stealer" and more of a star personality than an actor.

Newman gave it the old college try, at least, and has to be given points for that if nothing else.

12

A HITCH IN PLANS

WITH ONE BAD MOVIE CHOICE AFTER ANOTHER—ALTHOUGH *The Prize* at least made money—Paul and Joanne decided in 1964 that it might be time to get back to their roots and try the theater again.

To raise money for their operating expenses, the Actors Studio had started their own theater company and had already presented such plays as *Strange Interlude.* None of their plays had managed to break even let alone make a profit. When Newman told Lee Strasberg that he and Joanne were interested in doing something for the Studio and that they'd work for scale ($117.50 a week instead of the maximum $1000 that stars of their caliber were entitled to), Strasberg was ecstatic. Geraldine Page, who was heavily involved with the Studio at the time, suggested that a light comedy like *Any Wednesday* might be the perfect commercial choice, but Newman would have none of it because they had another vehicle in mind.

Joanne had stayed friends with most of her ex-fiancés, one of whom was playwright James Costigan. He had concocted a frothy, cynical piece entitled *Baby Want a Kiss*, which he took to Joanne with the suggestion that she appear in it. Joanne took it to Paul, who had reservations but again gave in to his wife's demands just as he had with *A New Kind of Love*. Joanne saw potential in the material and thought it would be fun, and she was all for doing a friend (whom she had once used outrageously) a favor. The Newmans were to play a married movie star couple—quite a stretch—who secretly hated each other and were as phony as ten-dollar toupees.

Many felt that Costigan was quite the sly one when he got the Newmans to appear in his play. Not only were the characters monstrous egomaniacs, but the husband was also a closet queen. It was as if Costigan were getting revenge on the two of them for events that had happened years before. Costigan cast himself in the third role, a down-on-his-luck writer friend on whom the famous movie star couple make a patronizing call. As the play proceeds, first the wife and then the husband make a pass at Costigan, both of them needing reaffirmation of their attractiveness since they've gotten insecure in middle age. (Actually both Newman and Woodward were a little young for the roles.)

The homosexual scene was a particularly lengthy one; one critic noted that during this scene Newman was "like an actor who has wandered into the wrong theater" while others thought it was a comical travesty of Brick from *Cat on a Hot Tin Roof.*

Frank Corsaro was brought in to direct the play and found it to be an unhappy experience. Like many, he felt it was not a good choice for the Actors Studio Theater, and he was irritated by Costigan's refusal to make any changes in the script. The play had possibilities, but it had no real ending. Corsaro spent his time working to help Newman create a convincing comic performance and, to a large degree, succeeded. Newman and Joanne both got good reviews, but the play was decimated by the critics when it opened off Broadway at the Little Theater in mid-April.

But the play had even more serious repercussions. Strasberg had been so anxious to raise money for the Studio that he hadn't given serious thought to what it would look like to offer a weak, glossy star vehicle to the public instead of the serious theater people expected from the prestigious Actors Studio. He'd thought the curse would be taken off *Baby* by presenting it almost concurrently with the worthier James Baldwin play *Blues for Mr. Charlie*, but the Baldwin piece only underlined the frothy mindlessness of the other play in people's minds.

Baby Want a Kiss did manage to make money for the Studio, but it did more harm than good. The Ford Foundation, which had given generous donations to Strasberg in the past, lessened its commitment to the studio. If bad plays bolstered by the participation of movie stars and featuring essentially superficial performances and substandard characterizations were to premiere under the auspices of the Actors Studio, what did that say about the Studio's commitment to art and great acting? Geraldine Page, who'd appeared in the formidable *Sweet Bird of Youth* with Newman, wasted no words in her opinion of *Baby Want a Kiss*. "I hated it!" she said. If nothing else, *Baby* proved what outright damage connections could do.

Around this time the Newmans went to New York harbor to bid bon voyage to their friend Gore Vidal, who was leaving on a cruise to the Mediterranean. He would link up with his friend Howard Austen in Palermo. As he sat alone at dinner in the cavernous dining room of the *Leonardo da Vinci*, he suddenly looked up and saw Paul and Joanne heading toward his table. At first he assumed that they must have failed to get off the boat before it set sail, but then he learned that at the last minute they'd decided to join him on the cruise. Apparently when it comes to double-dating—or taking cruises—Paul and Joanne's favorite fun couple were Gore and Howard. It practically turned into a second honeymoon.

In his next film venture, Newman was teamed with the voluptuous Sophia Loren in another comedy, entitled *Lady L* (1965), based on the Romaine Gary novel. George Cukor had actually begun filming this some years before with Tony Curtis and another Italian bombshell, Gina Lollobrigida, in the leads, but the project was shelved for one reason or another. Then some bigwig got the bright idea of teaming Newman and Loren in—of all things—a film adaptation of *After the Fall*, which explored playwright Arthur Miller's relationship with Marilyn Monroe. Saner heads prevailed, relatively speaking. The *Lady L* script was dusted off and handed to writer-director Peter Ustinov for revisions, and Newman and Loren were drafted to take over for Curtis and Lollobrigida. Newman was no longer an indentured servant to the studios and could pick and choose his own scripts, so one wonders why he ever thought *Lady L* would be appropriate for him. Perhaps, like most men, he wanted to work in close quarters with Loren at her loveliest. Newman, after all, became an old man of forty while making this film.

Newman plays a revolutionary and Loren a laundress. The convolutions of the plot have her marrying a lord (David Niven) in exchange for saving her lover (Newman) from the authorities. As the years go by, Niven allows Loren's relationship with Newman to continue. Many years later she is a widow whose aristocratic children have all actually been sired by Newman, who is now her chauffeur. A few laughs were squeezed out of these situations, and the picture was cute, but no one's career was advanced in the slightest.

Peter Ustinov once gave an interviewer this interesting observation about Newman: "He's overly cerebral about a role . . . a superb actor who has yet to hit his zenith. I believe Paul's true destiny is behind the camera, as a director. There he will have all the room he needs to buttress his intelligence with his instinct." If ever there was a double-edged compliment, this was it. Ustinov tactfully dismissed Newman as an actor while mapping out his future direction with uncanny prescience.

David Niven told me some years after making the film, "The picture turned out rather unfortunately. Paul seemed as downed by it as the rest of us. I think he was at his weakest in it—the material just wasn't there." With consummate humility, he then added: "But then we were all terrible in it."

The release of the picture was delayed for one year while the studio hoped Newman would have a hit picture, after which they could sneak *Lady L* in and hope to benefit from the hit film's publicity. This is exactly what happened. But even riding on the coattails of Newman's next film, *Harper*, which did exceedingly well at the box office, *Lady L* hardly registered record grosses. At least Newman got to go to Paris again for some location shooting.

Harper had its genesis in a novel entitled *The Moving Target*, the first of a series of mostly excellent mystery novels by Ross MacDonald, which featured private eye Lew Archer. Because Newman had had such success with previous *h* films, *The Hustler* and *Hud*, the character and the film were rechristened Lew Harper. Frank Sinatra was actually the first choice for the role; he wound up playing another private eye, *Tony Rome*, the following year.

One of the *Harper* producers, Elliot Kastner, flew to Paris with the director to meet with Newman while he filmed *Lady L*. Newman liked the script, but the director mentioned that he thought otherwise and wanted the script rewritten. Since Newman meant more to the film than the director did, Kastner fired him and brought in Jack Smight to helm the picture. The script was by a neophyte who had published a novel or two, William Goldman, later to be known as one of Hollywood's premier screenwriters. He was told he had better make the minor revisions Newman wanted, to his specifications, or they would find another writer. If Newman was more important than the director, he was certainly more important than a mere writer. Goldman came through and the success of *Harper* put him on the map.

To hedge their bets, the producers also hired Lauren Bacall, widow of Humphrey Bogart, who portrayed Raymond Chandler's Phillip Marlowe on the screen (Chandler was a big influence on MacDonald). Bacall played Harper's client. Joanne's old co-star from *A Kiss Before Dying*, Robert Wagner, was given a role, and pretty Pamela Tiffin was brought in as cheesecake.

Newman was returning to his old studio, Warner, to make the picture, but this time he was getting $750,000 against 10 percent of the gross, a big difference from the comparatively paltry salary he'd received as a contract player. He was still considered a big box-office attraction—*Harper*'s success would only add to his rating—despite the fact that several of his recent pictures hadn't made much money.

In fact, in his fortieth year, this weighed on his mind more than one might imagine. He did not consider himself wealthy. With five kids to support and another on the way, not to mention a wife and an ex, there was a lot of money going out. Newman was afraid he'd wake up and find all that he'd achieved taken away from him. "It isn't just the money," he told an interviewer, "but the fact that I've become accustomed to a certain kind of living and recognition that may be totally destroyed. I worry so much that I'm lucky if I get five hours sleep at night—even between films."

Newman worried about becoming a has-been as he got older primarily because he knew a lot of his success was due to simple good looks and good genes, and he was smart enough to know that such success could be stripped away by a stroke of fate as easily as it had been acquired. The Newman Luck did stand by him until he had become an icon, too famous and too well liked and too firmly entrenched in the national consciousness to ever be completely ignored by a public always wanting the new flavor of the month. But if a wealthy (by most standards) movie star like Newman would toss and turn at night with worry, how would he ever manage to deal with failure or ugliness or disease or disappointment or the things that most human beings go through?

Harper must have done a lot to shore up his flagging spirits because the film's publicity people promoted him not just as a tough private eye but also as a sex symbol, something they never did with the homely Bogie. Jack Warner even came down to the soundstage to greet Newman with—what else?—a smile and a handshake. Paul had a photo taken of the historic meeting and sent it out on his Christmas cards that year. One can only imagine the look on Jack's face when he got his.

Shooting the picture went along smoothly under the direction of the workmanlike, if hardly ultra-talented, Jack Smight, a director who barely leaves a personal imprint upon a picture. Goldman's script followed the basic story line of the novel—a woman hires Archer/Harper to find her missing millionaire husband, and he encounters strange characters at every step. Goldman did put skewered twists on things when he could. For instance, in the novel the sexy young Pamela Tiffin character puts the moves on and smooches with Lew Archer, but in the film the blowsy Shelley Winters flirts with and plants a big smack on Harper. Goldman also scripted some hilariously bitchy interchanges between Lauren Bacall as the wife and Pamela Tiffin as the stepdaughter. Too bad he couldn't have added some depth to the many stereotypical situations and characters.

Offscreen Tiffin's encounter with a visiting Joanne Woodward was almost along the lines of her on-screen scenes with Bacall. Tiffin was intimidated by Joanne, who "doesn't have a great sense of humor," as she told one writer. Woodward, now creeping toward middle age, was to be continually threatened by Newman's increasingly beautiful—and ever younger—co-stars. At least she could take some solace in the fact Newman had no love scenes with Tiffin and only got bussed by Winters, who at nearly 220 pounds was certainly no threat to her.

Another cast member's presence may also have given Joanne pause: Paul's first wife. By this time the bad feelings between Paul and Jackie had softened considerably, and Jackie was not above asking Paul if he could get her a small part in the picture; her attempts at building up her own career had not been very successful. Still plagued with guilty feelings over what had happened, Paul acquiesced. In truth, he would have done it sooner in previous films had he not been afraid of Joanne's reaction.

Billed as Jacqueline de Wit, Jackie Witte Newman played the part of a bar owner about midway through the picture. Harper comes into the establishment and starts to talk to the attractive lady in hair curlers. The lady gets flirtatious as he pumps her for information. The bit doesn't last long, but it was better than nothing. Paul and Jackie hadn't acted together since they'd first met in summer stock.

The bit was fun for Jackie on the surface, but one can imagine the deeper emotions that must have been reverberating through her while she was waiting on the set. Few of the people even knew who this extra was or what she had once meant to the big-time movie star who was appearing in the scene with her. According to a friend, "It was a hard time for Jackie. Once she had been closer to Paul than everyone else on the soundstage, but now she was just another one of the people surrounding him, *at* him, asking for things, although who was more entitled than she was? I think her hatred for Joanne, in particular, welled up in her a lot of the time."

Newman had a major hit with *Harper*, but his performance, though breezy and insouciant, left a lot to be desired. He never captured the essence of the character MacDonald had created, although one could argue that he was playing Lew Harper, not Archer. Actors often find a certain key or theme to help their performance, and in *Harper* Newman seems to have chosen smugness. Wearing a kind of bored, superficially cool expression throughout the movie, he never seems remotely real, as Archer is in the novels.

He borrowed one technique from watching Robert Francis Kennedy, which he called "listening sideways"—he would look in another direction from the person who was talking without actually missing a word they were saying. He claimed this was what Bobby did. His adoption of this technique did nothing to enhance his performance but only made him seem inappropriately languid and blasé, something that Bobby Kennedy was decidedly not.

Newman was caught up in intrigue again for his next film, the genesis of which was England's Burgess-MacLean spy case. Alfred Hitchcock, undoubtedly the greatest director Newman ever worked with, wanted to make a picture that would tell the story from the point of view of a Mary Burgess-type character. What was it like to have your husband betray your country and run off with another man on top of it? A gifted novelist, Brian Moore (*The Lonely Passion of Judith Hearne*), was asked to work on the screenplay, which he did because he needed the money.

Moore had daily meetings with Hitchcock where eventually they would get around to discussing the script. Moore found that Hitchcock often had trouble focusing; the story would switch from the wife's to the husband's point of view and back again. But the final blow came when Universal told Hitchcock that he *must* use Newman and Julie Andrews— both of whom were top box-office attractions—whether he liked it or not. He didn't like it.

For one thing, the stars' salaries would take up a huge

chunk—over 20 percent—of the $5 million budget, and Hitchcock did not like using stars in his pictures. While this was attributed to his ego—he was a star in his own right— Hitchcock also knew that powerful stars could be a nuisance with their demands and their attempts to take control of the screenplay and everything else.

There were other problems with the casting of *Torn Curtain*. Newman would not be believable as a Britisher, and apparently Hitchcock felt he wouldn't be believable as a gay because that aspect of the picture was dropped (despite Newman's gay role in *Baby Want a Kiss* and, more or less, in *Cat on a Hot Tin Roof*). Newman may also have used his star power to nix the homosexual subtheme. Apparently he got less, instead of more, comfortable with the idea of playing gay as he got older. (In January 1966 he had turned forty-one.)

Hitchcock was appalled by the decision to use Julie Andrews. He'd wanted to work with singing actress Doris Day in his remake of *The Man who Knew Too Much* and didn't even mind her warbling "Que Sera, Sera" midway through the picture, but the idea of the audience expecting Mary Poppins to break out into song in the middle of *Torn Curtain* was enough to give him the willies.

Slowly Hitchcock realized that there was no way he would be allowed to make the picture he envisioned. He had sleepless nights thinking of what the presence of Newman and Andrews would do to his picture, which was supposed to have been a departure for him, his milestone fiftieth film. Instead, he gave up the struggle and came up with set pieces that were similar to ones he had used in previous pictures. Since they wouldn't let him do something different, he figured he'd give them more of the same and hope for the best.

Therefore, as story meetings continued, the basic premise of the picture began to mutate drastically, although some vestiges remained. The woman—turned into a fiancée instead of a wife—became the main character for at least the first third of the film. The audience is kept in the dark as she follows her lover behind the Iron Curtain where he apparently plans to defect. The fiancé is only pretending so he can trick a Communist scientist into divulging a secret formula, an idea contributed by Moore. Moore also came up with the bit in which a pathetic Russian countess agrees to help the couple if they will sponsor her United States citizenship in return. He also told Hitchcock that people were not always as easy to kill in real life as they were in the movies, which inspired Hitch to come up with the movie's most memorable sequence. Many of the film's sequences were, in fact, developed by Hitchcock.

Although Moore suggested that Hitchcock should get some of the screenwriting credit, the latter refused, getting mad at Moore when the novelist told him the script wasn't very good and needed reworking. Hitch dismissed him and brought in two new writers to revamp the screenplay, but their revisions were minimal, and Moore received the only official scriptwriting credit.

Newman was initially thrilled to be working with the famous director on his fiftieth film, even if Hitchcock hardly felt the same. Relations between the two men weren't helped when Paul went over to Hitchcock's house to discuss the script. Hitchcock was a very formal man who wore a suit and tie on his movie sets and expected his crew members to do the same; therefore, he felt a suit was proper attire for a meeting between director and star. When Newman, a much more informal fellow, showed up in casual clothing, Hitchcock was affronted. Newman was not showing proper respect. Hitchcock offered Newman fine wine; Newman requested a beer and even strode into the kitchen to get it himself. The fine-mannered, epicurean, old-world Hitch found Newman to be utterly déclassé.

Newman never cared for the script that was finally hammered out. He felt it was a far cry from what Hitchcock had originally outlined to him at their meeting, which was probably a hybrid of the first Mary Burgess idea and the eventual, much more gimmicky, screenplay.

In *Torn Curtain* Hitchcock was essentially back in the territory of, say, *The Thirty-Nine Steps*. The problem was that styles had changed a great deal by 1966, and spy pictures were generally either of the outlandish James Bond variety or very realistic and gritty cold-war stories. Many of the situations in *Torn Curtain* were too absurd for it to be considered realistic and not absurd enough for it to be totally outlandish. It was an odd, out-of-time hybrid.

Although Hitchcock was diplomatic to reporters at the time of the film's release (he told me that although he had heard Newman was difficult, he was actually "easy to direct"), making the film was an unhappy experience for both of them. Once Hitchcock had finished a storyboard for his picture, the work was over as far as he was concerned. If an actor did his job, Hitch would sit back and say nothing. If he wasn't working out, Hitch would glare at him like a man suffering the worst case of indigestion in recorded history. From Newman's vantage point, Hitchcock must have seemed continually dyspeptic.

Newman was annoyed with the way this very cinematic director would move the actors about like furniture. In one sequence he falls down a staircase after being deliberately tripped by a doctor who needs to speak privately to him in her office. Newman had no patience with being put in front of a "bluescreen" (a kind of back projection used for special effects) so that he could wave his arms and appear to be falling. (The footage behind him simply showed the stairs going upward so he would appear to be falling downward.) This wasn't acting in his mind; it was special effects.

Hitchcock was so displeased with Newman that he dropped one sequence out of the movie in part because of the actor. This factory scene has Newman encountering the brother of a man he had just helped murder. The brother begins to slice sausages with a knife that is very similar to one employed at one point in the murder sequence. "I wasn't too happy with the way Paul Newman played it," Hitchcock admitted a few years later. "As you know, he's a 'Method' actor, and he found it hard to just give me one of those neutral looks I needed to cut from his point of view. Instead of simply looking toward Gromek's brother, toward the knife or the sausage, he played the scene in the 'Method' style, with emotion, and he was always turning away. Well, I fixed it somehow in the cutting, but finally I dropped the scene."

Newman was criticized for playing the part too seriously instead of using the light touch employed by Cary Grant in Hitchcock's masterpiece *North by Northwest*, but in this, Newman's instincts were correct. *Torn Curtain* is not a comedy-thriller like *Northwest*; there's not much comic relief, and in some ways there is much more at stake than in the more famous movie. The Iron Curtain was an exceedingly grim symbol, and there was nothing humorous about the citizens of East Berlin being denied their freedom and trying desperately to get out from behind the wall. Despite the fantastic nature of much of the situations, contemporary political events ground *Torn Curtain* in a somber reality.

Newman is actually rather good in the picture. When he cleverly tricks the Communist professor into giving up secrets by pretending to know more than he does and challenging the professor to prove his superior knowledge, Newman looks like he really understands and is reading those cryptic, gobbledygook formulas. He's also very effective when he reads the speech in East Berlin that explains why he's (allegedly) defecting. The audience, of course, knows that Newman isn't going to play an actual traitor (anymore than Cary Grant would turn out to be an actual murderer in Hitchcock's *Suspicion*), but Newman doesn't make it any more obvious than it has to be. Unfortunately, most probably disgusted by the whole experience, he looks rather bored at the climactic ballet scene—as if he's been dragged to a real-life perform-ance by Joanne (Newman is not much for culture)—which only helps to drain the sequence of needed tension.

Newman's reactions, however, are right on the mark when he and a woman are forced to kill the spy Gromek, superbly played by Wolfgang Kieling, at an isolated farm-house. Kieling has discovered that Newman's defection is phony and will not only expose him but also the organization that helps people get out from under the Iron Curtain. Hundreds of lives are at stake, so they have no choice but to dispose of him. Newman makes it clear that his character's heart and stomach aren't in it, but *he has to do it*. Remem-bering what Moore said about it not being easy to really kill a person, Hitchcock's macabre mind came up with a masterful sequence that is, unfortunately, usually severely cut when shown on television.

According to William Schoell, Hitchcock devotee and author of the seminal book *Stay Out of the Shower*, this se-quence is among the finest in any Hitchcock picture. "*Torn Curtain* may not be on the level of Hitchcock's greatest films," Schoell said, "but it's been unfairly dismissed as a stinker when nothing is further from the truth. The farmhouse se-quence alone is worth the price of admission. As Gromek uses the phone to call the authorities, Newman rips it off the wall. He can't use Gromek's gun to shoot him, because it will alert his associates waiting outside. The woman tries to stab Gromek but the blade of the knife snaps off. As Newman and Gromek grapple, she grabs a shovel and begins to bash him on the legs. Finally they have Gromek on his knees and slowly drag him over to the oven, where they hold his head in as the gas does its work. Newman's face mirrors both relief and dis-gust at what he's had to do. The whole sequence is breathlessly edited, beginning with extreme close ups of Gromek's finger stabbing into Newman's stomach as they talk before the murder. How *Torn Curtain* can be blithely dismissed when it contains a brilliant sequence like this—and others—is beyond me. The bus scene when Newman and Andrews try to stay ahead of the pursuing authorities, despite those background transparencies Hitchcock never cared for, is also very clever and suspenseful."

Julie Andrews found the experience as disappointing as Newman did. She arrived on the set only to hear Hitchcock announce that his work was done (with the storyboarding) and the rest was a bore. "He taught me more about film and lenses than anyone . . . but he was more interested in manipulating people and getting a reaction from the audience than he was in directing us," she said. In spite of that, Andrews etches a convincing portrait of distress and confusion over her lover's apparent defection. Hitchcock underlines this disorientation by alternating close-ups of Andrews as she stands at the top of the plane's gangplank with long shots of Newman surrounded by a mass of strangers welcoming him to East Berlin.

Newman's aversion to *Torn Curtain* is amusing when one considers the true stinkers that would be in his future. In spite of his dislike for the film, *Torn Curtain* made even more money than *Harper*. Considering the mixed nature of the reviews—in truth this basically good picture does have its flaws, including a lack of intensity and a *sustained* sense of imminent danger—Hitchcock might have wound up with a financial turkey had he not grudgingly accepted the participation of one of the decade's hottest movie stars.

13

THE DIRECTOR'S HAT

WHEN PAUL WAS MAKING *TORN CURTAIN*, JOANNE GAVE BIRTH to their third child, another daughter, on April 21, 1965. The baby was christened Claire Olivia Newman and nicknamed Clea. Like the other two girls, her day-to-day care was turned over to a nanny, although Joanne was an attentive enough mother when she wasn't working on a picture. As for Paul, he wouldn't even lift a finger to change a diaper. Like a lot of insecure men, Newman felt that anything that smacked of "women's work"—making dinner, washing dishes, changing diapers—was beneath him. Reportedly, Joanne was irritated by his attitude but knew there was nothing she could do about it. That was simply the way he was.

Jackie's children were frequent visitors to their Connecticut home, and they generally got along with Paul's other children. Of course there were bound to be occasional fights and misunderstandings, not to mention the resentment engendered by the fact that Joanne's three daughters had a much higher standard of living than Jackie's three children did. In particular Scott (as Alan Scott was now known), who was the oldest at almost sixteen, couldn't bury the idea that if his father had stayed married to his mother and not dumped her for Joanne, he and his sisters would be the ones with the swimming pools and all the rest of it. Full of bitterness, he would want to have all that his father was capable of giving Joanne's three girls. When it was clear that this was not going to happen, he included Joanne in his wrath and would often go for days without speaking to her. He would see her as the home wrecker until his death. Paul and Scott would never really resolve this conflict.

Susan also felt caught in the middle between Jackie and Joanne, loving her mother but also wanting the things her father and stepmother could do for her. Years later she said that being the daughter of a famous person meant only that "you have to work twice as hard to prove you're not just another spoiled brat kid. You have to establish a self for yourself." She had a difficult time doing so and became "impossible" to live with when she was a teenager—in other words, a spoiled brat.

When Newman finished his "ordeal by Hitchcock," he was ready to work again with the more simpatico Martin Ritt. But first there was some haggling with Richard Zanuck at Twentieth Century-Fox, who was suing Ritt because he had supposedly failed to honor an old contract. Ritt got Fox to drop the lawsuit by agreeing to take less money, and everyone was satisfied. Irving Ravetch and Harriet Frank were brought in to fashion their third screenplay with Newman as star, this time working from an Elmore Leonard novel. With each screenplay, however, their work seemed to get worse. *Long Hot Summer* was excellent; *Hud* was good but disappointing; and *Hombre* was, well, not very memorable. Perhaps going from Faulkner to Leonard by way of McMurtry provided too much of a culture shock for the screenwriting team.

The story of *Hombre* deals with a young white man (Newman) who is kidnapped by Indians as a child and is more of a "redskin" than a white. When his father dies, he exchanges the boardinghouse he inherits for a herd of horses and decides to make his way back home by stagecoach. His fellow passengers include the woman who used to run the boardinghouse (Diane Cilento), a pair of newlyweds, an ugly and unsociable gunslinger (Richard Boone), and an older couple named Favor. Mr. Favor (Fredric March) is carrying a great deal of money that he made by selling horse meat to the Indians and calling it beef. Boone, and some associates of his they encounter on the road, kidnap Favor's wife (Barbara Rush) and threaten to kill her unless March turns over the money.

Newman knows that Rush had just as much to do with fleecing the Indians as her husband did and doesn't think she's worth saving. Cilento, the bleeding heart to Newman's more practical voice, thinks it's not up to them to decide who's worth saving or not. When she determines to do something about the situation, Newman chivalrously takes over and gets shot for his trouble in a gunfight with the bandits.

This sudden character switch—Hombre was hardly the chivalrous sort and disliked and mistrusted most white men—came in for critical drubbing, as did Newman's performance. As in *The Outrage*, Newman was trying an outré character part and should be given credit for a certain bravery, but he was much too contemporary and white-bread for the role, even if he wasn't playing a real Native American. *Hombre* reminded everyone that although Newman could come across in roles that suited his unique personality and high-octane chemistry when he could relate to the characters, he had to fall back on tried-and-true superficial mannerisms when faced with something out of his range of talent or at least personal experience. He was a movie star constantly trying to prove he was an actor. But the only time he proved he was an actor was when he did something that was right for him. *Hombre* wasn't it.

The movie was basically a potboiler tricked up with a lot of psychosexual flavor—Rush even flashes Boone a seductive look as he kidnaps her!—but the tricks only serve to obscure the makings of a good story. Ritt's direction lacks pacing and suspense, and the picture has a solemnity it doesn't deserve. At times it even plays like a parody.

When he appeared in this film at age seventy, Fredric March, who'd once been as big a star as Newman, was a multimillionaire and didn't need to act. He did like to keep his hand in from time to time, however, which explains why he took the role of Alexander Favor. He didn't think much of the picture and frankly seemed uninvolved most of the time. He also didn't enjoy the scenes where he had to trek across the desert in the blazing sun after Hombre tossed him out of the party. When I was doing my book on March, he was lavish in his praise of Newman, however. "He's a professional all the way. The picture was not without flaws, and I personally felt that Paul's character was not that coherently developed, but even up against a handicap like that he got across the humanity and individualism of the character." March remembered Newman as courteous and understanding and "very respectful of my past performances, which I thought most kind on his part."

This was to be Newsman's last picture with longtime collaborator and onetime business partner Martin Ritt. Years later Ritt attended a retrospective of his work at Eastern Illinois University in Charleston. At the dinner party that followed the showing of one of his films, he shocked his staid Midwestern dinner companions by saying, "Paul always had that cool sexuality, what I call a great fuckability quotient. . . ."

In the late eighties and early nineties, Newman somehow got the impression that Ritt was angry with him and sent a letter complaining of Ritt's apparent neglect of their friendship, but the simple truth was that ill health made Ritt too weak to write letters or make a lot of phone calls.

His next picture seemed to offer him a part that was more appropriate, or at least seemed that way on the surface. *Cool Hand Luke* was a contemporary film about a prisoner on a chain gang. If Newman could do Rocky Graziano, who did time, shouldn't he be able to handle the part of a prisoner named Luke? He was at his best playing modern men at odds with a harsh society. At the time many thought he had given one of his greatest performances (me included) but the thirty-year-old picture—and Newman's performance in it—is long overdue for re-evaluation. Like *Hud*, neither Newman nor the film hold up well.

Cool Hand Luke, very popular in its day, is squarely in the genre of big bad cops versus heroic screw-ups, a genre prevalent in the antiestablishment sixties. Slickly made and fast paced, it was entertaining enough to fool audiences at the time into thinking it was better than it really was. "What we got here is a failure to communicate," intoned by jailer Strother Martin to a stubbornly resistant Newman, became a catch phrase of the day.

The picture was based on a novel written by real-life ex-convict Donn Pearce, who in turn based his antihero on a real-life safecracker named Donald Graham Garrison, whose Cool Hand Luke nickname had to do with his masterful ability to open safes. Garrison stole between $4 and $5 million during his career. When last heard from he had been released from the Federal Correction Institute in Lexington, Kentucky, in September 1980 and was living at a halfway house in Jacksonville.

The movie's Cool Hand Luke bears virtually no relation to Garrison. He's actually a poor sap who vandalizes parking meters on a drunken binge and winds up sentenced to a ridiculously severe three years of hard labor. In order to make his convict more palatable to the public and more of a hero, Pearce—in a twist oddly indigenous to the genre of books written by ex-convicts—turned him from a career criminal into a poor fool who doesn't deserve his punishment, making him morally superior to the authorities who incarcerate him.

Frankly, Newman is miscast as poor white trash. Although he was able to bury his nice-boy manners and up-bringing in the crudity of Rocky Graziano, Luke doesn't have enough larger-than-life characteristics for Newman to hide behind or use to build a characterization layer by layer. With Rocky, there was the low-class accent, the pugilistic mannerisms, the angry, bitter stance, but Luke is too much of a low-key, bland character. What Luke does makes him interesting, but the man himself is not. Moreover, movie-makers never seem to really understand poor people or what they go through, which is why Luke has such perfect white teeth throughout the picture. Either it didn't occur to Newman and company that poor people rarely get their teeth capped, or they didn't want to ruin his good looks. (With perhaps the exception of *The Battler*, Newman has never really played ugly.)

For once, even Newman's famed charisma fails him, for in *Cool Hand Luke* he completely lacks the charm that, say, Al Pacino in *Scarecrow* effortlessly exhibits when he plays a screw-up who also winds up (briefly) incarcerated. Newman is somewhat better in the second half of the picture, after he's been broken by the guards who keep dragging him back each time he escapes. When telling the other prisoners who hero-worship him that they can't keep living vicariously through him or when coming into the bunkhouse thoroughly exhausted from digging ditches (Newman undoubtedly dug an actual ditch just to look that way), he registers a bit more on the believability scale.

To be fair to Newman, he was trying his damnedest to play an impossible part, since Luke is a convict's rationalization fantasy and never a real character; we never learn nearly enough about his background to understand what makes him tick. We must consider the hero the filmmakers were asking us to root for. True, Luke doesn't deserve such harsh punishment, and he illustrates a certain indomitable quality in the human spirit when he cleverly escapes time and again, but he's not exactly a heroic member of the Paris underground escaping from the Nazis; he's an idiot who sawed off the heads of parking meters when he was inebriated.

Not only do Pearce, Newman, and director Stuart Rosenberg expect us to think of him as a great symbol of human courage, but Rosenberg even turns him—completely inappropriately—into a Christ figure. In case we don't get it, Rosenberg has Newman lie down on a bunk on his back and stretch out his arms, crucifixion style, at the end of the famous egg-eating scene (wherein he bets he can eat a hundred or so eggs at a single sitting and actually manages to do so). At the end we're even asked to endure Luke making a speech to God in a church where he is hiding from the authorities; Newman is perfunctory and rather terrible during this sequence. Maybe even he didn't believe it.

There are some things to admire about the film, including top-notch photography and editing—a fight Newman has with fellow inmate George Kennedy is particularly noteworthy in these departments. But despite some excellent supporting performances (Kennedy won a Best Supporting Oscar), the film is geared toward the most juvenile of mentalities. Because of—or perhaps in spite of—that it never really became a Hollywood classic.

Again Newman was nominated for Best Actor for *Cool Hand Luke*. Again, he did not deserve to win, regardless of how all of his fans may have felt at the time.

Certainly his performance in *Cool Hand Luke* was Oscar
material in comparison to his performance in his next film,
The Secret War of Harry Frigg, which made *Luke* seem like *Citizen
Kane*. In this World War II "comedy," a dumb private
(Newman) is made a major general so that he can rescue the
top brass being held in a commandeered Italian estate. His
plans to help them escape are temporarily delayed after he
meets the villa's sexy owner (Sylva Koscina) who has been
relocated to the gatehouse. In fact, he spends more time
sneaking in to see her than using his devious mind to get
himself and the others out of danger.

If Luke was an unreal character, Harry Frigg was positively unhuman. Newman hadn't the slightest idea of how to
play him. The director, Jack Smight, who had helmed *Harper*,
hadn't a clue either, so Newman was left with no recourse
but to mug shamelessly throughout the picture. He was so
bad that soon there was muttering on the set among the veteran character actors who were providing support. The gruff
James Gregory couldn't understand why Newman was playing it the way he was—like Rocky Graziano—when he was
supposed to be capable of sweeping a lovely Italian countess
off her feet.

In fairness to Newman, the character as conceived was
clever (he could always break out of the stockade) but not
book smart or especially sophisticated. Perhaps Koscina's
countess was bored with effete European playboys and wanted
an uncultured, American hunk. In any case, the blame for
this disaster was only partly on Newman's shoulders. The
screenplay was strictly on a bad sitcom level, and Smight's
direction could have been phoned in from the golf course.
Despite horrendous reviews and poor word of mouth, the picture still took in some money at the box office, undoubtedly
because of Newman's presence and the double-entendre title.
"Why not just call it *The Secret War of Harry Fuck*?" one wag
wanted to know.

Newman explained why he had made this picture and other stinkers. "If I worked in movies that appealed to me, I'd only make one picture every three years. I'm the type of guy who can't lay off for a long time. . . . It's important that I work steadily." Once Newman developed interests outside the motion picture business, he'd have no trouble staying off screens for years at a time.

Paul's first extracurricular interest didn't stray too far from what he was already doing—he simply walked toward the camera and kept walking until he was sitting in the director's chair.

The first film he directed, *Rachel, Rachel* (1968), began life as a novel by Margaret Laurence entitled *A Jest of God,* which won the distinguished Canadian Governor-General's Award. Joanne's agent at the time, John Foreman, who had worked at MCA with Newman's agent Myron McCormack, passed a copy of the book along to Joanne thinking she might be perfect for the role of the heroine, a woman in a small town who longs for love and excitement. Although this was not exactly typecasting, Woodward was often at her best playing characters with which she had nothing in common—something that was never true of Paul.

Joanne loved the novel and thought it would make a good picture. Paul wouldn't read it at first—which was fine as far as Joanne was concerned, because she didn't think he'd like it—but he agreed to go in with her and buy the film rights. Newman did his best to please Joanne when she got that certain look in her eye that meant she felt passionately about something. By now he knew better than to interfere. Besides, he had often spoken of her "impeccable judgment." To facilitate matters Newman started a new production company entitled Kayos (pronounced *chaos*) Productions. Apparently Jodell Productions had met all its commitments, and Ritt's and Newman's film interests had gone in different directions.

Newman had no intention of directing the film himself, although he had been toying with the idea of helming a motion picture for some time. Considering the critical reaction to some of his movies, he figured he could probably direct as well as anyone. Besides, he'd gone to Yale to study stage direction, so at least he knew he'd be good with actors.

The Newmans had been friends with the writer Stewart Stern since he'd written a teleplay Paul had starred in and particularly admired, *Thundering Silence.* (Stern also did the screenplay for *The Rack* as well as such notable films as *Rebel without a Cause* and *The Ugly American.*) He was their first choice to turn *A Jest of God* into a screenplay. They got in touch with him, and he agreed to take on the project, although there were times when he nearly came to regret it.

Stern would meet with Joanne and Paul at their home for story conferences, which is Hollywoodese for "let's bust the chops of the writer." Movie and television people can never understand that sometimes the writer should just be left alone to do his or her job and will in all likelihood come up with a fine first draft or even a polished product. But in the entertainment industry, everything is done by committee.

Stern found that Joanne had her ideas and Paul had his, and what he had to say made little impact. Soon the story conferences metamorphosed into polite disagreements, then arguments, then finally screaming matches. One afternoon the three of them had a quarrel about whether the heroine would "pleasure" herself in bed in the prone position or face-up. Stern told them that, in essence, too many cooks were spoiling the broth and that he would work on the script with Paul *or* Joanne but not both of them. He stormed out of the house and went home.

Paul and Joanne continued arguing after he left. Hashing things over, they determined that since Joanne would be the star and would therefore have enough on her plate,

Newman would handle the scripting and production end. (He was still not planning on directing the picture at this point.) The following afternoon Paul went to Stern's home and gave him a mock Nazi salute. "*I'm* the boss," he said, laughing. With an edgy, persnickety Joanne (after all, it was to be *her* movie) out of the picture, the two men were able to proceed with the rough draft of the screenplay.

Joanne read the rough draft and made some suggestions. Paul made further suggestions. Stern worked on a second draft and then a third. Finally everyone seemed to be satisfied.

Now came the difficult part of finding a studio that would be willing to finance the picture. Newman was a megastar at this point, and he could probably have gotten financing for just about anything he starred in, but his wife just wasn't as bankable. To his amazement and disillusionment, this major movie star found certain executives failing to return his phone calls. He was told by others that the story was too downbeat, that it wasn't commercial (which it wasn't), that Joanne wasn't a big enough name. "How about using another actress?" some inquired.

Newman knew that his wife's heart was set on making this picture, and by now he wanted it for her as much as she did. She may have pressured him into getting interested initially, but he loved her and didn't want her to be disappointed. As Stewart Stern put it with consummate insight born from years of friendship: "He is constantly trying to provide a setting where the world can see what he sees in her." Also, Kayos Productions was going to wind up with egg on its face if it didn't get the money to make the picture somewhere.

Paul has since claimed that he decided to direct *Rachel, Rachel* because he couldn't get anyone else to do it, but that seems unlikely. There were multiple reasons for his decision. First, Newman figured his name would still have marquee value as long as he was attached to the project in some capacity. If he couldn't star in it, he could certainly direct it. Second, he had wanted to direct a picture eventually so he might as well test the waters knowing he'd have a leading lady he could get along with. Third, as there was really no part for him in the picture and he wanted this to be Joanne's show (as did she), he had no choice but to direct the film if he wanted to participate on some level and satisfy prospective studios that it would be in some way a Paul Newman picture. Although he was also going to be producer of the film, Newman knew that the cult of film buffs who worshipped directors and felt they were the auteurs of their films did not quite have the same feeling about producers. No one would care if he only produced the picture, but if he directed it he was assured of the press's—and to some extent, the public's—interest.

For his trouble, Newman only got further lessons in disillusionment. Some years before he had made a commitment to do a picture for a studio that promised him he'd get paid even if the picture weren't made—they were hoping to get a particular actress to play opposite him and her participation was crucial. When they couldn't get the actress, the picture was shelved, but Newman told the studio he didn't want their money even though he was contractually entitled to it. The guys in the front office fell all over themselves thanking Newman for saving them half a million or more.

This was the first studio Newman approached once he'd decided to direct *Rachel, Rachel.* He told them they could have the entire package—Woodward, the screenwriter, Newman as director—for a total of $350,000 (chicken feed, even by 1967 standards). The studio turned him down. "So much for loyalty," he said later.

The trouble was still the same: Having Newman as director would not make up for the fact that he was not the star.

And it was still a project with as much commercial appeal as a film adaptation of *Othello* starring William Shatner.

Finally Warner Brothers, whom he'd kissed and made up with at the time of *Harper*, offered him a $700,000 plus 10 percent deal with a heavy price. He'd have to do two pictures at half salary, and Joanne would have to agree to do one more film for Warner at less than her market value. "They really had us over the barrel," he said. But he figured they had no other choice. They were determined to get the picture made come hell or high water.

But the Newman Luck held and neither he nor Joanne ever had to make those other pictures. Using his head, Newman had agreed to the terms with the stipulation that they would not apply if a new regime headed the studio. When this happened shortly afterward, he and Joanne were home free.

Now that Warner had put up the money, they wanted to have *their* say. They suggested the ending to the film would have more impact if Rachel were to leave town by herself instead of with the widowed mother to whom she has been a companion for many years. But the executives were missing the point of the story, which is that sometimes life does pass people by and that after the series of misadventures that the film details, Rachel might well have to resign herself to loneliness. Furthermore, it would not have been in character for Rachel to leave her mother behind. As Gore Vidal had discovered with *The Left-Handed Gun*, Newman was not always much of a fighter when it came to these things, but this time the circumstances were different: It was his wife's movie, and he told the studio that he was going to do it his way. Figuring they already had what they wanted from him, a two-picture commitment at half salary, Warner let him win this one.

Since *Rachel, Rachel* was not a typical Hollywood production, Newman decided to shoot it mostly in a converted gymnasium not too far from their Connecticut home, so the town of Danbury found itself host to mobile homes and toilets, out-of-town caterers, and a variety of crew members and actors. Newman's brother Arthur—the two had become friends over the years—was hired as an associate producer (a glorified assistant), and even daughter Elinor (as Nell Potts) was drafted to play Rachel as a young girl. Newman, Joanne, and little Nell spent the summer of 1967 commuting from house to gym and back again as Newman pieced together his first directorial effort.

Paul had acted with his wife before, but this was the first time he'd directed her. Years ago he'd said, "When we do a scene together, we both know we can't rely on tricks, and if one of us tries to, the other is sure to sound off about it." An older and wiser man, he knew Joanne was less likely to resort to "tricks" than he was, and he kept his directorial advice to a minimum. Now and then he'd tell her to "pinch it" or "thicken it"—let it out or pull it in—and she'd give him precisely what was required.

They were still tinkering with the script even as the five-week shoot proceeded. "Where does the genuinely poignant end and soap opera begin?" he wanted to know. Clad in a terry cloth shirt, stained shorts, and dark glasses, he would roam the set drinking beer and dealing with the crew in a positively gentlemanly manner—no Otto Preminger was he. Had Alfred Hitchcock caught a shot of him dressed like a beach bum and swallowing Schlitz, he would probably have gasped in *Psycho*-tic horror. Everything about the set was so *casual*.

Newman discovered one good thing about directing: He wasn't bored like he often was when acting. As an actor, he spent too much time sitting around waiting for everyone else to get ready, but a director had no such luxury. He had to check on everything from the costumes to the props and now and then say a word to the actors and cameramen.

Dede Allen, who had edited *The Hustler* and many other fine Hollywood films, was hired to cut *Rachel, Rachel,* but her job didn't end there. She reported to the Danbury gym-studio every day to provide helpful guidance. Newman had been in enough movies to know the rudiments of direction, but there were certain subtler things that Allen could help him with, such as making sure shots matched and shooting from different angles. She not only edited the film but in a sense had a hand in directing it. Still, Newman proved himself to be more than competent once he got the hang of it.

The first few rough cuts of the film—compiled over an eight-month period—were a disappointment to everyone, but finally Newman just left Allen alone and let her work her magic. When she was done, Joanne was the centerpiece of the film as she needed to be, and Paul had a picture he could be proud of.

Was Allen the true director of the film as some have claimed? While it's true that some films are better edited than they are directed—an editor can certainly help save a picture—it is also true that even the greatest editor can't make something out of nothing. Had Newman not turned in yards of usable footage, had he not known what to shoot and how to shoot it (admittedly with Allen's advice), Allen could have done nothing.

Before the film was released, Newman had one last battle with an unexpected opponent—the Director's Guild. Newman wanted to begin the film with "Joanne Woodward in *Rachel, Rachel*" and save the rest of the credits, including his directorial credit, until the end of the film. This was another sop to his wife and her ego. He didn't see why anyone would object, but the guild persisted in telling him that all credits *must* be at the opening of the picture. Newman told them he was afraid it would be too "distracting" for the audience—but surely they would know who'd directed the film even before buying a ticket. In any case, Newman got some powerhouse directors to

back him up, and the film was released just as he'd wanted it
to be—more Newman Luck. Peter Bogdanovich basically did
the same thing two years later in his *Last Picture Show,* and now
it's become quite the fashion.

Newman's directorial debut impressed virtually everyone, and his relatively sensitive work does add weight to
Stern's slight, if quietly powerful, screenplay. Woodward offers some of the best work of her career as the lonely, repressed woman who longs for some love and excitement and
in some ways gets more than she bargained for. In the story,
Rachel's best friend (Estelle Parsons) tells her she's in love
with her, and Rachel has an affair with a man who lies and
tells her he's married when she starts to take the relationship
too seriously. Thinking he's made her pregnant, she makes an
appointment at the doctor and discovers it's merely a cyst.
The best line comes after surgery when the nurse tells her
she's out of danger. "How can I be out of danger if I'm not
dead?" Rachel asks her. Although *Rachel, Rachel* is never
as devastating as it could have been, it remains a picture of
depth and meaning. Newman's instincts were right in revising
the screenplay and putting together so many rough cuts until
it was perfect, for *Rachel, Rachel* is often poignant and never
descends into soap opera as he was afraid it would.

Estelle Parsons enjoyed working with Newman and was
impressed by the self-effacing attention he gave to Joanne and
the other actors. "He wanted to showcase his wife's talent to
maximum advantage, and he succeeded," she said.

Newman and Joanne won Golden Globes and the New
York Film Critics' Award as Best Actress and Best Director.
Now it seemed there really was a conspiracy against Newman,
for Parsons, Stern, and Joanne got Oscar nominations (none
of them won), but Newman was ignored by the Academy in
spite of the prestigious Critics' Award, which usually carried
weight with the nominating committee.

However, some of the New York critics were reportedly so against Newman's winning the Critics' Award that they walked out en masse after the results of the voting were announced. Certain critics were probably unable to take a movie star seriously as a director. Although Newman may never be in the class of Fellini or Hitchcock, or even Spielberg for that matter, some directors who have been nominated and even won Oscars have demonstrated no particular talent except for manufacturing bad movies that make money.

Newman did receive a consolation prize, however. The modestly budgeted picture took in over $8 million at the box office.

He had directed a hit!

14

SPEEDWAY

SHORTLY AFTER *RACHEL, RACHEL* WAS RELEASED IN 1968, Newman got a strange, disturbing phone call. A woman's voice said, "You did it beautifully—what *is* your name?" The woman was apparently struggling to remember who she had phoned, even though she had placed the call. When a bemused Newman told her his name, she said, "Yes, *yes*," and told him it was Patricia Neal, his old co-star from *Hud*, calling to tell him how much she had loved *Rachel, Rachel*. Neal had suffered a massive stroke three years earlier and even then still had trouble remembering names of people she knew well. Newman was touched she had taken the trouble to phone him, even if he had as much difficulty expressing it as she did, albeit for different reasons.

Now that *Rachel, Rachel* was a critically acclaimed hit, Paul and Joanne were both the subject of even more public curiosity than ever. As usual, strangers would come up to Paul and ask him to take off his sunglasses so they could see his blue eyes. In Hollywood or Connecticut, people would start to talk to them as if they were close personal friends. Even the children were approached by fans seeking entree into the privileged world of the Newmans. Newman particularly hated it, understandably for once, when fans would come right up to him at a table in a restaurant while he was trying to enjoy dinner or when women would flirt with him or ask for a kiss right in front of a frosty, jealous, eternally insecure Joanne.

Joanne had nothing but contempt for their fans—and not just the pretty women. "[Those] tourists driving around on Sunday afternoon looking at movie star houses. They could get killed tomorrow and what do they have to show for it? They spent their last day on earth looking at Paul Newman's house."

Thinking that if he could direct a successful film and win some honors for it there was nothing he couldn't do, Newman turned his attention back to another arena: politics. He'd been disillusioned by Lyndon Johnson, so in 1968 he backed Eugene McCarthy, who impressed Newman with "his courage and his convictions." Paul traveled all over the country, from Milwaukee to Nebraska, for nine months, campaigning for his candidate. Heavily coached by McCarthy's team backstage, he was okay at delivering rhetorical speeches but not as good when he had to face the press on his own in question-and-answer sessions. He really didn't know enough about what was going on or have a great enough understanding of all the issues. He was simply against the war and nothing else mattered to him, even though there were many other issues involved in the presidential race of 1968.

Newman admitted that he often felt like a fish out of water—he still remembered his pointless trip to Alabama with Marlon Brando—but when he asked a cop who'd just lost his son in Vietnam if he resented a "Hollywood peacenik" being involved in the New Hampshire primary and the cop said "No," he figured he must be doing the right thing, that more

of the country was against the war than anybody realized.
Along with such serious Hollywood "intellectuals" as Peter
Fonda, Dennis Hopper, Arlo Guthrie of "Alice's Restaurant"
fame, and that *Midnight Cowboy* himself, Jon Voight, Newman
urged the public to boycott the very motion pictures each
gentleman was currently appearing in as an "act of con-
science" against the war. To say the studios were not amused is
an understatement. As the boycott would accomplish nothing
but deprive each man of profits from their own movies,
actions like this had some people thinking Newman gave
"thinking liberals" a bad name.

In the meantime, Newman started filming a picture that
was to have much impact on his life, a race car drama entitled
Winning (1969), which would also co-star Joanne. *Winning* was
supposed to have been a world premiere television movie for
NBC in 1967, but somehow it wound up as the first production of a new company, Newman-Foreman, that Paul and
Joanne formed with John Foreman. This company would last
a little longer than Jodell Productions and a lot longer than
the short-lived Kayos.

Newman had been a racing fan for several years and
tried to attend the famous Indianapolis 500 race every
Memorial Day. MCA, which had changed from a talent
agency into a production corporation and then had merged
with Universal, presented the race in select theaters via closed
circuit television. MCA figured they could somehow put a lot
of the footage together and make a television movie out of it,
but Foreman came up with the idea of getting Newman
involved. Newman's participation ensured that the project
would automatically be upgraded to a theatrical feature.
Foreman himself would be producer, which had been his goal
all along.

Unlike her husband, Joanne had no interest in racing—
her dislike would eventually turn into out-and-out loathing—

but she did like the idea of making another movie with Paul. Together they came up with the idea of casting Bob Wagner in the film as Newman's rival both on the racetrack and for Joanne's affections. For the part of Joanne's teenaged son, a young actor named Richard Thomas would be introduced. A relative newcomer named James Goldstone was hired as director.

Since Yves Montand and James Garner had attended the Robert Bondurant Racing School to prepare for their roles in *Grand Prix*, Foreman thought it would be a good idea if Newman and Wagner did the same. Bondurant found that he had much less time to instruct these two than he had with Montand and Garner, but Newman, in particular, was as avid pupil. He totally absorbed everything Bondurant had to tell him. Wagner went through the course like a pro but only for the movie. In truth, Newman was only doing the picture because it offered the opportunity to learn more about the sport and perhaps fulfill a fantasy he'd had for many years.

The first step of instruction consisted of classroom lessons where they learned the fundamentals of racing. There were two competitors, they were told: The other drivers and the clock. They learned the proper things to do to increase their speed and the things that could seriously slow them down, such as unnecessarily taking your foot off the throttle and putting it on the brake. A technique called "heel and toe" would save them precious seconds.

Next they were walked literally around the track as Bondurant told them what they would be expected to do as they hit each turn. Lessons continued at the exit line and the approach apex. Newman and Wagner were then put into the cars, where they were taught the controls, how to sit, how to steer, and everything else. Bondurant then took Newman around the track in a special training car and went over what

to do at the turns one more time, then told him how important it was to stay at the right rpm and not coast until the very
end of the race.

Newman was a quick study. Within a week, he was
driving a Lola 270, then switched to a Ford Grand National
stock car as Bondurant put him through his paces at the
Orange County Raceway and then the Riverside racingtrack.
"He looked so smooth," Bondurant said. "You'd think he'd
been driving for years." As Newman refused to use a double
or stunt driver for the racing scenes, the studio had him
insured for $3 million. Motion picture executives were never
to approve of his interest in racing, but Newman told them it
was his life to do with as he pleased and he would tolerate no
disagreement.

The film company chose a track in Elkhart Lake, a small
town in Wisconsin, for both location and indoor shooting,
converting a garage into a makeshift studio. Newman took to
the whole business with gleeful relish, hanging out at the
track and chewing the fat with the real-life racing drivers
every minute that he wasn't needed on the set. He went to the
local taverns and coffee shops where they hung out so he
could talk to them some more. At first Joanne assumed this
was just his usual way of preparing for a part, studying people
who were similar in some way to his character, but she later
realized, to her regret, that there were other reasons for
Paul's obsessive behavior.

Location shooting was also done at the Indianapolis 500.
This particular Memorial Day the thrill-seeking crowd was not
disappointed when a seventeen-car smashup occurred on the
track. Forman made sure the footage was used in the picture,
along with a lot of less sensational real-life racing sequences.

Newman took Joanne for a spin around the track in one
of the race cars, but she wouldn't let him go very fast and
squeezed his arm so hard that he finally gave up and took her

over to the pit. Later on she got behind the wheel herself but never went faster than forty or so miles an hour. She could never understand what Paul found interesting about competitive racing to begin with. His joy of zooming around the track at high speed seemed senseless to her.

The script should have seemed equally senseless, but she'd wanted to be with Paul, and this time he was the one who insisted they make the picture. In *Winning* Newman plays Frank Capua, a race car driver who meets and marries a divorcee (Woodward) with a teenaged son, Charley (Richard Thomas). Capua neglects his wife badly, and she shacks up with his friend-rival, Luthor Erding (Robert Wagner). After beating Erding in the Indianapolis 500 and decking him in the bargain, Capua realizes that he still loves Woodward and that he was partially to blame for her adultery. They and Charley will remain a family.

After the sensitive drama of *Rachel, Rachel, Winning* must have seemed just like the mawkish television movie it was supposed to have been, but Newman allowed his craze for the sport to overwhelm his good sense, and a loving Woodward went along with it.

Newman is okay in the picture, and he and Woodward clearly had fun playing the scene when they meet and he flirts with her as she works as a clerk behind a rental car counter. Newman is as youthful and "winning" as a teenage boy in this scene (he was forty-four at the time), but Joanne doesn't register enough nervousness with this persistent stranger, as a woman alone in a storefront realistically might; for all she knows he could be a maniac or rapist. Either she let her familiarity with the guy playing Capua dull her instincts, or she figured the picture wasn't worth pulling out all the stops for, or both.

Newman's best scenes are actually with Richard Thomas, a fine actor. These scenes ring true, particularly when

Newman amusedly and wryly watches Thomas get drunk on beer for the first time, watching over him as he gets higher and higher and listening to him pour out his teenage feelings all the while. However, Thomas out-acts Newman in their scenes together after his mother's indiscretion is revealed. Newman is too laid back compared to Thomas's more appropriate intensity. The picture picks up whenever Thomas is in view, which is why it's a shame he seems to vanish after some good middle scenes until practically the end of the movie.

The bit when Erding and Woodward's character go to bed together reportedly caused some embarrassment for Robert Wagner, who found himself sharing the sheets with a woman he had been friends with for over a decade, while her husband, another friend, was a few feet away waiting for his cue to burst into the motel room set and find them. Wagner looked up at Newman and winked. "How'm I doin'?" he asked Paul. The scene seems thrown in out of nowhere in any case. Woodward was neglected, yes, but not that much. It's as if scripter Howard Rodman had to toss something in just to wring some drama out of the story line. One the other end of the spectrum, Wagner being taken out of the climactic race so early in the game eliminates any drama that might have developed from his rivalry with Newman and undoes the suspense over which of them might win.

Wagner told me that he always found Joanne and Paul "a joy to work with" and that he was "privileged to be in their pictures." Wagner's name appears above the title with Newman's and Woodward's but in much smaller type.

If the script with its one-dimensional characters weren't mediocre enough, *Winning* is really sunk by James Goldstone's amateurish direction. Some of the racing montages try hard to capture the full flavor of the event— there are even shots of picnicking children and baton-twirling extras—but where's the thrilling ride we've been waiting for? The race scenes are arty when they should be cinematic and exciting. Apparently even two film editors working over the footage couldn't make much out of what Goldstone gave them. The inclusion of the seventeen-car crash seems more morbid than riveting.

Joanne had other reasons to wish they'd never made the picture. *Winning* created a racing fire in Paul that nothing could extinguish, turning him from a fascinated spectator, someone who only played a race car driver, into an actual competitive racer himself.

Whatever Freudian reasons one can ascribe to Paul's interest in racing at forty-four, he insists he just enjoys the thrill of the speed and the rush of competition. Certainly not all professional race car drivers are out to confirm their masculinity. But why would Newman—who had already proved he could race a car while filming *Winning*—need to risk life and limb time and again in such a dangerous sport when there were challenges enough in his own professional arena? His life thus far was never dull or unfulfilling.

Part of the answer lies in Newman's failure to ever really accept himself as a great actor, primarily because whenever he essayed a character part he was knocked down, deservedly so, by the critics. Acting was no longer such great fun to him. He'd reached the top of his profession, made millions, was a world-famous face. What was left? *King Lear*? *Othello*? He had sense enough to know he wasn't the kind of actor who could continually stretch himself by tackling classical or truly demanding roles. Behind the wheel of a race car, his good looks would be totally irrelevant.

Also, Newman had publicly and privately stated more than once that acting wasn't really "man's work." Proving that he was more like his father than his father was (Newman should have known better), he bought right into the "sissy" notion of artists and actors and never managed to shrug it off as he should have. What could possibly be more masculine than race car driving?

Last but not least, here was a way to stay in the public eye and win new fans without worrying about critical notices and the ugly eyes and ears of Hollywood. Early on, he never thought of racing as a second career, but as an all-consuming avocation that threatened to edge aside his film career if not entirely replace it. As the years went by, his co-stars often noticed that he talked more animatedly about racing than he ever did about the picture he was on.

For public consumption, Newman gave a very simple reason for his addiction to racing: "I couldn't dance, I couldn't play tennis, I did everything bad." Then he adds rather ambiguously: "The first thing I ever did gracefully in my life was in my car."

For her part, Joanne tried to accept this distraction, but it was worrying, not only because she was concerned for his welfare but also because it was something they could never really share like acting. Joanne and Paul had always been willing to give each other space, but this was much more than space—it was a gulf of ever widening dimensions. Joanne confessed to friends that if Paul had to get a new hobby, she wished it didn't have to be racing. She immersed herself in a world of art and culture, theater, ballet, painting, music, while Newman was captivated by a sport that to her was mind bogglingly anti-intellectual. She wouldn't have been human had she not ruefully pondered the fact that she was married to a man who could not really appreciate Balanchine, Puccini, or Rembrandt.

Although Paul Newman has remained in the public's eye for so many years primarily because he is a movie star, he became so caught up in the racing game that it is worth reviewing his alternate "career" as it proceeded after *Winning* and for several years afterward.

For one thing, the precedent for movie star racers had

already been started by Steve McQueen who, unlike Newman, admitted he did it at first to counteract the actor's unmasculine image. Anything McQueen could do, Newman figured he could do better.

Newman took part in a couple of celebrity races when he joined the board of directors of California's Ontario Motor Speedway in 1969. Driving a Porsche 914, he competed against other movie people such as James Garner, Robert Redford, and even Roman Polanski, as well as professional racers such as Mario Andretti and Graham Hill. Newman went out and bought himself a Stingray and even souped up his two Volkswagens like a high-school kid who thought hot wheels were the way to easy women.

Next he was driving various cars at various raceways. For instance, in a Datsun 510, he finished ninth place at the Road Atlanta runoffs. He competed in amateur races for five years. In 1974 alone (he was pushing fifty by then), he participated in over a dozen track events. He also roared across the Utah salt flats with a team of drivers practicing to beat the world speed record and put together his own racing team, which he called P. L. Newman Racing (the name he always raced under). After winning northeast division titles and doing well in the SCCA (Sports Car Club of America) runoffs, he managed to win their President's Cup in 1976. This trophy is the highest honor for an amateur driver.

Joanne figured that now that he'd won this cup, he'd be certain to give up racing—what more was there left to prove? She was haunted by an incident that had occurred in 1974 at Lime Rock Park in Connecticut. While P. L. Newman was racing, a frightened deer darted onto the track and caused a five-car collision. Joanne watched in horror as cars skidded and collided with each other, but no one—except the poor deer—was seriously injured. Later Paul nearly went off the track on the final lap of the race. Joanne was concerned only with his safety, but all he could think about was that he had come in second. Joanne felt it was her wifely duty to go and support the man she loved, but she was never to really become a racing fan and often braced herself for the inevitable accidents—which were to come with increasing frequency as Paul got older.

Now that Paul had won the highest honor awarded to an amateur driver, however, he was not about to rest on his laurels. To Joanne's consternation, he announced that he was going pro. While friends and relatives tried to be supportive, privately they felt he was overdoing it. He was fifty-one years old when he made this decision.

"Some guys need something to make them feel young and alive," an associate of his told me off the record. "It's very common with some men as they get older, even if Paul took it to extremes. He felt like nothing could stop him, he was charmed. If he could rise to the top of the acting profession, why not the racing world? Perhaps insecurity is tied up in it, but I think it also has a lot to do with simple boredom. Everyone pretty much felt the whole thing was silly, though. Although maybe he proved everyone wrong by doing so well in competition and really sticking with it. A lot of people didn't think he would."

At Daytona Newman made his debut as a professional racer. In competition with fifty-six other drivers, Newman approached speeds of 180 mph and managed to come in fifth out of the twenty-four drivers remaining when the race was finished. He drove around the track for six and a half hours that night in a car owned by another Hollywood racing fan, Clint Eastwood. Newman found the whole experience so thrilling that he immediately entered a twelve-hour race at Sebring. (At one point he asked Mort Sahl to write a screenplay based on *Stand on It*, a novel about a race car driver, which he would star in—a blend of his two vocations—but the project never materialized.)

His racing buddies mostly thought it was amazing how

quickly he'd taken to the sport and how well he performed, but not everyone was so enamored. Some drivers grumbled that he was too old and slow and was causing accidents, particularly one in 1983 in Georgia, and that he could afford to buy the most expensive, high-tech equipment. His buddies countered that he used virtually the same equipment everyone else did and that in racing it was the driver's skill that mattered more than anything else. Still, many racing Joes who were not so star struck thought Newman was a glorified dilettante, no matter how many professional races he entered, and thought he should retire from the sport before he caused any more harm or got himself and others killed.

They also resented a multimillionaire coming in and taking money—however slim his winnings might be—from working-class men who really needed it. But just as Joanne had let nothing sway her from her determination to land Paul, Newman would let nothing keep him away from the racetrack.

It's easy to understand how Newman was able to enthrall as many of the racers as he did. First, he was essentially a likable, friendly guy, especially with several beers in him, and as he frequently bought the beer, that just made him even more appealing to his buddies. Second, there are many people who are extremely flattered by the attention of famous people, who feel proud and somehow legitimized that someone the whole world knows is taking an interest in them. Could some of that fame rub off on them? The racers were no more immune to glamour than anyone else.

Paul had no trouble lining up sponsors, either, including Budweiser and Nissan Motor Company. (He has appeared in ads for Nissan, but only in Japan; it's common for major American stars to do commercials for the Japanese market.) But in other ways he refused to be exploited, such as the time a CBS sports crew showed up at the Bonneville

Speedway with the intention of doing a special on Paul Newman, race car driver. Newman was participating in the race and didn't mind CBS covering it, but he had no intention of being the focus of the report, especially when no one had informed him of what the network was planning. He ran off to a local tavern in a snit but was finally persuaded to give a brief interview with the understanding that CBS would cover the race itself and all the drivers, not just Newman the movie star. As far as he was concerned, when he was at or on the track, he was *not* a movie star. Many of his competitors would not agree, however.

After Daytona, Newman felt secure and fit enough to tackle Le Mans, where he was teamed with Dick Barbour and Rolf Stommelen. Barbour was the owner of the Porsche Newman was driving, and Stommelen was an expert racing professional from Germany. Dodging paparazzi who seemed to follow him everywhere no matter where he went, Newman rode in the race through pouring rain and managed to come in second. Newman was elated. His Newman Luck was with him all the way, and he felt—in his fifties, no less—that he could probably have conquered the world if he wanted. He may not have come in first, but considering how late in the game he'd gotten started, it was nevertheless remarkable.

Around 1984, Newman intimated to Joanne that he'd probably be retiring from the racing game, and she was relieved. Although he had for a time challenged the idea that competitive racing was strictly for the young, time was catching up with him. A medical exam revealed a dangerously high amount of fat building up in his arteries, so he underwent a surgical procedure to counteract the condition. After convalescence, instead of being sensible, he stated he felt more fit than ever for action. Whether he genuinely felt up to it, whether he felt it would keep Father Time at bay, or whether he merely wanted one final fling, he refused to retire.

Budweiser had been looking around for a new, younger celebrity spokesperson but stuck with Newman when he told them his decision. He also became chairman of the new Caesars Palace Grand Prix, which would be held at a new two-plus mile track built in Vegas by the hotel's owner.

As the years went by, Newman got many friends and coworkers—including Robert Redford and Tom Cruise—behind the wheel of a race car. He even got his daughters interested in the sport and attending classes at Road Atlanta Racing School. According to Joanne's claims—or at least the brave front she put up for the press—even she had gotten caught up in the insanity. If Paul would go to the ballet with her—she would intone in that rational, if defensive, voice of hers—why shouldn't she be a good wife and cheer him on at all of his races? Deep down, she might have wondered if her first impression of Paul as a mindless hunk wasn't all that unwarranted. Besides, nobody ever got killed at the ballet.

And Joanne had good reason to fear for Paul's safety because there were many more frightening incidents and close calls over the years. On one occasion, on a track outside of New Orleans, his car hit a rut in the dirt and went over on two wheels, throwing Paul violently to the right because he'd neglected to fasten his seat belt. The windshield shattered into powder (a safety feature), and Newman climbed out unharmed. In 1980 his brakes failed at 140 mph, and he had to seek a safety route wherein he could immediately slow the car to 80 mph. It was at this speed that he slammed into the wall and smashed the car into a pretzel, but miraculously he walked away from it in one piece while Joanne died a thousand deaths in the stands.

On Memorial Day in Lime Rock, the front brakes of Newman's car locked, and he found himself helplessly colliding with the rear of several of the other cars on the raceway, but he managed to get things under control and, again, walked away unhurt as his car was taken out of competition. Another time a car flipped over and landed right on top of his Datsun 510, crunching the roof, and in a later incident, his own car flipped over during a competition at the Golden State Raceway in California. Bloodied but unbowed, Newman crawled out of the upside-down window and walked off to get minor medical attention.

One of the more terrifying moments, as far as Joanne was concerned, was when Newman crashed in Braselton, Georgia, in November 1983. The track was slick with rain, and apparently he slowed down on a turn to make allowance for cars in front of him, who weren't going as fast. Doug Bethke, the defending champion, clipped the back of Newman's car, which sent it spinning out of control. A second later it smashed into the guardrail as the hood flew up and nearly off the rest of the auto.

Nick Aroyo, a photographer who was there, saw the confrontation between Woodward and Newman in the pit afterward. "One look said it all," recalled Aroyo. "It was like 'Thank God you're alive!' and at the same time 'Why are you doing this?'" Newman, always pathologically afraid of his strong (and in some ways stronger) wife making a public scene, grabbed her arm and hurriedly whisked her out of there. As they ran away from the crowd and reporters, "They were whispering to each other so no one could hear just what they said. Paul looked pretty grim about the whole thing."

According to news reports, many of the other drivers thought Newman's participation had made the whole thing a "slapstick" event. A veteran driver who observed the race told one reporter, "[Newman] tried real hard to become a smooth driver. But the fact is, he's not a natural. And he's not that young to be trying to do this." Bethke and Newman had words afterward, with each accusing the other of being at fault. A similar incident happened at the Riverside International Speedway in California in 1987 (Newman was then sixty-two); this time Woodward was not in attendance.

Newman felt that news reports always blew the incidents way out of proportion. More to the point, they stated that perhaps he was too old and too much of an amateur still to be in the driver's seat and even suggested that some of his wins had been flukes. As time went by, many more professional drivers became distinctly irritated by P. L. Newman and all he represented.

Over the years Newman had become friends with a professional driver named Jim Fitzgerald. The two men—the oldest drivers in the race—were competing in the 1987 St. Petersburg Grand Prix when Fitzgerald's Nissan crashed into a concrete wall coming into the third lap. The sixty-five-year-old Fitzgerald was killed instantly, his neck broken. Newman remained in his auto as the track was cleared, but when it was time for the race to continue, he was overcome with grief and anxiety and decided to drop out. He did not give up racing for good, however. Fitzgerald had claimed that it was racing that kept a man young, but that afternoon as Newman sat in his car after the accident, he must have wondered what the hell this particular old man was doing there and why another old man had to die. Undoubtedly afterward he rationalized his racing as some kind of tribute to Fitzgerald, who would have wanted him to continue and never give up.

Although some friends insisted that since Woodward didn't talk that much about the close calls she must have been taking it all in stride, it was more likely the opposite. She was so furious with the way Newman kept risking death that she was hardly able to talk about it. Each time he raced she had to brace herself for the possibility of either seeing someone she cherished die in front of her eyes or receiving a devastating phone call from someone at the racetrack.

"Can you imagine putting someone you love through

that?" an associate of Newman's once asked. "Newman kept racing even though he knew what Joanne was going through. A nice guy in some ways, but a very selfish man. His racing at his age was always ridiculous anyway."

Eventually Joanne was to do her best to put it all out of her mind and philosophize that if the famed Newman Luck had kept her husband whole and healthy through all those near disasters, it would probably hold for as long as he was determined to spin around a racetrack. She compromised with a kind of nonaccepting resignation.

When he was still only an amateur racer, Newman said, "It has its hazards, I know, but if I could drive competitively with the big time professionals, I would dump this movie business so fast it would make your head spin."

Luckily for Newman fans, it didn't quite happen that way, but considering some of the movies he was to make, it was clear that Newman's mind was often elsewhere, going 180 or 210 miles per hour in circle after circle after circle.

In his early twenties,
hot to trot. (Collection
of Lawrence J. Quirk)

His first movie, *The Silver
Chalice* (1954) embarrassed
him mightily. Virginia Mayo
is Lady in Attendance.
(Collection of
Lawrence J. Quirk)

In the 1956 TV drama *Bang the Drum Slowly*, with Albert Salmi. Newman always credited TV with giving him an excellent thespian apprenticeship. (Jerry Ohlinger)

Newman's strongly emotional performance as the traumatized officer in *The Rack* in 1956 impressed critics. (Jerry Ohlinger)

With Pier Angeli in *Somebody Up There Likes Me*, the 1956 film that made him a star. (Collection of Lawrence J. Quirk)

He won matinee-idol status as Ann Blyth's love-her-and-leave-her naughty boy in 1957's *The Helen Morgan Story*. (Jerry Ohlinger)

Until They Sail, also in 1957 with Jean Simmons, reinforced his romantic appeal with feminine audiences. (Jerry Ohlinger)

With Joanne Woodward in 1958, the year they were married, in *The Long Hot Summer*. Brash and cocky in this, he had the ladies "thrillin' and throbbin'." (Jerry Ohlinger)

In the 1958 *The Left-Handed Gun*, based on a teleplay about Billy the Kid by Newman's pal Gore Vidal, he pitched the woo to Lita Milan. (Jerry Ohlinger)

Newman at thirty-four, on top of the cinematic heap. (Collection of Lawrence J. Quirk)

Geraldine Page was his co-star in both stage (1959) and screen (1962) versions of Tennessee Williams's *Sweet Bird of Youth.*(Collection of Lawrence J. Quirk)

Exodus (1960), with an Israeli-action setting, was one of his less felicitous roles. (Collection of Lawrence J. Quirk)

Newman and Jackie Gleason struck strong histrionic sparks in 1961's *The Hustler*. (Jerry Ohlinger)

Particia Neal and Paul heated up the screen in the 1963 *Hud*, which won her an Oscar. (Jerry Ohlinger)

He was a racy anarchist (an intrigued, saucy Sophia Loren in the background) in the 1965 *Lady L.* Critical reaction was distinctly mixed. (Collection of Lawrence J. Quirk)

He enjoyed directing his talented wife Joanne Woodward; here they are on the set of *Rachel Rachel* (1968). (Jerry Ohlinger)

With pal and co-star Robert Wagner on the set of *Winning*, which got him thoroughly hooked on car racing (1969). (Collection of Lawrence J. Quirk)

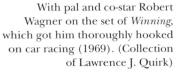

Newman and co-star Robert Redford contemplate that fateful jump into the rapids in *Butch Cassidy and the Sundance Kid.* They co-starred charismatically. (Jerry Ohlinger)

The famous bicycle sequence with Katherine Ross in *Butch Cassidy and the Sundance Kid* (1969), one of his biggest hits. (Collection of Lawrence J. Quirk)

Visiting Joanne Woodward and George C. Scott on the set of *They Might Be Giants* (1971). (Collection of Lawrence J. Quirk)

Paul and Joanne midway through their thirty-eight-year marriage, circa 1977. (Jerry Ohlinger)

Newman and Sally Field had a good mutual chemistry as co-stars in *Absence of Malice* (1981). (Jerry Ohlinger)

Relaxing with Ed Asner and Ken Wahl on the set of *Fort Apache, the Bronx* (1981). (Jerry Ohlinger)

Getting direction from director Sidney Lumet on *The Verdict* set in 1982. (Jerry Ohlinger)

Party-time on the set of *Harry and Son* (1984) with Joanne Woodward, Ellen Barkin, and Robby Benson, who played his son. (Collection of Lawrence J. Quirk)

With James Naughton, Karen Allen, Joanne Woodward, and John Malkovich on the 1987 Newman-directed *Glass Menagerie* set. (Jerry Ohlinger)

Looking happy and
contented as he prepares
for a 1983 race.
(Collection of
Lawrence J. Quirk)

Throughout his life
Newman has always
loved motorcycling.
(Collection of
Lawrence J. Quirk)

Newman, shown here in 1988, hale and hearty in his sixties. (Collection of Lawrence J. Quirk)

With Joanne and director Frank Corsaro at an Actors Studio benefit premiere in 1989. (Collection of Lawrence J. Quirk)

Making a speech as the politico in *Blaze* (1989). (Jerry Ohlinger)

"Making Middle-aged" with Joanne Woodward in 1990's *Mr. and Mrs. Bridge.* (Jerry Ohlinger)

Clowning with Tim Robbins on the *Hudsucker Proxy* set in 1994. (Jerry Ohlinger)

He and Joanne among the 1992 Kennedy Center honorees.
Ginger Rogers front center. (Jerry Ohlinger)

Schmoozing with Jessica Tandy on the set of *Nobody's Fool* (1994). (Collection of
Lawrence J. Quirk)

15

BUTCH AND THEN SOME

AS THE END OF THE SIXTIES DREW NEAR, NEWMAN FOUND himself with other interests besides racing. He was still a major movie star, still interested in politics, still married to a fascinating woman, and still the father of six children. Admittedly, none of these things seemed to absorb his interest as much as the racetrack, but they were at the very least obligations, and Newman was a man who tried his best to meet his obligations.

One couldn't necessarily blame him for fleeing when he could from the domesticity of Westport, Connecticut—little kids running around, toys and pet antics—although it was the perfect place to relax when he needed relaxing. The Westport house had been cobbled together by a Broadway scenic designer, Ralph Alswang. The property had a small apple orchard, a stream stocked with trout, and a private retreat for Paul that no one could enter without his permission.

This retreat was a separate building on the bank of the stream, and here he could read scripts in peace or just get away when he felt like it, perhaps imagining the next time he would get behind the wheel of his *vroom vroom* Porsche. Children, dogs, cats, and even wives were absolutely banned from this retreat, as were Joanne's many "artistic" friends. Since Paul had taken up racing at his age, Joanne had decided to take ballet lessons. Her sometime teacher was no less than Edward Villella. Many people thought she was being just as ludicrous as Paul was, if not quite so foolhardy.

Newman was also having difficulties with some of his kids, and he needed to get away from their problems whenever they threatened to overwhelm him. His difficult relationship with his own father ensured that he would never be comfortable dealing with his offspring. Therefore Joanne found she would have to be the mediator and disciplinarian and "bad guy" with not only her own daughters but Jackie's kids as well.

Speaking of which, these older children were now young adults, which meant new crises and problems every time they came to visit or whenever the phone rang. Despite the fact that he may not have had everything Joanne's three daughters had, Scott, in particular, had become spoiled and impossible. He was sent from one private school to another because neither parent wanted to deal with him or with his anger and resentment at them and at the world. His grades were terrible, he got into trouble for drinking, just as his father had, and in a couple of cases he was even expelled.

Jackie had remarried by now and was pregnant; trying to start a new life, the last thing she needed was Scott around making trouble for her and her new husband. "You created this mess," she, in effect, told Newman. "You take care of it." Scott was thrown onto his father, but his father had no idea how to deal with him and didn't really want to in any case. In time, Scott began taking drugs in addition to alcohol, and after graduating from motorbikes, he decided to follow in his father's footsteps, or go him one better, by taking up what many considered an even more dangerous sport than car racing: skydiving.

The Newmans startled people in mid-1969 by taking out an ad in the *Los Angeles Times* that read, "We Are Not Breaking Up." Were they reacting to the inevitable rumors, people wondered, or telling the world they were changing their minds? The Newmans' publicity machine quickly informed everyone that it was the former, but the truth was that Paul and Joanne's marriage had become deeply troubled. Partly it was Paul's insistence on throwing all the parenting onto Joanne's shoulders; partly it was her refusal to accept his racing and the emotional torment it inflicted on her. Then there were rumors about Paul having quickie, meaningless (to him) affairs on the set and on the racing circuit and that he was drinking too much. Paul and Joanne had many public quarrels and were perhaps too frank with interviewers. In any case, they have never come close to divorce in their lives.

When the couple has troubles, they heal themselves by throwing themselves into their work and private interests. In June of 1969, Newman formed yet another production company, First Artists, with Barbra Streisand and Sidney Poitier. (Later on Steve McQueen and Dustin Hoffman would also sign up.) First Artists' name was a homage to the original United Artists formed by Fairbanks, Pickford, and others and was intended to handle every aspect of the participants' pictures including distribution and financing. Much of the financing for the venture came from European banking interests. Newman-Foreman remained in business, producing Joanne's starring vehicle (with George C. Scott), *They Might Be Giants* in 1971, among others. Throughout his career, Newman has continued to form partnerships with studios and producers and other actors. It all began to seem rather dizzying and Byzantine, although all the maneuvering has been undoubtedly intended only to save on taxes and facilitate spending and funding.

In 1969 Newman also became interested in forming an

Actors Studio West because, it was pointed out to him, he and so many other colleagues from the old days in New York were now residing on the West Coast. He helped pick out a building site for the new Studio and contributed his time and money. And of course he still had his interest in politics.

He and several other movie stars—including Kirk Douglas, Jack Lemmon, and Dinah Shore—gave their support to the Center for the Study of Democratic Institutions in Santa Barbara. At the center, intellectuals from various fields, including sociology, mathematics, and education, would get together to compare notes and try to find solutions for world problems. For their financial contributions, the Hollywood elite were placed on the board of the center and allowed to sit in on the forums of their choosing. Newman always said that he felt great humility listening to these "prestigious" intellectuals ponder the issues of the day.

Newman stumped for George McGovern and became cochairman of the Connecticut Citizens for Joseph Duffey Committee in late 1969. (The "Reverend" Duffey was running for the Senate.) There were also people, including Gore Vidal, who thought Newman himself should run for office in Duffey's place, citing Newman's "good character." (Considering what Vidal thinks of politicians, which he has made clear many, many times over the years, saying Newman should run was perhaps a left-handed compliment coming from him.)

A few years later Newman was thrilled to learn he'd made Richard Nixon's enemies list, supposedly because Nixon was jealous because Newman made the cover of *Life* magazine when Nixon hadn't and because of Newman's support for Paul McCloskey, a Nixon opponent in 1972. Reportedly Nixon once told John Foreman, "Newman is a first-rate actor even if he thinks I'm a lousy politician." Newman would never had been as gracious as far as Nixon was concerned.

Now and then Newman had to bite the bullet and make another film, the latest of which was *Butch Cassidy and the Sundance Kid.* The script was by William (*Harper*) Goldman and was loosely based on exploits of two real-life bank and train robbers. Goldman had always envisioned Newman as Sundance and Jack Lemmon as Butch Cassidy (clearly the film had originally been conceived, not just as a bit of Western whimsy but as an out-and-out comedy). Twentieth Century-Fox, which paid a then record amount for the screenplay, $300,000, nixed Lemmon and wanted Steve McQueen as Sundance. McQueen had always carried on a one-sided competition with Newman, since his bit part in the latter's *Somebody Up There Likes Me,* and watched Newman's progress both as movie star and race car driver with envious interest. McQueen would not accept the part when he learned Newman was to get top billing.

A further complication occurred when George Roy Hill, hired as the director, insisted that if Newman played anyone, he should play Butch Cassidy, not Sundance. Hill also had somebody else in mind for Sundance, someone who'd only cost the studio half as much money as McQueen. When he tossed out the name Robert Redford, no one was much impressed, however. Redford's only (relatively) hit project to date was *Barefoot in the Park,* and he was not yet a major player. The studio wanted Marlon Brando. When Brando expressed his disinterest, they next planned on asking Warren Beatty until Newman intervened and told them to go along with the guy the director wanted and hire Robert Redford. Redford got the part.

It was a wise decision (and a career-making one for Redford); although Newman is good in the film, he's not quite as good as Redford. While neither actor is exactly convincing as an old-time outlaw, they offer charismatic, spirited, and entertaining performances in what amounted to a perfect date movie (Redford and Newman for the ladies, action and outlaws for the guys) and little else. The audiences had so much fun with Butch and Sundance that no one seemed to realize at the time that the picture wasn't all that good. Like many of Newman's movies, it doesn't hold up years later. Even the popular musical score is forgettable, with the mediocre *Raindrops Keep Fallin' on My Head* and awful "yabba dabba" vocalizations churned out like elevator music during action sequences. (Burt Bacharach did the dishonors.)

Goldman claimed he based his screenplay on official files of the Pinkerton National Detective Agency while Hill assured reporters that in real life Cassidy, at least, was not that bad a guy. "He never killed anybody until he and the Sundance Kid were in South America," he told one interviewer without a trace of irony. In truth, both men were vicious killers who thought nothing of robbing payrolls, depriving hard-working honest men of a hard month's wages. In the film's final scenes, they shoot and kill dozens of Bolivian soldiers who are only doing their jobs, which is to put an end to the two outlaws. To be fair to Goldman and Hill, they don't really ask us to feel sorry for these two outlaws as they die (offscreen) in a hail of bullets, but to accept that this was essentially what Butch and Sundance asked for and was completely expected. Because the movie Butch and Sundance were never more than one dimensional, *Butch Cassidy* often played like a tedious *Mad* magazine parody.

Katharine Ross, as the teacher involved with Redford and who the two guys take with them to South America, seemed like window dressing much of the time in the film. "The picture is a love affair between two men," Newman would admit. Newman was referring to the kind of male camaraderie that he felt in the bars with his racetrack buddies like Jim Fitzgerald or that he'd felt in the navy or at Kenyon, a male camaraderie that not even Joanne could share. Butch and Sundance seemed to have everything that goes into a relationship except sex. (Even if the outlaws did have sex in real life, it's unlikely they would have put it in a big Hollywood movie in the late sixties or in the files at Pinkerton.)

According to Katharine Ross, "Working with Paul and Bob was a double-whammy, a double-charge of creativity and dramatic tension. Getting into a scene with them always felt right. George Roy Hill understood the necessity of letting Paul and Bob play up to their own great instincts, and did they deliver!"

Hill and Newman did not always get along and nearly came to blows over the interpretation of a particular scene. Newman felt he could throw his weight around (Hill was hardly a big name at the time), but it was Hill's picture, too, and he was not about to buckle under. Things got so bad that there was talk of shutting down production until the matter was resolved or possibly by hiring a director more to Newman's liking—that is, one he could control. If Newman had told directors how he thought things should be done when he was a Hollywood neophyte, one can imagine how bossy he could be once he was a megastar. Luckily, the two men compromised instead of butting heads, and filming continued as Newman waffled away some of the tension by playing one childish practical joke on Hill after another (such as sawing his desk in half).

Still, the incident left an impression on Hill, who later said, "Charm is not one of Paul's big points." Hill seemed to admire, however, the way Newman got a *Butch Cassidy* stuntman fired by performing a bicycle trick the stuntman thought was too dangerous to do. Reportedly at the time, both Hill and Newman thought the other was a "prick," although that didn't stop them from working together later on in the strange-bedfellows manner of Hollywood, nor did it stop Hill from coming to Newman's aid when the latter needed help directing a picture.

Newman's next film was one that was to remain close to his heart—his political heart, at least—for several years to come. He thought of *WUSA* as an outcry against the creeping fascism of America, a battle cry to Americans to overcome their inertia and indifference, to care once more about the future of their country, and to fight against corporate greed and other national evils. Unfortunately, as he was to admit years later, the picture didn't make its points with any great clarity. "The producer, the director, and I loused [it] up," he told *Time*. They had made a political picture instead of a strong human drama. But until he saw the light, Newman declared war on all critics who dared attack the picture (which was most of them) and even went so far as to go on talk shows and a press tour just to have his say.

At the time of its release in 1970, I commended Newman and Woodward for making a picture that at least *attempted* to be thought provoking when most films of the time were merely mindless, even though I didn't necessarily share the views of the Newmans or *WUSA*. Nearly three decades later the film seems only a muddled, confusing mess and a waste of much potential. But if Newman himself can reverse an opinion of one of his films, certainly we critics can do the same.

WUSA is a plodding bore about three lost souls who are thrown together in New Orleans. Newman becomes an announcer for a right-wing radio station, Joanne Woodward (who shared her husband's politics but only did the picture because he wanted to and because she loves New Orleans) plays a whore that Newman moves in with, and Tony Perkins is a worm who turns psychotic—yet again!—for the picture's finale. The slick direction that Stuart Rosenberg evidenced in *Cool Hand Luke* is entirely missing, and the film has so little style it's pitiful. To his credit, Newman underplays and represses certain of his by now overly familiar movie-star mannerisms.

Tony Perkins had met the Newmans back in Hollywood in the fifties—they would all hang out at the pool at the Chateau Marmont with Gore Vidal and company—but became good friends with them during this picture. It was to have tremendous impact on his future private life. Perkins told me in 1972, "Paul and Joanne are two of the best friends I ever had. They've really tried to help me, as an actor and a man." Three years later he admitted rather cryptically, "Maybe their good intentions exceeded the results."

In 1972 Perkins was a lonely middle-aged man whose many relationships with handsome actors and other men had come to nothing. (One fairly long-term lover left him for a woman.) The trouble wasn't in Perkins's homosexual nature but in the fact that he was a public figure with his career on the wane, and he feared exposure of his sexual orientation and how it might impact on his professional life. (After his marriage, he discussed his early gay involvements rather frankly in a *People* magazine interview and elsewhere.) Other movie stars have managed to have discreet homosexual relationships, but for Tony, always high-strung and neurotic to say the least, it was simply impossible.

Seeing how lonely and unhappy he was, the Newmans—Paul in particular—began a campaign to bring out his heterosexual side, a campaign that did not reach fruition for some years. Although liberal on the subject of homosexuality and gay rights, the Newmans still felt it was better to be straight than gay, particularly if you were miserable. Still, they had a rather old-fashioned attitude for a couple who prided themselves on their open-mindedness. "Why didn't they convince Tony he could be *happy* as a gay person?" some Hollywood insiders asked. Largely at their suggestion, Perkins sought psychotherapy that would allegedly "turn" him straight.

Others in the *WUSA* cast included Laurence Harvey and

veteran actor Bruce (*King Kong*) Cabot. Harvey was enchanted with Woodward and socialized with the Newmans because of it, but he had problems with Paul. As Harvey told me, "Our chemistries clashed. We had different approaches to our work—and certainly different outlooks on life in general!" Bruce Cabot thought little of the picture and less of Newman's Method acting. "This Actors Studio dig-into-yourself approach is a lot of *shit*," he told me. "I just get out there and do it—say the lines and *get the hell out!*"

Newman wound up directing his next picture, *Sometimes a Great Notion*, although that had never been his intention. Newman-Foreman Productions had decided to mount an adaptation of Ken Kesey's novel and hired a young, inexperienced director, Richard Colla, to helm. Trouble began when Henry Fonda, playing Newman's father, told Newman that Colla was too preoccupied with camera setups and not preoccupied enough with the actors. An Alfred Hitchcock might be able to get away with this but a Colla couldn't. Then Newman broke his ankle and shooting had to be postponed until he was able to walk around without crutches. The picture was now over budget, and there was some doubt in Newman's and Foreman's minds that Colla could finish the job in the time that was left.

Newman did not want to direct a picture he was also starring in, so he was reluctant to get rid of Colla, despite grumpy Fonda's complaints. But as the coproducer, he did not like the idea of losing even more money. He asked George Roy Hill to take over, but Hill was not anxious to work with Newman so soon after their arguments on *Butch*. Hill did agree to look at Newman's footage if he needed some advice at a future point. Other directors turned the assignment down as well because they feared the picture had "bomb" written all over it, wanted to show solidarity with Colla, or were just afraid they'd be blamed if it went way over schedule and even more over budget.

Finally Newman decided to take over himself. Later he took Hill up on his offer, and the latter flew up to Newport, Oregon, where they were filming to pore over the footage. Just as Dede Allen had reportedly done, Hill not only told Newman what was missing and which shots would need to be inserted to properly cover the action but even put several long sequences together when Newman told him he was too busy just trying to finish the film to take time out to look at the dailies. Covering—if not saving—Newman's ass, Hill then flew back home. The actual editor of the film was Bob Wyman, but even Allen herself might not have been able to save it.

If Lee Remick had found Newman a bit moody on the set of *Long Hot Summer* years ago, now she found him even more preoccupied—but she understood. He was not only trying to build a performance but also to get the film in the can before it turned into a financial disaster for Newman-Foreman. "He was wearing two hats this time," Remick told me, "and I could tell it was nearly driving him crazy. I just tried to do my bit and stay out of his way." His direction of the actors was minimal. Newman and others noticed that Remick looked a little too pretty as Paul's wife, showing none of the signs of wear and tear that her forlorn, neglected character should have exhibited, but Newman was too busy with more important matters to pay attention to such niceties. Besides, even Newman might have had problems getting Remick to wear makeup—or none at all—to make her appear haggard.

Although *Sometimes a Great Notion* does move at a brisk pace, Newman just covers the action in the more intimate scenes and other sequences play like dull home movies. As for his acting, he's playing a hard, callous character, but he still could have shown some emotion under that external malevolence. Otherwise he's perfectly convincing in a role that doesn't call for him to do much more than look stoic.

The characters of *Sometimes a Great Notion* in John Gay's

screenplay are what Hollywood thinks all rednecks are like. With Fonda, Newman, Richard Jaeckel, and Michael Sarrazin playing lumberjacks, they almost seem more like male models (in various stages of dissipation) than they do tough loggers. At times the picture is comically macho. If an old-style movie publicity man had gotten his hands on it, one could imagine the ad copy that might result: *See* Newman cut a tree! *See* Newman ride a motorcycle! *See* Newman play touch football!

If *Sometimes a Great Notion* was meant to be a tribute to rugged individualism, it backfired badly. Fonda and company are a family of independent loggers who decide to keep working with the local timber company even though the other loggers are striking for better wages and benefits. As townspeople starve, worry about losing their homes, and threaten this monstrously selfish family, they stubbornly continue to resist and do "their own thing." After Fonda's arm is dismembered in an accident and he dies from loss of blood, Newman attaches the arm—its middle finger pointing rigidly upward—to his tugboat so it can give everyone in town the finger as he sails by. These people are so utterly loathsome that one has to wonder: Who are we supposed to be rooting for here?

Following the leftist *WUSA* with this picture, however, may not have been as screwy as it seemed. It may well have been a calculated attempt to win back those members of the audience—the Moral Majority and Heartland USA types—who saw Newman as some kind of commie pinko. No matter how many times he was asked, he never gave a satisfactory answer for why he did *WUSA* or exactly what message he was trying to get across. Ironically, in some ways, the Stamper clan of *Sometimes a Great Notion* are more un-American than the liberals of *WUSA*, but if this was Newman's point, he certainly muffed it.

There is one unforgettable sequence in the movie, though. Unlike the infamous murder scene in *Torn Curtain*, it holds up more because of the acting and situation than any great editing or directorial skill. During the accident that kills Henry Fonda, Richard Jaeckel is caught under a log in the river and can't extricate himself. Newman tries to move the log, but it is also beyond his capabilities. There seems no urgency at first because Jaeckel is not in pain, but the water level is slowly rising, and it is entirely possible that unless help comes in time, Jaeckel will drown in only a couple of feet of water. As the water rises and Jaeckel's head is submerged, Newman keeps him alive temporarily by giving him mouth to mouth, drawing in great gulps of air and exhaling it past Jaeckel's lips. But he can't keep it up long enough and Jaeckel dies.

The entire horrifying sequence, ending with Newman's scream of despair over Jaeckel's death, is completely believable, totally original, very well acted, and powerful. If every scene in the movie had been detailed with such loving care, *Sometimes a Great Notion* might have surmounted its script problems and emerged a memorable product.

Newman had bought the rights to the novel because of this scene and was quietly insistent that Jaeckel be given the part. Newman had seen Jaeckel act in Los Angeles in *The Desperate Hours* and liked the way he played the part Paul had originated on Broadway. Casting Jaeckel was Newman's idea from the first. (According to one Hollywood wiseguy, "If Newman had to plant his lips on another guy's, he figured it might as well be a reasonably good-looking younger blond like Jaeckel instead of, say, George Kennedy!")

Ironically, Jaeckel never thought that audiences would buy his death scene. As he saw it, no one would believe that Paul Newman couldn't just pull the guy out from under the log or that anybody would actually drown in two feet of water. But the scene does work, in spite of the fact that one might wonder why Newman doesn't look for a straw or tube Jaeckel could use to breathe through or why he just kind of gives up after a while and stops feeding him air. In any case, Jaeckel received an Oscar nomination for Best Supporting Actor. He told me, "Paul got the performance of my life out of me in that scene."

Henry Fonda was not as happy about the whole experience. A survivor of Hollywood's golden age, he was playing an old man for the first time and was used to high production values and studio niceties. The film is never mentioned in his memoirs because he couldn't stand it, even though he admired his own performance in it. When I pointedly asked him about the film, he grumbled that he did not have a good time making it. Not only was the first director inexperienced but even Newman was too busy to discuss the part or give much direction.

According to Fonda, Newman's style was "far removed from my own. I didn't understand what was going on half the time, but I did my best to match up to it." He added that his role was badly written. "I wasn't sure of who the hell I was supposed to be half of the time, a hero, an old prick, God knows what . . . Paul seemed to know what he was doing, I guess, but I wondered if he ever wondered about his character—or mine." He also disliked the scene when his bloody arm falls off. "Yuchh," he said, "movies show too much these days."

Sometimes a Great Notion was both a critical and financial failure. Newman began to think more carefully about what projects he should get involved with. Wisely he never made *Hillman,* in which he was to play a man living in a mound of garbage, and *Where the Dark Streets Go,* in which he would have played a priest. He also never got to do something with the intriguing title *Madonna Red.* Other projects he turned down later on included the starring role in *Ragtime* and a juicy part in *A Bridge Too Far,* as well as the lead roles in such films as *All That Jazz* (Roy Scheider), *Romancing the Stone* (Michael Douglas), *Missing* (Jack Lemmon), and even *Bobby Deerfield* (Al Pacino), in which he would have been cast as a racing pro.

He did make *Pocket Money* (1972), which started out as a project entitled *Jim Kane*. Martin Ritt was supposed to be the director, but he backed out early on. John Foreman was the producer, but the picture was made for First Artists and not Newman-Foreman. This confusion settled into John Gay's screenplay, which was even worse than the one for *Sometimes a Great Notion*. The plot had Newman and co-star Lee Marvin as cowboy con artists who bumble their way across the country with a herd of horses, getting into one scrap after another. It probably seemed funny enough on paper. Marvin had won an Oscar for his funny dual role in *Cat Ballou* seven years earlier, but in this, his comedy timing seemed off and his persona too menacing. Newman was so busy letting Marvin dominate the action that he seemed positively self-effacing and even devoid of his usual charm and chemistry. Director Rosenberg, who'd apparently learned nothing from his *WUSA* debacle, continued his downward plunge after *Cool Hand Luke*. It was a misfire on every level.

Marvin and Newman did not become good friends. Marvin had never been a pretty boy. He was a talented character actor, and he had absolutely no need to prove his masculinity or anything else. He and Newman were coming from entirely different places. "Newman—he was okay" was all I could get out of him when we talked about the film in 1973. He thought teaming with big-star Newman would have been a smart career move, but the picture did nothing for anyone.

Part of the problem with Newman's choices is that he tries his best to be a friend to everyone and give people a break when they need it. He undoubtedly allowed Rosenberg to direct these pictures (and one to follow) because Rosenberg needed the work, and he probably made *Pocket Money* because Foreman wanted him to make it. He had yet to learn the lesson that friendships and wise business and career decisions did not always go hand in hand.

But Joanne had a project that it might behoove him to get involved in and might just compensate for the failure of his last two movies.

16

GAMMA DELTA

THE NEWMANS FIRST GOT INVOLVED IN *THE EFFECTS OF Gamma Rays on Man-in-the-Moon Marigolds* when the play's author, Paul Zindel, was suggested as someone who might be a good bet to write a screenplay of a novel, *Mrs. Beneker*, which Joanne wanted to adapt. Out of curiosity, and to see what kind of talent they were dealing with, she took Paul with her to see Zindel's play. While Zindel was working on the *Beneker* script, they told him they wanted to turn *Gamma Rays* into a movie and paid him $65,000 for the film rights. The play later won a Pulitzer. Because Zindel was busy with the *Beneker* screenplay, Alvin Sargent was brought in to adapt Zindel's play to the screen. Newman would produce as well as direct, and John Foreman would be executive producer.

As *Rachel, Rachel* had earlier illustrated, there was an odd dichotomy in Newman when it came to scripts he chose to appear in and those he chose to direct. (*Sometimes a Great Notion* had been basically forced on him.) The movies he starred in were usually macho fantasies devoid of the more positive human values while the films he directed showed a more sensitive side that he seemed determined in all other aspects of his life to keep hidden. Since Joanne was the star, he could pretend he was doing it for her, that left to his own devices he might have chosen far different subjects, but there was a deep core of feeling in Newman that he could not express in any other way.

Newman chose the more rundown sections of Bridgeport, Connecticut, to film the story of Beatrice Hunsdorfer and her two daughters so that he, Joanne, and their daughter Nell, who had a big part in the film, could commute from home to work with relative ease. Besides, filming on Staten Island where the story took place would have presented them with too many union headaches. The headquarters for the film company was set up in an abandoned church, where some indoor scenes were also filmed in reconstructed chambers.

Newman was not thrilled when Zindel showed up at the set one day, dragging along a weird character who was desperate to meet Newman. Paul thought Zindel was rather prissy—someone you couldn't use four-letter words in front of—and a bit dippy on top of it. He had lunch with the two and then sent them on their way.

Paul and Joanne had a tougher time filming *Gamma Rays* than *Rachel.* The rather loathsome character of Beatrice did not come as easily to Joanne as Rachel had, and she and Paul had blistering fights on the set as they argued on the correct approach. Making matters worse—and the real reason for all the underlying tension—was that Joanne was expected to be mother, housemaid, and cook at the same time she was working and trying to construct a powerful performance. The Newmans had servants, of course, but Paul was the kind of old-fashioned husband who expected a wife to do as much hands-on work as possible when it came to husband and children. Also there were things that a servant just couldn't do, times when there could be no substitute for a mother. Although Joanne would tell people she liked Paul's "Victorian" attitude, that just being a good wife to him was her full-time career and she loved it, she was again putting up a brave front, hiding the fact that she was actually furious.

Before long the fights on the set transferred home, where Joanne became, as she put it, "a monster." She claimed shortly after that her behavior occurred because she was living inside Beatrice and that the dreadful woman's character came home with her. As the more informed knew, this explanation was specious, because Joanne—who could summon up tears at will when they were required for a scene—was not the kind of Method actress who had to walk around in character both on and off the set. As usual, the problem was that Newman expected her to keep house and play movie star at one and the same time. He was only directing. Weekends he was off to the races for some relaxation, while Joanne would have to attend to her children's—and often her stepchildren's—assorted needs and demands. It was an exasperating—and exhausting—situation.

Somehow the picture was finished with the odd result, considering the circumstances, that Joanne offered a polished performance but Paul's direction was a little off. Many, including myself, deemed *Gamma Rays* a masterpiece at the time of its release, but fresh viewings reveal it is simply a good picture but not a great one. Woodward offers one of her best performances as the frustrated, disappointed, entirely negative mother who takes out her problems on her daughters (and vice versa), although some scenes border on the comically grotesque, such as when Woodward drunkenly stumbles into an auditorium where her youngest is receiving a science award. "My heart is full," she mutters. When another young recipient, a bitchy girl who boiled and skinned a cat, starts to laugh at her, Woodward again snaps, "*My heart is full!*" The scene is vivid but perhaps more amusing than dramatic.

Still worrying about crossing that fine line between poignancy and soap opera, Newman prevents the film from being a sappy tearjerker but at the same time keeps it from being truly moving, this in spite of the many sad aspects of the story line. The picture has a lackluster look (probably intentional) that detracts from the result instead of enhancing it, and Newman's direction isn't really knowing enough to give the proceedings a significant impact. The *Los Angeles Times* pointed out part of the problem when its critic wrote, "everyone seems to be acting, reciting dialog, rather than living his part under Newman's stagy direction." As for the playwright, Zindel hated the picture when he attended the first screening but would reverse his opinion of it years later.

In the meantime, both Zindel and the Newmans had lost interest in *Mrs. Beneker* and Zindel's screenplay for same. Woodward instead began work on a property entitled *Death of a Snow Queen*, written for her by *Rachel* screenwriter Stewart Stern. When the film came out under the title *Summer Wishes, Winter Dreams* (1973), Zindel was astonished to see that it was, in his opinion, basically the same story and character as in *Mrs. Beneker.*

Newman would next film two collaborative efforts with director John Huston, who became good friends with the actor. The first was a sorry mess entitled *The Life and Times of Judge Roy Bean*, which John Foreman produced for First Artists. The picture was supposed to play around the legend of the judge but only managed to give heroic stature to someone who was, as the film suggests intentionally or not, an irredeemable idiot. According to this film, Bean, an outlaw, simply shows up in a small Western town and declares himself judge, jury, and on occasion, executioner. There are some funny scenes, but others, such as when a desperado shoots some hapless guy's toes off, are not only unamusing but even offensive. The movie has no impact and little to say or offer. It was Paul Newman in his macho, insensitive, butch mode again and nothing more.

At the time of the film's release, I wrote that, in effect, *Judge Roy Bean* tolled the death knell for popular culture, that in their desperate—and contemptuous—attempt to appeal to youth, the filmmakers had dumbed down the picture so that only a moron could enjoy it. They blithely ignored the fact that in the seventies particularly, there were many intelligent, aware, and seriously thoughtful young people in the country. It's sad that when you consider some of the films that were to debut in later decades (the *Friday the 13th* and *Porky's* series, for instance), *Judge Roy Bean* may now seem like a feast for the intellect.

The set was built in a desert outside of Tucson, Arizona, and every few days a new building would be erected as the film's town of Langtry, Texas, would spring up around the single saloon seen at the beginning of the picture. Director of photography Richard Moore created some stunning shots of the town through creative use of lighting, and the whole darn thing made a lovely weenie roast when burned to the ground at the big finale.

Huston, who had directed such masterpieces as *The Maltese Falcon* (his first) in 1941 and *In This Our Life* with Bette Davis, was in his declining period at the time of *Judge Roy Bean*. But he was anxious to work with Newman. Discussing different actors and the way they approached their careers, he said of his *Judge Roy Bean* star: "Paul Newman . . . is venturesome, he hits and misses. He likes playing dissimilar roles; this reflects his imagination and his willingness to take a flier."

Young *Judge* screenwriter John Milius, who was paid $300,000 by Newman-Foreman Productions, wanted to direct the picture himself and was furious at the "caricature" they were making of his movie. Huston countered angrily that he had "to make a turd smell sweet" by making changes and that Milius had better shut his mouth. Newman dismissed Milius's script as boring and said Huston had given it some "class."

What happened on the set of Judge Roy Bean while filming proceeded would have made for a far more entertaining and much more grotesque motion picture. For one thing, Huston strode around the set continuously drinking straight vodka, which he called water, and showing off—and chasing—his new young wife, Cici. Huston was sixty-six years old at the time, and his fifth wife was, as Newman put it, "a functioning voluptuary." According to someone who worked on the production, "When we saw this gal, no one could believe Huston had actually married her. We thought he had just brought a hooker to the set to have quickies with between set ups!" Several years later Huston would write about this marriage in his memoirs. "It was tantamount to putting my finger in the sea-snake's mouth. I survived—but barely!" But now he was in lust and spent every minute he could running off with Cici to his trailer, letting actors and crew members fend for themselves.

Another cast member was a big trained bear that stole a lot of scenes from the actors. His trainer also kept a pet lion on the set, which got away one afternoon and proceeded to investigate Jacqueline Bisset's trailer. Bisset soon came screaming out of the trailer, while the lion ran into the saloon set and had at least one extra climbing up the drapes in abject terror. For an encore, the animal urinated all over a visiting journalist who undoubtedly neglected to mention this incident in his exclusive from-the-set reports.

Almost as bad as the lion was Ava Gardner, who played Lily Langtry. Like Huston, she was drunk most of the time, throwing fits and liquor bottles in equal measure. When she wandered off the set one day in a stupor and headed straight into the desert, no one wanted to bring her back. Milius was elected, but the screenwriter was too angry at what was happening to his movie to be an errand boy on top of it and told everyone to go screw themselves. Presumably Gardner made it back on her own.

Newman found himself directing some of the picture and offering guidance to some of the less experienced actors such as Victoria Principal. One day when Huston stumbled out of his trailer to temporarily take charge of the movie, he told Principal how he wanted her to handle a particular scene. When she protested that Paul had told her to do it otherwise, Paul grabbed her, took her to a corner, and chewed her out. "Don't ever turn to me in front of *John Huston* and do that. *John Huston* is the director and don't you forget it!" Other than that incident, Principal had no problems working with Paul.

She was also spared being harassed by dirty old Huston because he was otherwise occupied with Cici, but most of the men on the set wanted to have their way with her. She was too busy dating Frank Sinatra at the time, but reportedly she did have at least one unexpected dalliance with an actor working on *Judge Roy Bean*: Tony Perkins! This was all Newman's idea. He was fully aware that many gay men could more accurately be described as bisexual and felt that Tony shouldn't give up on a straight life until he gave heterosexuality a try. The full-lipped, full-bodied, very ambitious Principal was only too happy to do a favor for Newman; besides, she saw Perkins as a challenge to her ultra-femininity.

Whatever she did, it must have worked—for a time. Perkins wound up married to Berry Berenson and had two sons by her, but he never fully neglected his gay side and caught AIDS from a male prostitute he met at a Manhattan hustler bar called Rounds. Apparently Newman had been only too right that Perkins was bisexual. Ironically, Perkins was probably more of a loving father to his own sons than

Newman ever was to Scott. In spite of this, as the years went by, Perkins would often turn to Paul and Joanne for advice on raising his own children, among other, unfortunately less prosaic matters.

Tony Perkins told me that Paul also served as a buffer between him and Huston, "who could be rough. Huston always made me nervous." He would not go so far as to say Newman had directed him in the film but did admit, "Paul got me to open up more than usual in that." Or was he referring to the business with Principal? Huston told me, "In some cases, friction on a set breeds more excitement." But the hard-living director wasn't specific as to which kind of friction.

Newman always felt that *Judge Roy Bean* would have been a great motion picture if it had only had a better ending. To explain away the film's weaknesses, Huston claimed that he had "made deliberate use of a technique that has since become much more popular, letting all sorts of events occur without logical justification." (To put it mildly!)

Newman found Huston to be "a graceful man" and once said of him that "when John was at his peak, he was royalty, the last of a breed." For his part, Huston gave Newman a poetic tribute in his memoirs, calling him "one of the most gifted actors I have ever known" and the "Golden Lad," suggesting that "among the gods he would surely find a place as Hermes of the Winged Heels, forever in motion—graceful, stylish, with an inborn rhythm." He felt Newman had made the picture work and praises his insights and instincts and "quick transformation of personality that amount to the change of a mask." Newman and Huston shared similar political and artistic views, and this alone was enough to cement their friendship—plus the fact that they both liked their liquor. But Huston's final words on *Judge Roy Bean* were telling: "It didn't take off, as they say."

Newman's next project with Huston, which he did immediately after *Bean* primarily because of the friendship he had with the director, was better than *Bean* but wasn't much more successful at the box office or with critics. In *The Mackintosh Man*, which came out under the auspices of Newman-Foreman in conjunction with Huston Productions, Newman played an undercover agent who pretends to be a jewel thief so he can get the goods on an organization that breaks felons out of prison in exchange for big bucks.

The project began life as a script that Walter Hill wrote just to fulfill a Warner Brothers contract he wanted to get out of because he felt they'd stabbed him in the back on an earlier project. Huston did not want to do the picture—he was ill at the time—but when he learned he'd be working with Newman, he changed his mind. In effect, both men agreed to do the film because they thought the other guy wanted him to do it. Huston also needed the money. Perhaps in deference to Huston's health, Newman deferred to his judgment on everything. "He was a real Boy Scout," cameraman Ossie Morris claimed. But Newman and Huston normally saw eye to eye on things anyway, and Newman had great respect for Huston as a director, even though that respect was based more on past successes than current product.

The Mackintosh Man is very Hitchcockian in plot and structure—which Hill apparently intended—but not in style, of course, since the Master was not in attendance. Huston wanted the script to be more intense and serious, so he rewrote the last 40 percent or so. He later stated that everyone involved was demoralized because no one could think of a decent ending—the filming was almost over before they did. "I suspect that if we had been able to start shooting with it in mind, *The Mackintosh Man* would have been a really good film."

The lack of a strong ending is the major weakness of the

picture, which actually begins very well and has a perfectly absorbing middle section. Since this was the era of anti-heroes, we're almost willing to believe that Newman really is a diamond thief until we learn otherwise. Newman basically plays his part like he did in *Torn Curtain,* and it's an effective enough performance. Huston's direction is crisp this time out—without the distractions of a new wife and too much liquor he was in better form. Some moments, such as the escape from jail and a later break out from the evil organization's eerie estate, are real standout sequences. Ossie Morris's photography is handsome, but Maurice Jarre's otherwise pretty music does little for a suspense item like *Mackintosh Man.* The movie was well made but perhaps too low-key for audiences used to graphic mayhem and gadget-laden spy flicks.

The script has some gay humor in it, such as when a cop tells Newman, "I'd like to get you alone, just by myself, for ten minutes," and Newman purses his lips at him. In a later scene a fellow convict makes a pass at Newman in the prison cafeteria. "Ask me again in a couple of years," Newman tells him. Newman also has some sexy banter with a woman who gives him a fake passport at the aforementioned estate and winds up kicking him in the privates.

Newman's leading lady in this was Dominique Sanda, who had made her mark in brilliant foreign films such as Bernardo Bertolucci's *The Conformist* and Vittorio De Sica's *The Garden of the Finzi-Continis,* where her glacial beauty and Italian charm could be seen to good advantage. *Mackintosh* was her attempt to become an American film star, but apparently her appeal didn't weather the crossing of the Atlantic. Although a fine actress in the right milieu, Sanda's accent was too off-putting to critics, and the film, frankly, was far below the material to which she was accustomed. She and the much older Newman did not generate the right chemistry in any case. Sanda was used to working not just with Italian actors but great talents, and a comparatively superficial American film star with limited range was too much out of her range of experience. The film's failure put an end to her plans to take the United States by storm.

The inestimable James Mason was also in the film, as the traitor who's behind the whole secret organization. "Ah, that one," he grimaced when I asked him about the film two years after its release. He smiled and said, "It rained a lot when we were shooting, that's really all I remember." As for Newman? "A nice fellow, nice to work with."

The only strain between Paul and Huston during the filming occurred because Newman tried one of his endless practical jokes on Huston and nearly gave the already ailing director a stroke. Paul and a stuntman staged a violent argument and shoving match on a sixty-foot high balcony. After some moments of shouting, the two men stepped into the room behind the balcony, after which Paul's body seemed to go crashing out of the room, over the railing, and onto the ground beyond a fence. There were several moments of tense horror until Newman stepped out onto the balcony and waved to everyone; he and his buddy had thrown a dummy onto the ground. Huston found none of this amusing and told Paul to cut out the juvenile antics.

Newman once admitted that at thirty he had the emotional maturity of a thirteen year old, so what can one say about a man—two years short of fifty at the time—who pulls pranks like a college kid? In some ways Newman has never grown up, and the heavy drinking he did even when he was working (which was to get worse before it got better) didn't help matters any.

Huston wanted to make *The Man Who Would Be King* with Newman and Redford, but Newman was smart enough to see that the parts required English actors. When he suggested

Huston hire Michael Caine and Sean Connery for the roles, Huston was relieved. Instead Newman and Redford did a picture that was much more appropriate for them.

George Roy Hill and Robert Redford, who'd had no quarrels while making *Butch Cassidy*, had not planned on making *The Sting* (1973) with Newman. The original script had only one star part, Redford's, and the role Newman eventually played was for a supporting character actor. But everyone wanted to re-create, and if possible surpass, the box-office grosses for *Butch*. So Newman, like Redford, got a half million dollars for doing *The Sting* as well as a percentage of the profits and the higher billing. In exchange, Hill and Redford had more tiresome practical jokes played on them, and Redford received a needlepoint (done by Joanne) whose message admonished him not to be late. Redford's lack of punctuality on the *Butch Cassidy* set had been a sore point with Newman. In spite of this, the two became pretty good friends.

The Sting is about two 1930s con artists, an older veteran (Newman) and a comparative neophyte (Redford), who team up to pull a "sting" on a nasty racketeer who was responsible for the death of a friend and partner in crime. Like *Butch Cassidy*, *The Sting* has a cartoon approach to crooks of the world, although this time the script was by David S. Ward and not William Goldman.

Tired of being told that he was no Cary Grant and shouldn't do light pictures or comedies because he hadn't a light touch, Newman got ahold of some William Powell movies such as *The Thin Man* to see if he could pick up some tips from that fine old master of ultra-suave. But what William Powell had couldn't be bottled or imitated; it was unique, part of his whole make up. Powell had the greater talent and the light touch Newman lacked.

Still, the Newman charisma is much in evidence in *The Sting*, and his performance certainly isn't bad. He's convincing playing drunk (something he was much too familiar with) when he enters the club car to play cards with villain Robert Shaw, but most of the time he's like a dandy masquerading as a grifter instead of the other way around. He was still the well-bred college boy playing at being a comparative crud.

As in *Butch*, Newman and Redford play well together, with Redford in somewhat better form than his famous co-star. Redford may not agree; he once told an interviewer, "It's admirable that [Newman] sees himself in that context of not being that good. But he is good. And he's gotten better through the years."

By this time Redford and Newman were the two most famous male sex symbols in the world. Is it odd they are prettier than the female cast members of the *The Sting*, none of whom are raving beauties by Hollywood standards, giving one the grotesque, but unlikely, suspicion that their contracts called for the exclusion of anyone who was better looking than they were. Naturally, the two of them being teamed together, and their outside friendship (Redford eventually moved closer to where Newman lived after divorcing his wife), led to much speculation about how close these two gentlemen really were. For months the Hollywood rumor mill churned with alleged eyewitness tales of their affair backstage on the set of *The Sting*. If anything of such a nature did happen between these two actors, it much have been the most discreet affair in tinsel town, because no authenticated reports have ever surfaced.

Throughout his career, rumors about homosexuality have plagued Newman, which is one reason he kept choosing macho roles and took up racing. In the entertainment field, out-of-closet types frequently offer details of their intimate encounters with whichever male star they've slept with, and Newman is frequently mentioned. Most of these stories are self-serving and totally suspect, but occasionally one will ring true. A prominent character actor who was in the film version of *The Boys in the Band* and later became a soap star startled me when he insisted that Paul Newman was gay.

"How do you know?" I asked him.

"I only say someone is gay if I've slept with them," he told me, offering details that made his story very credible and explaining that even someone who is essentially homosexual (like Tony Perkins) can function with women and therefore father as many children as he wants. Whatever Newman's sexual orientation—gay, straight, or bi—he would probably be the first to admit that it makes no difference as to what kind of person you are and, more importantly, is nobody's damn business.

At least Newman has kept his sense of humor about the whole alleged Newman-Redford "love match." Many years later a radio interviewer asked if he and Redford would ever do another picture together and suggested a sequel to *Indecent Proposal*, the film in which Redford offers Demi Moore a million dollars to sleep with him.

"Would you sleep with Redford for a million dollars?" the radio jock asked Newman. "For a million dollars I'd sleep with a gorilla," was Newman's response. "A *male* gorilla?" the interviewer goaded. Not to be outdone, Newman shot back: "Add ten percent." When Redford was told about this exchange, according to Newman, his droll response to the million dollar price tag was, "Not enough."

Newman had his run-ins with one of the producers of *The Sting*, Julia Phillips, who said in her memoirs that Newman "was seriously weird. He once said hello to the back of my head and took umbrage when I didn't respond." She also claims that George Roy Hill told her "the thing to remember about Newman [is] that he has holes in his head." Many Hollywood types saw Newman as a bit of a nut because of his practical jokes and his often loopy political opinions.

Newman's fans, which seemed to outnumber Redford's, followed him everywhere they could. Filming in Chicago's Union Station one afternoon, Newman walked off when the scene was finished and had no less than three hundred people following behind him. The crowd was so large and confusing that some of the actors in the film were denied entrance to the area where the film crew was to lunch. A police escort was required for Newman at all times.

Robert Shaw had injured his leg before filming and liked the way Newman, if not Redford, was always solicitous toward him. One of the finest character actors around, Shaw had to watch and graciously put up with all the fuss made over the pretty boys. "It was mostly Newman that everybody wanted to see," he told me. "I think Paul has developed his talent very conscientiously. If it has its limits like you say, he's taken it all the way, and what more can the man do?"

George Roy Hill told me he basically liked working on the picture. "What puts Newman and Redford over so well together," he said, "is as much chemistry as acting. When they're in the same frame something exciting happens even when they're not talking or even moving."

In truth, it's this "chemistry" that puts *The Sting* over. Like *Butch Cassidy*, the film is entertaining if overrated, high on production design and handsome photography, and filled with flavorful atmosphere (though never as flavorful as the great gangster pics of old). Hill's direction keeps things moving along from one twist to the next, but the picture has a surprisingly abrupt and rather flat windup. It picked up $69 million and garnered Oscar nominations for Best Picture, Best Director, and Best Actor—Redford, not Newman. It's a fun movie but nothing really major, except at the box office.

But in Hollywood, the box office reigns supreme.

Newman's next project would go after that box office with a vengeance.

17

DROWNING

THE TOWERING INFERNO CAME INTO BEING WHEN BOTH Warner Brothers and Twentieth Century-Fox realized they were planning film adaptations of two novels, *The Tower* and *The Glass Inferno*, that had the exact same premise: A towering high rise, with offices, apartments, and a restaurant on top, catches fire. Rather than have competing pictures, the two movie giants used sense for a change and went into coproduction with a script that combined elements from both novels. Irwin Allen, who had produced the previous disaster megasuccess *The Poseidon Adventure*, was given $13 million for *Inferno* and directed all of the action sequences. (The nominal director was John Guillerman.) Newman was paid $1 million up front. Steve McQueen was his co-star— though the two didn't particularly hit it off—and Bob Wagner was in the supporting cast along with William Holden and Jennifer Jones.

When detailing the horrifying results of a skyscraper fire, *The Towering Inferno* was positively gut wrenching and harrowing, but it suffered from one-dimensional characters and the cold-bloodedness that permeated most pictures in the disaster genre of the day. As I wrote at the time of its release, "It evokes a great deal of terror, but not one ounce of pity." Newman was okay as the architect of the world's highest building in San Francisco who's told by fire chief McQueen that disastrous fires like this will keep occurring until the builders consult with them before erecting such monstrosities. The most grotesque and disturbing scene was when Jennifer Jones falls to her death from a glass elevator many stories in the air.

Despite their similar insecurities and mutual obsession with racing, McQueen didn't care much for Newman and told me rather ambiguously, "Paul is always 'on' as an actor." William Holden put up with being a star turned supporting player with as much grace as he could muster and described Newman's talent as "first-class; he can make trash look classy."

Newman's son, Scott, was given a small part as a fireman in *Inferno*. He had worked on the second unit on *Sometimes a Great Notion*, but now he would get his own handsome puss on screen as an actor. Though he was supposed to return to college after finishing his duties on *Notion*, he decided to drop out and try to make it as an actor instead. He got as much publicity value out of his brief appearance in his father's movie as he possibly could.

When it came to Scott, Paul had basically thrown up his hands and given up. Paul's father had not helped him become an actor, and he had no intention of doing much to help Scott; he wanted his children to make it on their own. While many would agree that this was the right way to raise a child and to help him feel responsibility for his own fate, Newman forgot that Scott had the burden of being in the shadow of a superstar father, not the easiest of fates for anyone. Paul's father had been a prominent citizen in Cleveland, true, but his face and name had not been known to everyone in the country, and he didn't have women of all ages throwing themselves at him constantly. Scott was a good-looking young man, but he knew many girls went out with him only because they were hoping to meet his famous father.

Demanding (even if silently) and difficult, Scott would show up in Connecticut and create tension. Joanne had always harbored resentments of her own when it came to Scott. First, he was Jackie's child, and she knew he still blamed her for the break up of his parents' marriage. Second, she saw how Scott was depending on Paul to get him jobs and take charge of his career and life for him. She felt Scott should stand on his own two feet. For years the two of them would not say one word to each other even when they were in the same room.

After awhile, in part due to Joanne's interference, Scott stopped coming to Paul for handouts; he put the touch to friends instead, who didn't care what he needed the money for and wouldn't ask him. By now he was heavily abusing liquor and drugs. Based in his own apartment in Los Angeles, he attended acting classes where he only managed to alienate most of the other students. He was too drugged out half the time to remember appointments or to show up for rehearsals on time. People there got the impression that he wasn't even that interested in acting (and certainly not in actually learning his craft) but needed to do something and might as well try acting if only because he was in constant competition with his father. Some acting classmates got the impression that Scott would have happily lived off his father and forgotten all about a career had Paul been willing to support him.

Scott made a few stabs at independence. He became so experienced at skydiving that he was briefly hired as a parachute instructor at the United States Naval Academy, where he coached fresh young cadets on their jumps. At one point he was reduced to digging ditches, though whether this was because he refused his father's money or Paul refused to give him any more is moot. Completely severing a professional relationship with his father at one point, he adopted the stage name William Scott and tried to start a career as a singer. He managed to secure showcases at various Los Angeles night spots, but his plans to cut a record with singer Don McClean never came to fruition.

After taking full advantage of the publicity generated by *The Towering Inferno*'s tremendous success, Scott thought his film career would take off. He helped it along himself (just as his father had once done) by using every contact he could, such as Robert Redford and George Roy Hill. These latter two got him a part in their *Great Waldo Pepper*, where Scott's experience as a parachute jumper came in handy. Scott's biggest part was in Thomas J. Tobin's film *Fraternity Row* (1977), a picture about the evils of hazing set in the 1950s at an upper-class college. Scott played a nasty fraternity type who believed in tradition no matter who got hurt and played it convincingly, drawing upon all those years of bitterness and resentment. He looked well, if a little chunky and full in the face, which may have been due to his heavy drinking. But he wasn't quite as handsome as his father, and most of the other actors in the film, such as Gregory Harrison, looked like walking advertisements for *Gentleman's Quarterly*. *Fraternity Row* started out as a University of Southern California project but looked more polished than a lot of studio movies, although it's perhaps too glossy to get across its important points as vividly as it should have.

Like his father, Scott had a lot of charm and sex appeal, but he seemed to undermine all that with his hostile antics with friends when he'd been drinking too much or the weird things he'd do when he was under the influence of illegal drugs. He went from one strange California thing to another, be it out-of-body experiments or going for days drinking nothing but nutritional joy juice meant to purge his system of its poisons. His problem? He was the only son of an incredibly successful, charismatic, fantastically famous father who hadn't a clue as to how to talk to him.

But there was no real excuse for the often self-destructive and moronic things Scott did. Just as his father had gotten involved in a drunken brawl at Kenyon College, Scott did the same thing at the Mammoth Lake ski resort in 1974. Hauled off by police, he was being driven to the station house when he lifted his leg from the backseat and whacked the officer who was driving the car in the back of the head. The officer lost control of the vehicle, the patrol car smashed into a snow-bank, but luckily no one was injured. Scott was charged with resisting arrest and assaulting an officer.

When Paul heard the news, his conviction to let Scott deal with his own messes and fend for himself flew out the window. He exerted all of his influence and got the police to reduce the charges. Scott was only charged with a misde-meanor. He got off with two years' probation and a $1,000 fine that Daddy paid for him.

By doing this, Newman sent mixed signals, and for all the wrong reasons. Newman remembered his own youthful excesses at Kenyon and felt the police and the press—who played up the whole sordid incident—were too hard on his boy; plus Paul, still a heavy drinker himself, admired a little hell-raising. Therefore he behaved the same way his own father had when he had gotten kicked off the football team and nearly expelled from Kenyon: He got mad but not mad enough.

Still, the incident convinced Paul (temporarily, at least) that he could no longer simply sit back and let Scott make a complete mess of his life. Because Paul had found therapy helpful when he'd been married to Jackie (and afterward), he put two psychologists on retainer to be available to Scott whenever he needed them and also got Scott to seek counseling for his alcoholism. But again Newman was really shunting the problem of his son onto other people, just as he'd let Joanne take care of all his children's problems for decades. But Joanne was not Scott's mother and had little influence over him in any case; besides she had her own children to worry about. Jackie also had little influence over Scott, who did not get along with his stepfather.

Paul would simply not accept that in many ways he had helped shape both his son's character *and* his characteristics and that Scott was only emulating his father when he took up risky hobbies and drank excessive amounts of liquor. Newman's disassociation from his son's troubled psyche would in part lead to a later tragedy. He and Joanne rationalized that there was nothing they could do for Scott at this point but wait for the inevitable phone call.

Meanwhile Newman's film work continued, even if his mind was more on racing than making pictures. *The Drowning Pool* (1975) was an adaptation of the second of Ross MacDonald's Lew Archer novels, with Newman again playing the role of Lew Harper. His wife and Tony Franciosa, from *Long Hot Summer* and the infamous trip to Alabama, were also on had. Three writers, including Walter Hill of *Mackintosh Man*, worked on the screenplay, and Newman insisted Stuart Rosenberg, who needed the work, be given the picture even though Newman had already promised it to another friend who was, apparently, in less desperate circumstances. The plot had Harper coming to the rescue of an old girlfriend (Woodward), who was being blackmailed when murder intervened. The drowning pool of the title was a flooded hydrotherapy room that Newman and a woman got trapped in until he effected a heroic rescue of them both.

William Schoell summed up the movie expertly in his

write-up: "Director of Photography Gordon Willis keeps the movie looking good most of the time, but it moves at a plodding pace. All the spice of the original, which in itself was no masterpiece, is missing, and the script is so dumb and predictable that even ol' Blue Eyes can't make it work. Newman once again portrays Harper in that 'cutesy wutesy' wiseacre style of his—how much longer can he get away with it? Or does he?"

Ten years had passed since *Harper*, and Newman was a bit long in the tooth to play the part as if the character were twenty years old. *The Drowning Pool* was a critical and financial bomb. At least Newman enjoyed running into his mother in *From the Terrace*, Myrna Loy, who was touring with *Don Juan in Hell* in New Orleans. Newman ran up to her, swept her in his arms, and gave her a kiss while several college girls standing nearby practically shivered and screamed with envy. He later sent her a whole pecan pie when she asked him where she could find a good one in response to his "What can I do for you, Myrna?"

Perhaps partly due to all the tension over Scott, not to mention Paul's racing and heavy drinking, the Newmans were having marital troubles again, only this time a new factor was added—another man. Still fascinated by the world of ballet as much as Paul was by motor oil and dipsticks, Joanne was financially backing a ballet company called Dancers, which put on experimental recitals in New York. No one was surprised when the pushy, generous Joanne wound up on the board of directors, but eyebrows were certainly raised when she spent much more time than fellow board members felt was necessary with the creative director, a handsome young heterosexual named Dennis Wayne.

Soon Joanne and Dennis became the stuff of mildly and merrily malicious cocktail party chatter. Wayne had received mixed grades as a choreographer, but Joanne was determined to keep him as creative director. Others observed that Wayne seemed the type who could play women like a flute and his friendship with Joanne was only typical of the networking that went on in the artistic world between creative types and ladies with loot. Struggling dance companies needed funding, and in this case it was Joanne Woodward to the rescue. "But the way she looked at him," an observer commented. "Like Dennis was a bowl of cream and she was the cat."

Before long the Newmans were having nasty public quarrels. There was one at Sardi's, where they shocked the sophisticated theater crowd with their bitter sallies, and then another at the Rainbow Room before the world premiere, at Manhattan's Rivoli theater, of *The Great Waldo Pepper*, in which Paul's son appeared. To keep tongues from wagging, they resorted to a ploy similar to what they had tried before when they took out an ad in the *Los Angeles Times*. This time their public relations people let it be known that the "loving couple," who despised the press, would be only too happy to be interviewed, provided they were interviewed together. In these interviews they made it clear that no marriage could last as long as theirs had without there being some difficult moments.

Whatever the relationship of Woodward and Wayne, sources say that Joanne could not help but be attracted, unrequitedly or not, to a man like Wayne who personified all of the things she missed in Paul: romance, tenderness, a true love and understanding of art and culture. Who could blame the woman if for once she indulged in a little harmless flirtation and fantasizing, if not more?

Joanne also raised a lot of eyebrows by the attention she gave to one of her protégés, Dylan McDermott, whom she directed in four plays off-off-Broadway and in workshop productions, favoring him over other, better actors. Observers noted that McDermott was hardly a great talent, but he had a lot of hunky, dark sex appeal and possibly reminded Joanne of Paul in his younger days. "It was pretty clear to everyone she had a kind of puppy dog crush on Dylan," an associate of hers commented, "but who didn't? Joanne sort of covered it up with this layer of maternal concern that didn't really fool anybody except maybe Dylan. He wasn't at all interested in her in that way and if he had made a move on her she probably would have run for the hills!" Joanne did her best to get McDermott some film roles.

In any case, there were no visible signs of friction between the Newmans when they attended a Lincoln Center gala in their honor given by the New York Film Society. Although it was meant to be quite a tribute, the egotistical Newmans were pleasant enough but didn't seem terribly enthused, probably because they were not quite as ossified and ready for retirement as the previous honorees. More vain about his age than he would ever admit, Newman in particular found it a mixed compliment. An inebriated Tennessee Williams, who was one of the celebrity hosts, told the glittering assemblage that he was delighted to pay court to "Paul Goodman." (Williams's mistake can be forgiven as Paul Goodman was a prominent writer of the period and probably a friend of his.)

Newman next got a call from gnomelike Mel Brooks. Newman probably would have jumped suicidally at the chance of doing a comedy for Brooks, but the director was only asking if Paul would join a number of other movie stars who were doing cameos in his next feature, *Silent Movie*. "It's a great idea," he told Newman. "Just trust me." He got Newman and the others to do it for scale.

In the finished film, which mirrored the real-life situation, Brooks goes around asking stars to appear in his silent movie which he's making in 1976 despite protests from the studio. Newman shows up briefly in a plaster cast and a wheelchair. An honest-to-goodness silent movie, there are only subtitles in the film, which is sporadically amusing and no more.

If critics had had reservations about Newman's professional relationship with John Huston, they were positively appalled when he hooked up with director Robert Altman. The first picture together was *Buffalo Bill and the Indians* (1976), which was based on an Arthur Kopit play. Newman-Foreman paid a rather large half million for the film rights, but Newman was intrigued by the piece. It debunked Buffalo Bill the same way *Judge Roy Bean* had trashed another legendary Western character.

Apparently Newman's mind was on other matters, or he just never learned from his mistakes. When it came to Buffalo Bill, he thought the American public should never have made a hero out of a guy "who was really a butcher," but as fuzzy minded as ever, it didn't occur to him that he had appeared in films like *Butch Cassidy and the Sundance Kid*, which made heroes out of outlaws.

Still, the theme of the picture was dear to his heart. "What it does is shoot down all those legendary people. That includes Buffalo Bill and me and Redford and Muhammad Ali and Churchill and Stalin and Roosevelt. There's simply no way that any human being could be anything like what legend makers try to convince the public he is."

Buffalo Bill was more excoriated than *Judge Roy Bean*, with critics finding it dull and one-dimensional and so sloppily put together that it blunted its points about how the white man treated the red man and how the heroic Wild West was all a hunk of mythical bull. Although there were those who found Newman's performance amusing, most agreed that it was one of his all-time worst. Clad in a long blond wig and beard that couldn't disguise his pretty features, he pranced around in a farce that was more tedious than illuminating. At the press conference, Altman was typically defensive, for good reason. Even Newman quipped to the reporters, "I hope you left your grenades at the door."

Burt Lancaster also appeared in the film as Ned Buntline, who helps create the whole Buffalo Bill legend. "It was always interesting to watch Paul Newman work," he told me. "He always gives it all he has." This time it wasn't enough. Altman wanted great soprano Beverly Sills to play the opera singer who appears in the movie, but she declined. She would have loved to have worked with Newman, but one look at that script—not even Newman was worth it.

Having given Native Americans a fair shake (or at least having attempted to), Newman next turned his attention, surprisingly, to the gays. A popular novel entitled *The Front Runner* had come out that detailed the love affair between a male track coach and a younger male runner. The author Patricia Nell Warren had originally had two lesbians in mind but was told by the publisher that if the protagonists were gay men, it would sell better. With no pretensions to art and full of cliches about gay men, *The Front Runner* was a least a good read and came along at the right time. Newman optioned the book, and Warren went on to write several more gay potboilers.

There's no indication, as an apocryphal story suggests, that Newman ever asked Robert Redford to play his lover in the film, although it's certainly an irresistible anecdote. Redford would actually have been too old since the runner is supposed to be quite a few years younger than the coach. The true front runner for the part was Richard Thomas, who'd been Newman's son in *Winning* and could have certainly handled the part. Robby Benson was also in contention. Benson had sensitively played a gay part in the rather dated if engaging *Ode to Billy Joe* and later also played Newman's son in *Harry and Son*. Although there was hardly as much specula-

tion as there had been when Selznick sought his Scarlet
O'Hara, the many fans of the novel anxiously awaited the
announcement of which actor would be necking with
Newman on the big screen. Many pointed out that Thomas
and Benson were hardly handsome enough to play the
runner and that it would stretch belief that gorgeous
Newman would be attracted to either of them, so it was
assumed a third party would eventually emerge.

When asked about the picture, which intrigued a great
many of his fans, Newman would always refer to script
problems. The screenplay did go through several drafts,
none of which were satisfactory. Finally Newman let it be
known that he was backing out of the movie. He claimed that
no one would find him believable as a homosexual (though
there are many gay athletes and though he would be portraying a manly gay guy, not a queen) and that the age difference between the lovers presented an insurmountable
problem. He seemed to intimate that no one would believe a
young runner would have the hots for his middle-aged coach
(even if he looked like Paul Newman). He followed this up
by mentioning his continuing commitment to gay rights. It
seems Newman's old homosexual panic would simply not let
go of him.

Instead of *The Front Runner*, Newman ran in 1977 to the
safety of one of his macho mindless movies, this one entitled
Slap Shot. Newman played a coach all right, but not a gay one
and not for a "sissy" sport like running. He was a coach and
sometime player for a down-and-out hockey team. Once more
we have an attempt by Newman to be hyper-masculine as an
apology for being an actor and as a means of washing away all
the renewed rumors about him that had sprung up since he'd
said he'd do *Front Runner*. (Why, they'd even had his picture
on the cover of a gay magazine, *The Advocate*!) It was as if he
felt he had no choice but to do *Slap Shot*, with its dialogue

littered with all manner of "fag" and "dyke" jokes and remarks, which taken in context were all quite realistic.

Newman had another good reason to do the picture. He'd followed two blockbusters, *The Sting* and *Inferno*, with two pictures that barely registered at the box office. Newman was still frightened of become a has-been and of not being able to meet all of his considerable bills, what with six children to support. Despite all the publicity it engendered, *The Front Runner* was a risky financial proposition, whereas the crude, more visceral *Slap Shot* seemed like a sure thing. Newman traded in his sensitivity and liberalism for dollars and, as he saw it, common sense. At heart he was still a boy afraid of being called names by the bigger boys.

The shame of it was that *The Front Runner* might have done a lot to humanize gays in the public's eyes—Hollywood movies tended to make them either victims or villains—and his participation undoubtedly would have attracted viewers who might otherwise have avoided the picture. Newman had stated that he could never understand why people wanted to go beat up on gays, but a part of the reason stemmed from their depiction in popular motion pictures. Instead of doing his bit to redress this wrong, Newman traded in his vaunted social activism for a hockey puck.

By this time movies to Newman mostly represented money to support his family and, especially, racing and other activities and little else. "I think Paul is bored with acting," said George Roy Hill, who was reunited with him on *Slap Shot*. Newman did not want to have to stretch himself, although if he'd stopped stereotyping gays himself, the coach in *Front Runner* might not have been that big of a stretch. But he liked the part in *Slap Shot*, saying that it was closer to his true character than most roles, "vulgar, on the skids." The film was shot mostly in Johnstown, Pennsylvania.

Slap Shot is actually not a totally mindless picture. When

Newman decides to make his team winners by playing dirty and violent, the movie makes the point that the team attracts more fans that way than by simply playing good hockey. Nancy Dowd's script tries to play it both ways by appealing not only to hockey fans of that type but also to those who have contempt for them—it hardly portrays a world that is flattering to the athletes or their fans. The trouble is that the film is too heavy-handed, too brutal and realistic to make good satire. There are decades-old movies that have made the same cynical points about human nature but done it with much more zippy flair and pace. Still, *Slap Shot* does have its funny scenes, such as when a disgusted player, Michael Ontkean, does a striptease on the ice to illustrate just how much of a burlesque the game has become to him.

Considering his comment about how much the character in *Slap Shot* is like him, Newman plays the vulgar coach much too charmingly, completely blunting the effect. (Just because Paul uses cuss words now and then doesn't take away his good breeding.) He's frequently self-conscious and wears a jacket with a fur-lined collar that even *The Front Runner* coach probably wouldn't have been caught dead in. Still, his performance emerges as one of the more energetic of his later work.

Since Newman did this film instead of *Front Runner*, it's interesting to note the picture's attitude toward homosexuality. As earlier noted, the players frequently make antigay jibes, but taken in context, these are in character and realistic. There's an interesting scene when Newman learns of a lady bedmate's bisexuality. "Who knows? Things being the way they are, maybe I'll wind up sleeping with old goalies," he says unfazed by her admission, but later he taunts a rival player with his wife's lesbianism to get him off his game. When he confronts the woman owner of the team, who is a bitchy hypocrite, he looks at her young son and says, "That kid's gonna be sucking dick before you can say Jack Robinson," or words to that effect. Since Newman is the hero of the film and the woman is so totally unlikable, the audience is clearly supposed to roar with laughter at these remarks. Whether or not Hill and Newman made changes to Dowd's script, which is a distinct possibility, is unknown.

Gore Vidal threw a fifty-second birthday party for Paul shortly before the film's release. One can only imagine what Gore thought of it when—and if—he saw it. Reportedly Newman once tried to deck a man who referred to Vidal as a fag, but whether it was because the man had used a pejorative term to describe a gay friend or had dared to imply that Vidal was homosexual is not known.

Susan Newman, one of Paul's daughters by Jackie, has a small part in *Slap Shot*. A pretty young lady whose head is a perfect oval (like Merle Oberon's), she stands behind the pharmaceutical counter of a drugstore and says to a hockey player with a headache, "I'll make you a double dose and you won't feel *anything*." She was smitten with quite a few of the real hockey players employed as extras on the film and caught the acting bug if nothing else.

Susan got through the terrible teen years more successfully than her brother Scott, though her career as an actress didn't amount to much more than his. Like Scott, she used her father's contacts and got herself a small part in Robert Altman's film *A Wedding*. She then got a much bigger part in *I Wanna Hold Your Hand*, a comedy about Beatles fans. Her father posed for publicity shots with her, but the publicity splurge didn't really help Susan anymore than the *Inferno* push did Scott.

Susan got to know her father better when she was an older child. They would get together for weekends in New York, which she later described as a fantasy frequently interrupted by Newman's persistent fans. Later she said,

"Other people's fantasies of what my life as Paul Newman's daughter is like are just plain wrong. They assume my father writes me a check for $5,000 every week or something. Wrong!"

But Susan also discovered that her father could be just as unrealistic. When she got the part in *I Wanna Hold Your Hand*, her father in all seriousness asked her how many points of the film's grosses she was going to get. She realized that her father had become so successful, so quickly, that he was completely out of touch with the life of the ordinary actor.

But Paul and Joanne were often out of touch with the average citizen. When they told interviewers about the amount of time they spent picking up trash in Central Park in an attempt to beautify New York (when they still spent most of their time there), they bemoaned the fact that no one else ever joined them. Apparently it never even occurred to this multimillionaire couple that most New Yorkers have nine-to-five jobs.

18

THE END OF THE WORLD

SINCE NEWMAN AND ROBERT ALTMAN WERE SIMPATICO, IT wasn't long before they were embarking on another picture together. Altman had a strange dream one night, in which emotionally sterile people kept obsessively playing a bizarre game in an icy barren world. He called up veteran screenwriter Lionel Chetwynd and asked him to write a novella—in essence a lengthy screen treatment—based on elements from this dream, and Chetwynd complied.

Altman read the novella but wasn't satisfied. First he told Chetwynd to revise it, but after the screenwriter had already begun, he got a call from an International Creative Management (ICM) executive telling him Altman had fired him. This might not have been a problem except Chetwynd had yet to get paid for his substantial work on the project. When he tried to secure payment for his services, Altman called Chetwynd himself and told him, in effect, that he'd never get work in Hollywood again. (Considering that Chetwynd makes no secret of his conservative political views, is it a stretch to speculate that perhaps Newman had a hand in his troubles with Altman, who needed Newman's participation in the picture more than he did Chetwynd's?) The director hired Frank Barhydt and Patricia Resnick to fashion a screenplay and then added a few finishing touches of his own. This didn't stop him from trying to get sole screenwriting credit, which was denied him.

Chetwynd had the last laugh because his name was never mentioned in connection with the abysmal film, perhaps the very worst that Newman has ever appeared in and decidedly the most tedious. Again, Newman chose to do the film because he liked Altman; the two had a similarly gross and juvenile sense of humor. Newman wanted to have fun while making his movies, but he showed great irresponsibility in not caring about the final product. Heavy drinking and family problems only contributed to his lack of judgment.

The film, entitled *Quintet*, takes place in an apparently futuristic, unspecified Ice Age, where old buildings and subways and roads are dilapidated and covered with frost. Even the walls inside buildings are sheathed with a layer of ice. The cast roughed it on location at Montreal's Man and His World and Frobisher Bay during a winter shoot where the temperature would sometimes go down to forty degrees below zero. Some fun. There wasn't much relief when the cast and crew went "indoors" because the sets were built outside to accommodate all that ice on the walls.

Newman plays a mysterious fellow who goes after the unknown person responsible for the death of his lover, brother, and the brother's family, in an explosion. Their deaths are all tied into a game being played by several characters, in which the winner will be whomever murders all of the others. Newman takes the place and identity of another victim and joins the game, eventually emerging the winner. He learns that there's no prize; the game was played for no purpose other than to keep the game going. Apparently

Altman needed nearly two hours of time to unfold a pretentious allegory that supposedly illustrated the point that when people try to ruthlessly survive and beat all competition, they lose sight of the things that really matter in life, such as love and family.

With no real character to play, Newman just walks through the movie. *Quintet* is like bad avant-garde theater directed by schlock director Albert Pyun; it makes Arnold Schwarzenegger movies seem Oscar worthy in comparison. Laughably awful and somnambulistically directed by Altman, *Quintet* should have savaged the director's reputation for good. There are so few extras milling about that this never looks like a community of any kind, even a decimated one. It is never explained why, if it's so cold that ice forms on light bulbs inside a "hotel," everyone doesn't just freeze to death, parkas notwithstanding. The dullness is occasionally punctuated by a dead body, some of which are intentionally comical, such as Nina Van Pallandt with an ice pick through one eye and the other raised as if to ask, "How did I get into this?" (Van Pallandt's sole claim to fame, aside from appearing in bad Bob Altman movies, is that she was once the girlfriend of Clifford Irving, the writer imprisoned for faking an autobiography of Howard Hughes.)

The film has a multiplicity of accents from an international supporting cast, some of whom fare much better than Newman. Bibi Andersson (as another player) was not for one minute fooled into thinking she was in another vastly superior Ingmar Bergman film—*Quintet* was no *Sawdust and Tinsel*, or even a *Seventh Seal*—and Vittorio Gassman just wanted to complete his stint and go somewhere to get warm. "Yes, the picture was dull, but Paul did his best to keep us all in there making the most of things," he told me. Leon Ericksen's production design was also interesting (if a bit nonsensical, in keeping with the general theme), and Jean

Boffety's photography was generally first rate. The single highlight of the picture was a sequence full of striking images that showed Newman dragging a corpse to a river with ice floes on it while several hungry dogs (who probably would have attacked him long before) follow after him.

With *Quintet* Newman and Altman had themselves another megabomb. Chetwynd should have counted himself lucky. "I've never been able to sit through it all," he said.

The fact that Newman was screwing up in virtually every area of his life—making bad movies, acting antediluvian and indifferent as a husband and a father, risking life and limb on one racetrack after another—did not stop politicians from paying homage to him. This time it was the president, Jimmy Carter, who wanted to meet with Newman. Once they were settled, Carter spent half an hour grilling Paul about the movie business, then finally told him he wanted to appoint him a delegate, along with George McGovern, to a United Nations session on disarmament. The more lucid members of the press pilloried Carter for this bit of silliness, wondering if Carted expected the Soviets to simply dismantle their intercontinental missile system because Paul Newman asked them to. Head in the clouds, out of touch, frequently inebriated, and racetrack dizzy, Newman was as out of place at the UN as Joanne would be at a Pesmo Beach wet tee shirt contest.

While their mostly absentee father used his celebrity in ways that were inappropriate, his children did their best to grow up and find their own place in the world. Susan had her acting career and later would become a producer. Her sister, Stephanie, was more interested in photography and horses. Although their half sister Nell had already appeared in *Gamma Rays,* she didn't seem cut out for life as a thespian. Many people, playwright Paul Zindel included, felt Newman should have restrained his nepotistic instincts and cast a real

actress in the picture. Even her mother admitted Nell was not
really an actress in any true sense of the word. With no
central focus in her life, Nell, like her older half brother,
began abusing drugs, totally uncertain of her place in the
world. Her school, work, friendships, and self-esteem suffered
a beating from her chemical experimentation, and for a time
it appeared she'd become as difficult a case as Scott. Eventually she would straighten herself out and resign herself to
behind-the-scenes jobs, such as production assistant on the
upcoming *Fort Apache.*

Joanne's other daughters had diverse interests, with
Melissa taking a stab at acting (playing Woodward's daughter,
quite a stretch, in a made-for-television movie) and also
taking an interest in art. Clea and her mother became avid
horsewomen, as did Stephanie, but Clea became so advanced
that at sixteen she entered the competition at the National
Horse Show held at Madison Square Garden. Her gelding
tripped and rolled over on her, but she was uninjured.

The girls were okay, more or less, but Scott was as badly
off as ever. He had not been able to keep up the rent on his
apartment and had temporarily moved into a cheap room at
the Ramada Inn in West Los Angeles. Acting opportunities
seemed to have dried up, and his second career as a singer
was going nowhere. With or without the great Newman name
to back him up, he was convinced he was a loser. Added to his
emotional anguish was the physical pain from injuries he had
recently sustained in a motorcycle mishap. Although he was
generally inured to most of the pain he might get from the
sprains and contusions engendered by his stunt work and
skydiving, the motorbike accident was a little more serious.

On a Sunday before Thanksgiving in 1978, Scott went
over to a friend's apartment to watch football on television.
Reportedly, his shoulder and his ribs were troubling him so
much that he tried to drown the pain in alcohol, but by this

time Scott actually needed little excuse to start drinking. Scott also took a total of eight tablets of Valium, presumably to help him deal with the stress he was under and relax his muscles. As the day proceeded, he only got more and more depressed, and by the time night rolled around, he was on the phone to one of the psychologists his father had put on retainer for his needs.

Scott went over to the psychologist's office where he proceeded to lament on how troubled he was that his career was amounting to nothing when his father was so famous, how he felt insignificant beside his father and scared of being a nobody, just another also-ran in Hollywood despite his famous parent. Complaining of increasing pain in his shoulder, Scott was given a sample of Darvon to take along with him. He went back to his friend's apartment instead of to his lonely room at the Ramada Inn and had several more drinks. After awhile the doorbell rang; it was the psychologist's associate, who had been sent to keep an eye on Scott.

Unaware of exactly how many drugs Scott had taken or how many drinks he'd imbibed, the associate got Scott to go back to his hotel room where he planned to watch over him for the rest of the evening. Once there, Scott went to the bathroom and took a lethal combination of Quaaludes and cocaine, although the associate had no idea of what had transpired. When Scott returned from the bathroom, he announced that he was tired and going to bed.

An hour or so later his watchdog noticed that Scott was breathing funny and became alarmed. He immediately called the paramedics, who tried their best to revive Scott before bundling him into an ambulance. He was dead on arrival, his last moment being 1:07 AM on Monday, November 20, 1978. He was twenty-eight years old.

Although his death was officially ruled accidental, there are strong indications that it was actually a suicide. It is generally difficult to tell from the physical evidence in a drug overdose whether a death was accidental or not, especially in this case with quantities of different drugs consumed over a lengthy period. Therefore, the victim's emotional state and other evidence must be factored in. Scott's depression, his pathetic current circumstances, his desperate call to the doctor, and the fact that someone was sent to essentially keep a suicide watch over him pretty much tell the story. Friends of his acknowledge that not only was Scott a suicidal personality, but his whole lifestyle—the drugs, the drinking, the skydiving (not opening his parachute until the very last second)—all added up to someone who was seeking an escape from life, probably on a permanent basis.

Reliable sources indicate that Scott had yet another motive for ending his life. He had never really forgiven his father for leaving his mother and altering his young life so dramatically, and he still harbored terrific resentment over his father's failure to help his career in any concrete way or to even be there personally when he needed him. For years Scott had felt as if his own father was threatened by the idea of there being another famous, successful male in the family, someone who was younger and was therefore a potential replacement, someone who could have more help from his family in career terms than he, Paul, ever did.

The evidence suggests Scott Newman *hated* his father. It's possible his death was as much a way of punishing Paul for his neglect as it was an escape from his own misery. There were psychologists on call, yes, but his own father was too busy, too preoccupied, to speak to him. The tacky hotel room was light years from his father's retreat in Connecticut and from the life the great Paul Newman led. Drunk and drugged up, with a complete stranger watching over him as if he were a naughty eight year old, Scott Newman must have felt as if his life had reached rock bottom. Had he been

sober, thinking more clearly, he might not have taken such a
drastic, unalterable step, but sadly such was not the case. So
Paul Newman's only son, the first of his six children, the boy
who should have been his pride and joy but wasn't and never
had been, killed himself.

When the news came, Newman was at his alma mater,
Kenyon College, which by now had gone coed, directing a
play by Michael Cristofer entitled *C. C. Pyle and the Bunion
Derby*. Newman had offered to do it some time ago, when
Kenyon announced they were building a beautiful new
theater. He was busy enjoying the rapport he had with these
young actors, which he had ironically never attained with his
own son, when he got the phone call from police during a
rehearsal. When he came back, he was visibly shaken, but he
had no intention of postponing the show or flying from
Ohio to see either Joanne or Scott's grief-stricken, hysterical
mother, Jackie. He simply told the cast that he needed to
keep busy, to lose himself in the play. "I need the rowdiness,"
he told them. When he went back to the room he was rent-
ing on campus, some of the cast showed up quite late at
night, a bit snookered and carrying a bottle of Jack Daniels.
Newman took the proffered Daniels and told them he hadn't
had hard liquor in years, but maybe it was time. He took a
long slug from the bottle and held back tears. Then he
quickly excused himself.

Paul flew to California for the funeral, which was
attended only by the immediate family. Jackie, now Mrs.
Robinson, was too distraught to say much to Paul, but later
she raged at him and blamed him for their son's death. It
took years for her to get past the assignment of guilt. Many of
Scott's friends, who felt they were his true family, were put out
that they had not been invited to the funeral and held their
own memorial service at Actors Studio West. In fact, Scott's
friends, not his family, put a memorial notice in the trade

papers. Meanwhile, Newman's public relations people sent out carefully composed press releases talking of the warm and close relationship that had been enjoyed by father and son.

Paul did not let Scott's death interfere with his plans. A little over two weeks after the night of the suicide, he headed to Washington, DC, to try to head off the end of the world: It was a one-day nuclear conference that he had been involved in from the first and had even paid for. As he sat at the podium listening to panelists debate the disarmament issue in front of television cameras, he must have felt the irony that he was trying to save the world, as he saw it, but had been unable to save his son's world from suddenly ending with crushing finality.

People react to grief in different ways, and the fact that Paul continued directing a foolish play and bothered attending the conference (where he had little to say in any case and could hardly summon the energy to say what he did) does not mean he was inhuman when it came to the fate of his only son. Some people who have suffered a great loss often throw themselves into doing things, just as, conversely, other people can only get by under heavy sedation and a doctor's care. Paul felt the loss deeply; he felt he had failed his son. He also felt angry at Scott, the way people feel angry at loved ones who throw their lives away either through suicide or through foolhardy habits, the way Joanne would have felt if Paul were killed during one of his stupid races.

"We were like rubber bands," Newman said about his son. "One minute close, the next separated by an enormous and unaccountable distance. I don't think I'll ever escape the guilt." Years later he tried to explain to Leslie Stahl why he had done so little when Scott was figuratively drowning. "I've always been a terrible risk taker," he told her, "a terrible volunteer—*nuts*—I expect that [kind of behavior] to be kind of normal . . . just part of getting through the day. At some

point you gotta recognize that someone's in danger."
Whether he genuinely believed that Scott's recklessness and
addictive personality were normal, at least as far as he was
concerned, is debatable. He might have only been rationaliz-
ing to deal with his guilt. He added: "It's an event that never
gets better. It gets different but never gets better. It will come
to completion, it will come full circle. It hasn't yet, but it will."

Shortly after Scott's death, when he'd been consuming
quite a lot of beer, he reportedly startled one interviewer by
telling her his chief memory of Scott was "how *handsome* he
was" and bursting into tears. How ironic that Newman, whose
warmest relationships through the years have been with men
like A. E. Hotchner, should be completely unable to bond
with his own son.

Newman had two major reactions to Scott's death. He
spent much more time at the racetrack in what some considered an orgy of self-destructiveness, pushing himself to go
faster and harder even though he was fifty-three at the time
and often the oldest man on the track. And he consumed
much more liquor than ever before.

Newman had always enjoyed getting high on a six-pack
or two. As he got older, he often drank Jack Daniels and other
hard liquor, so much in fact that it took a lot of it to have an
effect on him. He called this having "discipline" over drink
until he realized that just because it took a lot to get him
drunk didn't mean he wasn't drinking way too much. He
came from a generation that equated manliness with how
much booze you could consume before passing out or
vomiting. Newman drank a lot to celebrate and drank a lot
when he was stressed out or depressed. He may never had
been a bona fide alcoholic, but he was imbibing more than
was good for him.

In the early seventies, with Joanne's admonishments
ringing in his ears, he temporarily gave up hard liquor and

drank only beer and wine. Some saw a difference in his personality, which had been more jovial and outgoing before. On the set of *Pocket Money*, Newman was more reserved with the crew and other cast members than usual, keeping to himself more often than not and avoiding parties. Partly, he wanted to avoid temptation; partly he was a somewhat different Paul Newman without all the liquor. Paul Newman, people realized to their surprise, was a little bit shy. He always had been, but without all the alcohol in his system, it was much more apparent.

Still, Paul went through about a six-pack of beer a day, until his son's death drove him back to the bottle with a vengeance. His picture commitments, races, and political activities weren't enough to help him deal with his guilt. He did all that he had to do, never missed meetings and never wound up flat on his face—he could still handle his liquor—but he did everything under the cushioning of alcohol. "I was out of control," he admitted. Everything was just so much easier when he was a little high, and he drank throughout the day so that the high wouldn't ever go away.

Gradually it got easier for him, but the real slap in the face was when he noticed what the drinking was gradually doing to his appearance. Newman had always kept age at bay and held off the effects of alcohol by sticking to a strict regimen of exercise, using the sauna and pool on a daily basis, and being careful with what he ate. (Food was not his problem.) He also jogged every day to keep in shape. But now the drinking was so heavy that it was starting to show in his face; he was beginning to develop a paunch, and at times he was too tired and hung over to work out. He intensified his physical activities, cut off the hard liquor, and limited himself to about three beers a day, maybe some wine on special occasions. Fortunately, the minor physical changes the liquor had wreaked were reversible. If his binge had continued for some years, however, the effect would not have been so easily neutralized.

Not long after Scott's death, Paul's publicist, Warren Cowan, among others, came up with the idea of the Scott Newman Foundation to combat drug abuse. Paul was not actively involved in the formation of the group, whose initial members were actually friends of his such as Stewart Stern and John Foreman, but it was quite a public relations coup—most people thought Paul began the foundation as a tribute to his son. Joanne did eventually join the group's board of directors, and Susan Newman, Scott's sister, became its spokeswoman. (Later Jackie Robinson got on board.) When it was decided that the foundation would award $150,000 to the writers, producers, and directors of outstanding antidrug television programs, Paul agreed to put up the money, as well as to underwrite any antidrug films the foundation produced on its own. By 1985 the foundation had evolved into the Scott Newman Center for Drug Abuse Prevention and Health Communications Research by merging with a research institute at USC. It boasted such board members as Betty Ford, Tom Bradley, Fay Kanin, and Wallis Annenberg. Paul gave a speech and dedicated the new center, hoping children in the future would be spared the terrible scourge of drug abuse.

Newman had always been rather intolerant of dissenting political viewpoints, but some thought he was carrying it to extremes when he allowed his opinions to get in the way of his—or at least the foundation's—antidrug crusade. For instance, when he was contacted in 1987 by First Lady Nancy Reagan during her "Just Say No" campaign, he refused to tape a public service announcement with her because he disagreed with her husband's policies. Newman's spin doctors claimed it was really because he was "too busy" to do it, but no one was fooled by this specious explanation. On another occasion he committed an unforgivable act of rudeness by demanding Charlton Heston be replaced as the person who was going to introduce him at a Scott Newman Foundation dinner, because Heston was too right wing. If Newman were ever discriminated against or disinvited because somebody didn't like his politics, one wonders if he wouldn't be the first to cry bloody murder.

His next picture was appropriately titled *The Day the World Ended*, although it was released as *When Time Ran Out* (1980). Irwin Allen of *Towering Inferno* fame was the producer while James (*Winning*) Goldstone directed. (Allen undoubtedly worked on the action sequences as he had done with *Inferno*.) This time the disaster was a volcano exploding on a tropical island resort, and some scenes played like a remake of Mervyn Leroy's 1961 *Devil at Four O'Clock* with Frank Sinatra and Spencer Tracy. Although the critics savaged the movie, it actually emerged an entertaining time-passer with a couple of standout sequences, such as when a kind of scientific cable car descending into a crater nearly drops into the lava or when the cast makes a harrowing trek over a lava flow on a collapsing bridge. As usual, however, the human drama was extremely weak, and on the whole the film was not as effective (or perhaps as callous) as *Inferno*.

Anesthetized by the alcohol that dulled his grief over Scott's death, Newman managed to come out with a competent performance as the man who leads the hotel guests— most of them, anyway—to safety. He was reunited with former co-stars William Holden and Jackie Bisset, both of whom enjoyed working with him again. James Franciscus was also in the cast as a guy who thinks the hotel will be spared by the lava flow and everyone is crazy to run off with "Chicken Little" Newman. "We all knew we were in a thriller-trash type thing, but Paul had a way of making all of us feel we were in something meaningful and important," Franciscus told me. "He did it by taking it all so seriously and professionally we followed suit."

Joanne came to Kalaleu, Hawaii, for the filming with

Paul, and they celebrated an anniversary while they were there. Paul made special arrangements to have a romantic dinner served for two at a shady spot by the sea on a deserted golf course. As they were eating, Kalaleu was hit by an earthquake that measured 5.0 on the Richter scale. "Gee, Paul—you pick the nicest places," Joanne told him when it was over. Later on when they were filming in natural caverns on the island and Allen wanted the special effects men to fix up some fake geysers for him, the earth itself obliged before they had a chance to begin work, and steam burst from underground as if on cue.

Though Mount Saint Helens erupted right around the time the film premiered, *When Time Ran Out* didn't make any money. With the exception of *Slap Shot*, which had done okay if not spectacularly at the box office, Newman hadn't appeared in a really successful film since *Inferno*. Most actors who appeared in movies like *When Time Ran Out* (the disaster genre had pretty much petered out by then) were considered utter has-beens, but Newman somehow was spared this fate. He was still considered a big name; it was a coup to get him for a film. Perhaps the difference was that Newman wasn't only offered scripts like the Allen film; he just wound up making them because his judgment was poor (and because, in this case, he was paid $2 million).

If that had not been the case, he would have undoubtedly been labeled box-office poison.

19

SHADOW BOXING

MANY HAVE WONDERED WHY NEWMAN CHOSE TO MAKE A television adaptation of Michael Cristofer's play *The Shadow Box* in 1980 because it deals with death and terminal illness. His son, Scott, had not been dead for very long, and Newman's mother was to die of cancer two years later (it might already have been diagnosed at this point).

The truth was Joanne was friends with Cristofer and wanted to do the movie, and Newman would do virtually anything to please Joanne. Joanne got in touch with stepdaughter Susan, who by this time had started a small production outfit with a woman named Jill Marti. Susan was thrilled that her stepmother wanted her and Jill to produce *The Shadow Box* for television, although she may have been a bit taken aback when Joanne told her that her first order of business was to get her famous father to do the directorial honors.

Paul agreed to do the picture. If Joanne ever wondered about the emotional effect this might have had on her husband, she didn't let it bother her for long. Justifying as she

always did, she concentrated on what a good part the adaptation would offer her and the millions of people who might
tune in to see it.

Susan and Jill approached ABC armed with the positive
reviews the play had received, and pointed out how many
critics had noted that it was ultimately uplifting about the
subjects of life and death. The major selling point, however,
was the participation of Newman and the on-screen appearance of his wife. When ABC officials were told that Newman
himself would foot the bills if the costs on the modestly
budgeted television feature went overboard, they figured
they had nothing to lose. The production was penciled in on
the fall schedule, and filming began on the family affair that
summer in California. No one figured there would be any
problem in getting a major sponsor to present the movie
later on.

The Shadow Box takes place at a retreat for the terminally
ill and tells three stories concurrently. First there is a woman
(Valerie Harper) who arrives with her young son but can't
accept her husband's (James Broderick) illness, then there is
an elderly, dying lady (Sylvia Sydney) who is cared for by her
self-sacrificing daughter (Melinda Dillon). And last a gay man
(Christopher Plummer) is spending his final weeks with the
young lover (Ben Masters) he left his wife for when the ex-
wife comes to pay her last respects.

Woodward at first wanted the drabber parts eventually
played by Harper and Dillon, but was talked into the more
glamorous role of Plummer's ex-wife. Not blind to the persistent stories about her own husband's alleged bisexuality
over the years, she had tremendous difficulty coming to grips
with the part and all it intimated. Despite this, she almost
manages to evoke a certain pathetic characterization of a
woman deeply hurt, essentially abandoned, still in love, trying
to accept the unacceptable on several different levels.

Newman's direction as far as the camera is concerned could be best described as unobtrusive. By going from one extremely long take into another, he overestimates the viewer's interest in the actors, characters, and dialogue of a very talky drama that doesn't begin to build up power until almost half of it is over. Although the basic premise of the purgatory on earth is compelling and poignant, dying people aren't necessarily interesting people and not until the powerful dramatics and emoting of the second half does *The Shadow Box* come fully alive.

Newman's direction of the actors was more rigorous, but one senses that the best actors simply give the best performances and Newman's notes have little to do with it. Plummer is much too over-rehearsed, acting all over the place, which may have had a lot to do with Newman's insistence on rehearsing all the scenes for two weeks ahead of filming. At first Valerie Harper comes on like Rhoda at the hospice, all cutesy and giggly, but Newman succeeded in toning down the gifted comedienne's effects so that she's much more convincing in the final sequences. Melinda Dillon, who won great acclaim playing the friend who commits suicide in *Absence of Malice,* has a fine scene when she tells the doctor how she reads made-up letters from a sister who died a long time ago to her ailing mother. It's one of the few times the film's complete lack of cinematic elan doesn't seem to matter.

Some of the best scenes focus on Plummer's lover, played superbly by Ben Masters. Whether drunkenly giving a soliloquy about how he first met Plummer while hustling on Market Street or bantering with Woodward (the script wisely avoids the cliché of a bitter confrontation between wife and gay lover), Masters is, in a word, masterful. He exhibits the kind of strong, simple, passionate, intense, basic acting ability that has always eluded Paul Newman, who so often resorts to effects and methods and mannerisms when he isn't simply playing a cool variation of himself.

Newman was troubled when he was told by ABC that no major company would sponsor the broadcast of *The Shadow Box*, undeniably because its subject matter was far removed from the mindless sitcom level of most of television's offerings, and especially because of the frank, sympathetic treatment accorded the gay lovers. (Arguments that Newman was trying to make up for his dropping out of *The Front Runner* by directing *The Shadow Box* don't really hold water because Joanne was the basic instigator of the telefilm.) Even the more daring sponsors were afraid of the effect the movie might have on Middle American consumers. So instead of coming off like a prestigious "Hallmark Presents" or the like, it would seem no different from any other run-of-the-mill telefilm.

ABC executives enjoined Paul to do something he was loathe to do under most other circumstances: meet the press. He was booked on some lightweight talk shows, as well as for a major interview with Barbara Walters, all just to stump for *The Shadow Box*. Walters tried to dig for some personal nuggets amid the publicity soundbites but was too charmed by Newman to do much damage. The movie won a Golden Globe Award and got decent, if unspectacular, ratings.

The experience of two ex-police officers named Thomas Mulhearn and Pete Tessitore at the Forty-first Precinct of New York provided the fuel for Heywood Gould's screenplay and Newman's next project, *Fort Apache, the Bronx*. The screenplay was revised time and again as one big name after another, including Nick Nolte and Steve McQueen, turned it down. Newman was paid $3 million to essay the role of a world-weary officer at the precinct nicknamed Fort Apache because of its high crime rate and the general mayhem inflicted by some of its citizenry on the more helpless members of the populace.

Newman wanted John Travolta to play his younger partner, but Travolta was nixed when he asked for too much money. The part went to a newcomer, Ken Wahl, later to become semifamous as the star of the exciting television series *Wiseguy.*

Newman was driven around the area of the Forty-first Precinct by Tessitore and Mulhearn and marveled at how they could ever have dealt on a daily basis with the poverty and violence that he saw, or at least was told about. Newman had led such a sheltered life (even before he became a movie star) that seeing this underprivileged section of the Bronx was a real eye-opening experience for him. His naiveté had prevented him from ever realizing that there were people whose life styles and living arrangements were far, far below Shaker Heights, Ohio, let alone Beverly Hills, California. "It was a revelation, a shock to me," he said at the time. "The acreage, the size of the blight." The two ex-cops thought he had terrific powers of observation but noted that Newman seemed much more "out of it" than the average person. Newman had little in common with Tessitore and Mulhearn but bonded with them as he had with the race car drivers because of their star-struck attitude and his broad, somewhat juvenile sense of humor.

When the film crew set up in the actual neighborhood to do some location shooting, word got out to certain activists that *Fort Apache, the Bronx* presented only negative portraits of the inhabitants, most of whom were either black or Hispanic. Before long self-appointed leaders of the community, as well as politicians, were denouncing the film and organizing protests. On one occasion, several youths jumped onto the roof of a car Newman was filming a scene in and began to stamp their feet and scream obscenities at him. Another afternoon the director, Daniel Petrie, inadvertently set up his cameras right outside a storefront that was serving as headquarters for

the hastily formed Coalition Against *Fort Apache*. Every time
one of the actors in the scene tried to say something, the
group's few members would start shouting and screwing up
the soundtrack. The batty William Kunstler, ever hungry for
publicity and any cause that would ensure him loads of press
clippings, even filed a libel suit against the picture on behalf
of the protesters. When the film opened, some Upper East
Side theaters refused to show it for fear that residents would
be angered at the presence of picketers, the wrong element
for the neighborhood.

In truth, most residents of the South Bronx had more
important things to worry about than the movie, and some
were even glad the film company was there. Politicians
looking for votes and newspapers looking for readers did
their best to keep the controversy going for weeks, however.
Mayor Ed Koch denounced the film and labeled it racist,
adding fuel to the fire. Petrie, Newman, and company held
many a press conference hoping to persuade everyone that
their movie wasn't racist or inaccurate. When the protesters
argued that not everyone living in Fort Apache was a criminal
or drug addict, Newman countered that the film was about
cops and that the people they ran into while on the job would
hardly be the nicer, more law-abiding denizens of the area.

Only one major minority character appears in the film,
a Puerto Rican nurse, played by Rachel Ticotin, who is
Newman's love interest. A heroin user, she dies of an overdose inflicted by a dealer because of her relationship with
Newman. On the other hand, we are also shown many decent
blacks and Puerto Ricans who are cops, doctors, other nurses,
waitresses, and just plain ordinary citizens living in Fort
Apache. The new station commander (played superbly by Ed
Asner) even says, "I can see people out there, not just the
pimps and hookers and junkies, trying to build something."
At the time of its release, *Fort Apache* may have seemed to lack

balance, but now it seems like a fairly accurate portrayal of a neighborhood where the majority of good citizens are held hostage by a minority of bad.

Still, superliberal, civil rights supporter Newman might have realized the minute he read the script that the lack of positive portrayals of minorities in major roles would make the picture seem unfairly slanted to many viewers. Although the situation has changed dramatically, there were not that many sympathetic, heroic parts for minority actors in the early 1980s (even the popular blaxploitation movies, made mostly by whites who concentrated on seedy portrayals—but at least the heroes were black).

Cartoons depicting the limousine liberal Newman as the oppressor of the people appeared in print as Newman accused the press of highly exaggerating the opposition to the movie and fabricating stories of riots. The whole experience proved highly embarrassing to the actor. Even archenemy right-wing Charlton Heston (who actually had always had a strong commitment to civil rights himself) had never been involved in such a humiliating brouhaha.

Ironically, the behind-the-scenes instigator of the whole controversy was not the protesters, Newman, Ed Koch, or even William Kunstler, but the production company who made sure sections of the script were leaked to the proper inflammatory parties. Their motive: publicity and profits. No one knew that it would get out of hand, that the papers and politicos would really run with it, that Newman would practically be branded a Nazi, or that it would take more than one press conference to end the whole conflict after all the publicity value had been siphoned away. Even Newman, eternally out of touch, was surprised that people didn't just take his word that *Fort Apache, the Bronx* wasn't racist. Paul Newman in a racist picture? Come on!

The trouble with *Fort Apache* is not so much its alleged

racism but the fact that the filmmakers seem determined to take serious situations and go cute at every opportunity—just like a television show. The script and production in general are full of dirt and grit but very little depth or insight. Worse, the movie is full of the kind of implausibilities that nearly sink this supposedly hard and realistic picture right off the bat. When two rookie cops are found dead in the patrol car, their colleagues need to be pep-talked into scouring the South Bronx to find their killers. As any New Yorker knows, members of the NYPD go ballistic when one of their own is shot and make getting the killer their top priority; the cops in *Fort Apache* don't even seem to care. For long stretches it's as if the Hollywood filmmakers are simply using the neighborhood as a backdrop for highly suspect episodes of comedy drama, such as when Newman and Wahl commandeer a city bus to take an assemblage of small-time offenders to the jail house or when a drag queen tries to throw himself off a roof, a sequence that plays like outtakes from *Dog Day Afternoon*. The film is half over before we arrive at the main story line: Newman sees a colleague throw an innocent Puerto Rican boy off a roof and can't decide whether to keep silent and not be a stool pigeon or to turn the creep (Danny Aiello) in for murder. It comes as no surprise when he does the latter.

Newman is never really believable as an Irish cop, named Murphy no less, but his performance is more a problem of miscasting and his limitations than bad acting per se. His lower-class accent comes and goes, but he does have an excellent scene when he refuses to accept his nurse-girlfriend's death and carries her dead body around the emergency room, finally exploding in a paroxysm of grief. As if to prove to everyone that he was still in tip-top shape at fifty-six, there are alot of scenes where he's running after suspects and keeping pace with the much younger Ken Wahl.

Many have noted that the scene when Newman and Aiello come to blows is the most frighteningly realistic scene in the picture. "Danny really threw himself into that scene," said one observer. "I mean, he really threw himself at Paul. They got along okay, but I think Danny kind of resented Newman, the whole pretty boy movie star thing. Danny is a much more talented actor and like a lot of actors he sometimes resents having to support the 'stars.' Anyway, he wasn't kidding in that scene, it wasn't just great acting. Danny was dead serious when he was punching Paul around. It made a lot of us nervous."

Ken Wahl enjoyed working with Newman. "Paul took a real interest in my work," he said. "Just being around him was exciting; we all wanted to do our best." Perhaps the most vivid performer in the film was Pam Grier as the psychotic hooker who shoots the two rookies and slashes a few other victims, but she didn't have any scenes with Newman. *Fort Apache* remains an entertaining but sadly minor film that with proper treatment and execution, could have been so much more.

Still stinging from the sorry way he felt he had been treated by the press during the making of *Fort Apache*, Newman decided to take on the print establishment in his very next picture, *Absence of Malice* (1981). George Roy Hill had originally optioned the property, but it eventually found its way to director Sydney Pollack, who trimmed the script of its fat and hired old pal Al Pacino for the lead. When Pacino dropped out of the film without warning, Pollack sent the script to Newman in desperation. The timing could not have been more fortuitous. When Newman read Kurt Leudtke's screenplay, he knew he had to make this picture. Leudtke had been a reporter for the *Detroit Free Press*, but his script didn't let newspaper people off the hook and, in fact, examined that very question of press responsibility. Leudtke had been inspired by *Washington Post* publisher Ben Bradlee's famous statement: "We don't print the truth, we print what people tell us."

Newman did the film because it excited him morally and

politically, not just for the money, which is in part why it emerged as one of his better latter-day films and one of his stronger performances to boot. In it he plays a liquor dealer who is wrongly implicated in the disappearance of a union leader. The authorities hope that if he's properly squeezed, he'll use his own contacts to get to the bottom of the disappearance, so they deliberately leak alleged facts about his involvement to an ambitious young reporter (Sally Field). The rest of the story resonates with repercussions and unexpected plot twists, such as a brief romance between Newman and Field.

While consistently absorbing and entertaining, *Absence of Malice* never really explodes with passion, except for a scene when Newman physically attacks Field after a friend commits suicide due to a story Field printed about her. This particular scene wasn't easy for either actor. According to Field, "[Paul is] such a decent, loving guy that the difficult part of the role for him was being mean to me. In the fight scene, he had to push me around and he really didn't want to do it. He was so afraid he would hurt me, he could have cared less what the scene was. I had to act like such a booger, and he finally did it. I was completely black and blue, but I couldn't let him know so he wouldn't feel bad."

Before the film opened, Newman, Pollack, Field, and others held a press conference at Tavern on the Green in Manhattan, which was sort of along the lines of a Nazi war criminal addressing a meeting of B'nai Brith. Right from the first, everyone in the room was on the defensive. Newman was especially rude to entertainment reporters from the *New York Post*, even though they were not necessarily the same who'd written the articles he'd disliked about *Fort Apache*. Many of the reporters understandably were enraged that Newman expected them to write yards of copy about him and his projects yet did absolutely nothing to disguise his contempt for these very people he wanted to use. For his part, Newman lambasted the press's methods of making up stories when there was nothing sensational to report, burying apologies for inaccurate reports on the back pages, and closing ranks whenever somebody dared to attack one of them.

When the film opened, the controversy continued, with some reporters claiming that no one in the press would act as irresponsibly as the Sally Field character does in the movie and others countering that, yes, they themselves knew plenty of reporters who were, unfortunately, just like that character. Carrie Rickey in the *Village Voice* laughably whined that the picture really seemed to be asking if women had a place in the newsroom, although it was clear to everyone that the reporter and villain was made a female not out of sexism but to provide a love interest (and the resulting plot configurations) for the male protagonist. Rickey's tiresome political correctness—which was not at all the issue of *Absence of Malice*—was fortunately ignored by all of the more prestigious New York critics.

When he wasn't taking on the press, Newman was immersed in a continuing variety of political causes, some old, some new. He went to Washington in December 1981 to help form a group called Energy Action, which planned to lead the fight against decontrol of natural gas, then debated old foe Charlton Heston on the nuclear freeze initiative on an ABC show entitled *The Last Word*. He stumped for a wealthy department store heir named Mark Dayton, who wanted to become a senator and had already spent $10 million of his own money to help himself get there. But when Newman called a press conference to talk about Dayton, very few reporters bothered showing up, their patience at being used by Newman at an all-time low. In any case, Newman's support for a particular candidate has always been the kiss of death, and it was no different for Dayton, who was thoroughly trounced by his opponent. The public may have flocked to certain of Newman's films, but his political opinions did not influence them when they went to the polls.

In August of 1982, after a long battle with cancer, his mother, Theresa Newman, passed away at eighty-three. By ordinary family standards, Newman had badly neglected his mother during her protracted illness; the two had had a relationship that could be best described as cordial rather than close. Not only did his film, political, and racing interests keep him away from Theresa for long stretches of time, but he never really knew what to say to his mother. Comforting people, confronting his own emotions over a situation, had never been easy for him. He could tell actors how to feel as they emoted on the set of *The Shadow Box* but hadn't a clue as to how to "direct" his own mother. Because she had not been a big part of his life for many years, he was saddened but not devastated by her death.

In any case, Newman was soon in the middle of shooting his next picture, *The Verdict* (1982), for director Sidney Lumet. He was not the first choice for the role. It was to have been played by his buddy Robert Redford, who had two directors, Arthur Hiller and James Bridges, fired because he wanted to work with Sydney Pollack (not to be confused with Sidney Lumet), the director of *Absence of Malice.* But then Redford started grumbling about David Mamet's screenplay: The main character was too grizzled and cheap and disreputable for him. Could they make changes?

At this point the producing team of Zanuck/Brown, who had worked on *The Sting*, threw up their hands in exasperation. The project was heading in an entirely different direction from where they had wanted it to go. They approached Newman, figuring he would welcome a grittier part as a way of going against the grain of his pretty, movie star image, something he was always more than willing to do.

Newman agreed to step in when Redford bowed out and had no objections to the seamier aspects of the lawyer, Frank Galvin, he was playing.

The Verdict began life as a real-life tragedy suffered by a doctor in Great Barrington, Massachusetts, and his pregnant wife, who wound up brain damaged and paralyzed due to medical incompetence. Although medical practitioners generally close ranks in such situations and don't dare take on their own, the grief-stricken doctor decided to sue. Barry Reed, who worked for the law firm representing the woman's husband, turned the whole sad story into a novel, fictionalizing many of the elements (the doctor versus doctor element was dropped, and the equally controversial element of the Archdiocese's involvement was added). Playwright David Mamet's screenplay further turned a real event into a rather formulaic story: An alcoholic underdog (Newman) gets one last chance to make good, but this time he's up against the big boys and the odds weigh heavily against him.

In the film Newman has been hired by a young couple to represent the wife's sister, who has been turned into a vegetable because she was given the wrong anesthesia. He rejects a hefty settlement from the Archdiocese (which owns the hospital where the incompetence occurred) because he wants justice for the girl. But bit by bit his case starts falling apart.

The whole trouble with—and basic truth of—Newman as an actor is illustrated in this film. He genuinely gives one of his best performances, yet at the same time there are other, better actors who would have been much more effective without even working up a sweat. Newman was up to his usual Method tricks: When one scene called for him to be out of breath as he arrives late for a meeting with the judge, he literally ran around the entire studio twice so he'd be huffing and puffing realistically as he delivered the first of his lines.

Newman, at least, had sterling support from the other

male actors, including James Mason (who'd been with him in *Mackintosh Man*) as the lawyer for the Archdiocese, Milo O'Shea as the judge, and Jack Warden as Newman's associate. Alas, the almost token female, played by Charlotte Rampling, is pretty much wasted. Newman beds her then belts her in a bar after she is revealed to be a stereotypical female betrayer—a misogynistic cliché if ever there were one. (And the *Village Voice* critic thought *Absence of Malice* was bad.) Because of Mamet's perfunctory script and Lumet's slow direction (he tried too hard to be stately and powerful without ever really getting there), *The Verdict* emerged as a surefire audience pleaser but hardly great drama.

The most inspired moment is Lumet's use of slowly developing Polaroid pictures to illustrate Newman's dawning sensitivity towards the plight of his comatose client. Unfortunately, that same client is pretty much forgotten by the end of the picture. (In real life she "lived" in that state for seventeen years in a nursing home before dying, and her son eventually turned into a drug addict.) *The Verdict* is too cold and manipulative to be art.

Although the film got generally fine notices, as well as a score of Oscar nominations (including one for Newman), it too, became embroiled in controversy. This time it was because of lawyers' reactions. Clearly Lumet and Mamet believed in the old writer's maxim, "Never let the facts get in the way of the story," for lawyers argued that not even an ambulance chaser would turn down a settlement (for nearly a quarter of a million, no less) without first consulting his client. Scenes when Newman breaks into a mailbox and the judge's obvious deference to the defense were also called into question. "On the law, the movie was a disaster," one attorney intoned.

Newman was determined to win his Oscar that year and decided to go all out in publicizing *The Verdict* and hence himself. He posed for covers of everything from *Time* to *Rolling Stone* regardless of what he thought of their politics or how they had treated him in the past. He went on more talk shows. In short, he did everything he and his public relations firm possibly could do, but in the end it just didn't work. Ben Kingsley won the Best Actor award for his brilliant (and clearly superior) work in *Ghandi.*

In January of 1983, Paul and Joanne celebrated their twenty-fifth wedding anniversary by renewing their vows in a private ceremony in Westport, Connecticut. The couple managed to keep the whole thing secret—their public relations firms sent out no media releases and no reporters got wind of it until later. Close friends and relatives were in attendance, but there were no members of the press and hardly any lawyers.

20

OSCAR x 2

As mentioned previously, Newman often allowed friendship to interfere with his common sense, which is why he wound up working on his next film project, *Harry and Son* (1984). Newman had a friend, a Los Angeles entrepreneur named Ronald Buck, who had been trying for years to get Newman interested in a script he'd written based on the novel *A Lost King* by Raymond DeCapite. Newman was constantly plied with scripts from would-be screenwriters, but apparently Buck was more persistent than most, or else Newman was fonder of him than the other "friends," merchants, and professional acquaintances who tried to force upon him their fledgling efforts. "Buck used Newman, it's as simple as that," said a source involved with the film project. (But one might say that Newman got even and ruined Buck's movie.)

Once Newman consented to do the film, however, Buck discovered it would not be as easy as all that. Newman insisted that Buck rewrite the script dozens of times according to his specifications, throwing out scenes Buck cherished and adding sequences the neophyte screenwriter didn't care for at all.

Still, Buck figured Newman knew more about the whole process than he did and kept quiet about it at the time. Too
much squawking from him and Newman might figure it
wasn't worth the bother. Newman kept telling Buck that there
was too much emotion in the script and that the audience
would overload on it just when it was most important that
they respond. He was still concerned about crossing the line
from pathos to soap opera—and that's where he made his
fatal mistake. Although the script and characters had little to
do with either Paul or Scott Newman or the relationship
between the two, even Buck noted that Newman had to be
drawing on certain aspects of that relationship when working
on the script.

Newman had always intended to direct the film, but he
had no desire to repeat his experience on *Sometimes a Great
Notion* and act in it too. He wanted Gene Hackman to play
the father, but no studio would bankroll this iffy project—a
relatively quiet family drama in an era of big-budget special-
effects movies—unless Newman himself would star. This
would have given him the perfect out from the project, an
out he should have taken, but he had spent too much time
in preparation and there was faithful Buck anxious for his
first screenwriting credit. Besides, Joanne told him he'd be
a fool to turn down what was shaping up to be a great
character part.

Joanne, as usual, had underlying motives. It was time for
another location vacation, and she wanted to go down to
Florida where they'd be shooting. To justify her being there,
Newman expanded a three-line part into a small supporting
role and cast Joanne. She was also to be an uncredited co-
director, working on the more difficult scenes focusing on the
father, leaving Paul the freedom to concentrate on his acting
and not the camera angles. She wound up directing only one
or two scenes.

Now that Newman would play Harry, they needed an actor for the son. Tom Cruise was one of several young actors who tested for the role, but he was deemed too young. (*Top Gun*, which made Cruise a major star, was still two years in the future.) The name of Robby Benson came up, as it had when Newman was mulling over the possibility of doing *The Front Runner*. Benson was clearly the front runner for the part of Harry's son, which he won.

Newman did not enjoy wearing two hats again on *Harry and Son*. His experience on *Sometimes a Great Notion* notwithstanding, he hated the extra long hours and full work weeks he had to put in as an actor and director, let alone as coproducer and cowriter. The script was being rewritten even as it was being shot, which shows in the finished product. Editor Dede Allen was on hand to offer helpful suggestions and to work some magic when it was discovered in the rushes that Newman occasionally lapsed out of character to watch another actor in the scene in his role as director. To ease up some of the tension, he resorted to his usual practical jokes. At one point he had Benson hold up a real live baby while standing on the beach. Unbeknownst to the crew, Benson then substituted a large doll for the baby before hurling the doll into the ocean. "You heard the gasping of the entire crew," Benson said.

In *Harry and Son* Newman plays a construction worker who has a difficult relationship with his loving son, Robby Benson, who wants to be a writer. When Harry develops headaches and vision problems, he's let go from his job working the crane and becomes, if anything, even more irascible. (What he manages to live on is never delineated, more evidence of how out of touch Newman is with the common folk.) Benson has an ex-girlfriend (Ellen Barkin) who's pregnant with another guy's child (seems she slept with everybody but Robby), while her mother (Woodward), who has a parakeet that can sing along with *Madame Butterfly*, seems to have a mild hankering for Robby's father. It all ends with Harry dropping dead suddenly and the others consoling each other.

Newman's direction is professional and workmanlike, if nothing more. Even Gene Hackman, however, would have had trouble convincingly playing the part of the distinctly unpleasant, overly macho construction worker, a part that seems tailor-made for no less than Charles Bronson. Newman isn't bad as Harry, but he's always Paul Newman as construction worker rather than a construction worker who happens to be played by Paul Newman. He never plays it any more deeply than on a sitcom level, possibly because the script rarely rises above that.

In fact, it is as a screenwriter that Newman really sinks his own movie. He was so afraid to overdo the emotion that he removed all emotion from the film. Trying not to over-sentimentalize the main character, he rarely explores the reasons Harry is so dreadful to his own children. (The film could easily have been subtitled "Why Children Leave Home.") Therefore, we see Harry deliberately and cruelly breaking an entire box of his late wife's beloved china just so his daughter and detested son-in-law can't have it, but there are no scenes showing his panic over his age and illness, anything that might make us feel for the man on any level. Newman intended the most emotional scene in the film to be when Harry keels over at the end of the movie, but why should anyone in the audience be remotely moved when we've only come to know him as a miserable old bastard? (Actually the only moving scene and the only one that humanizes Harry, too little too late, is when he gives his son a warm hug when the boy gets his first check for a story he's written.)

Newman put a lot of his own life into the movie. Harry

looking down on his son the wannabe author is Arthur Newman looking down on Paul the wannabe actor. Harry's brother has a job very similar to Arthur Newman's in sporting-goods, selling surplus, and he keeps asking both Harry and his son to join him in his store to their patronizing dismay. Benson's first real job, feeding boxes into a machine, is the kind of dehumanizing work that Newman would have hated. One also senses that Harry is very much the kind of bitter, unlikable person Paul Newman could have turned into had he not become successful as an actor, had he muffed a teaching post and wound up doing manual labor for a living. He also drew upon his own fear of heights for a scene when Harry, looking for work, starts to cross an exposed beam, loses his nerve, and has to crouch and be helped by the other workers to the edge. (The film was shot twenty stories high for verisimilitude, but of course there was a safety net or the insurance for the film would have skyrocketed.)

In an attempt to be sexy and trendy 1980s style, Newman also inserted some scenes with Judith Ivey that seemed dragged in from a *Porky's* feature. In the first of these, Ivey invites Benson up to her office to offer him a job and improbably winds up having sex with him after he snaps her picture. It's almost as if Newman felt it necessary to let the audience know that the sensitive, artistic Benson character was heterosexual. In a later scene, Benson brings his father to see Ivey, who has a thing for older men. Introduced in this picture, the talented Ivey was given the most undignified debut of any actress, because her character is never remotely believable, no fault of hers. No matter how she played the part, there was no way she could make it three-dimensional and no way to convince producer-director-writer-star Newman how absurd the whole bit was.

In a sequence when Benson is briefly employed as a repo man, civil rights supporter Newman brings in a tough-looking character played by Ossie Davis who only reinforces the "Big Bad Black Dude" stereotype.

Since we don't find out that Harry's illness is fatal until the very end of the movie (Newman wanted to avoid soap opera again), the fact that Benson continuously puts up with the old man's nasty acts and attitudes makes him seem like a total sap, and his uncanny resemblance to Liza Minelli never helps matters. Benson has some good scenes, screaming at Newman, "If you want to fight, let's fight, now I can finally do something you want me to be good at." But he's not nearly angry enough at his father after he breaks his mother's china. Woodward was behind the camera for Newman's death scene, which only consists of Benson running into Newman's room and finding him lying on his side. In an implausible moment, Benson never checks his pulse or breathing, attempts CPR, or calls the paramedics.

Ellen Barkin has the small role of Benson's girlfriend, and she's very good in the part but hardly recognizable as the sex symbol she would become five years later in *Sea of Love* with Al Pacino. In the intervening years, Barkin lost at least twenty pounds and either learned some makeup tricks or had some cosmetic surgery done, because the change in appearance from 1984 to 1989 is startling to say the least.

The final hilarity about the ill-advised *Harry and Son* is a scene when Benson opens a letter from a magazine he's submitted a story to and finds a $1,500 check inside. Magazines that pay that kind of money for stories never send a check before informing the author of their decision and getting them to sign a contract to boot. (Only in the movies!) It isn't these small details that make the movie such a disappointment, but Newman's completely misplaced insistence on rooting all the emotion out of the screenplay and most of the scenes in the movie, a by-product of his own emotional sterility. *Harry and Son* could have been a powerful and

important masterpiece instead of the eminently forgettable—
and mostly unseen—fiasco that it is.

Luckily, another project that Newman started with a
friend, this time A. E. Hotchner, turned out to be one of the
most successful of his career. Together with Hotchner's wife,
Ursula, the two men put a Newman's Own olive oil-based
"kick-in-the-derriere" salad dressing on the market complete
with a picture of Paul's face on the label. The dressing was at
first available only in selected outlets in New England but
within six months had gone national. Newman was such a
famous figure that what would normally have been the hard
task of promoting a new product was made incredibly easy.

Setting up an office in Westport with Ursula in charge,
the trio decided which of their other homemade recipes
could be converted into Newman's Own products. Following
the salad dressing was a spaghetti sauce that Newman had
come up with by revising Ursula's basic recipe, then an "old-
fashioned roadside virgin lemonade," which Newman
claimed could even restore Joan Collins to virginity. Next
came an "old-style picture show popcorn." Paul got daughter
Nell into the act, having her and Ursula edit a book of
Newman's Own recipes. The profits from this business were
to become staggering.

After finishing *Harry and Son*, Paul and Joanne returned
to New York where they had bought a new penthouse
apartment overlooking Central Park. There they learned that
they were to jointly receive the Screen Actors Guild Annual
Achievement Award for "fostering the finest ideals of the
acting profession," as well as for their charitable works,
political activities, and antidrug work via the Scott Newman
Center. There had been quite a bit of discussion among the
powers-that-be at SAG on whether to give the award to
Joanne (the better actor) or Paul (the bigger star) and if
either would refuse if the other wasn't included. In the end

they decided to honor both husband and wife and hedge
their bets.

Next Paul learned he was to be given an honorary Oscar
by the Academy of Arts and Sciences, a consolation prize that
he felt was usually ladled out to overlooked actors who were
on the edge of retirement, if not worse. Paul's reaction was
publicly bittersweet, privately just bitter. Although he had
always been seemingly self-effacing about his acting talent,
that self-effacement was a sham in which he was fishing for
compliments, hoping people would say, "You're a terrific
actor," in response to his protestations of luck and limitations.
He very badly wanted a *real* Academy Award, and this seemed
like an insulting sop patronizingly and dismissively offered to
a second-rater. He barely reined himself in when talking to
the press about it, but to his friends and associates he complained that the Academy was treating him as if he were "old
and through."

A list of some of the other actors who have received
honorary Oscars because they never actually won one in
competition reads like a luminous Who's Who of Hollywood:
Cary Grant, Barbara Stanwyck, Kirk Douglas, Charlie Chaplin,
and even the legendary Greta Garbo. Newman should have
been honored to be is such company, but his ego was simply
too affronted. He felt he was too young, that the Academy was
implying he was a washed-up has-been.

Newman raged about this prestigious snub and decided
to snub the Academy right back. He wouldn't accept the
award. Joanne and others prevailed on him to be gracious (if
he couldn't be mature) and to accept the honor. He agreed
to do so but wouldn't attend the ceremony. Like a baby de-
prived of his rattle, he went about whining in a constant snit
for days, secluding himself as he tried to compose just the
perfect speech to get across his true feelings without seeming
like a total ingrate. Having been informed of his feelings, the

Oscar committee contacted his *Absence of Malice* co-star Sally Field and asked her to give the presentation. She was given a special speech to read in which she mentioned that, unlike most recipients of the honorary award, Newman was hardly retired but was "at the height of his career." This wasn't enough to keep Newman, via satellite, from rather ungraciously quipping: "I'm grateful this award didn't come wrapped as a gift certificate to Forest Lawn." Afterward he joked that he had always wanted to show up toothless and ninety and on a stretcher to tell the Oscar audience, "Finally!" Newman wouldn't have to wait too long before his "real" Oscar dream would come true.

When the honorary Oscar contretemps was erupting, he had already started work on the picture that was to garner him his Best Actor statuette, *The Color of Money* (1986), which was a sequel to *The Hustler*. (If one were to include the films he directed but did not appear in, including the television film *The Shadow Box*, *The Color of Money* was Newman's fiftieth film.) Although the original writer of the novel upon which *The Hustler* was based, Walter Tevis, had written his own sequel, once the Hollywood people got a hold of it there was little chance of it being used. As usual, the Hollywood types were quick to come up with their own idea for the character of Eddie Felson and what he might be up to twenty-five years later.

At this point Newman's only contact with the man who would eventually direct *The Color of Money*, Martin Scorsese, was a letter Newman sent, addressed to "Michael" Scorsese, telling Scorsese how much he admired *Raging Bull*. (Newman was confusing Scorsese with *The Deer Hunter* director Michael Cimino.) Scorsese was a big fan of Newman's—it was said he even cherished *The Silver Chalice* and other lesser-known Newman vehicles—and was so thrilled to get the letter he didn't care if the name was a little off. Unlike actors such as

Robert De Niro, whom Scorsese had known since the days when both of them were unknowns, Scorsese thought of Newman as a real movie star and the first of such he'd ever worked with.

As is often the case in Hollywood, Scorsese decided to direct the film for reasons that had little to do with Newman. At this time, Michael Ovitz was still head of Creative Artists Agency, and Newman was one of his clients. Scorsese wanted to be represented by Ovitz himself, not only because Ovitz was a Hollywood superpower but also because Ovitz had been supportive of Scorsese's future plans to make *The Last Temptation of Christ* and the director figured the agent could help him bring these plans together. Scorsese had previously only worked on films he himself had originated. But when he was asked by Michael Eisner and Jeffrey Katzenberg at Walt Disney's Touchstone Studios, which now owned the rights to *The Hustler* sequel, to direct the film with Newman as star, he wasted no time saying yes. His association with the picture and with Newman led to Ovitz signing him up as a client, which had been his goal all along.

In Tevis's sequel, Eddie Felson falls for a college teacher and retires from the struggling, always on-the-edge, catch-as-catch-can existence he'd been living for so long. "I didn't believe what went on in the novel and I didn't believe what went on in the script, either," Scorsese said, "so I had to come up with another idea. I didn't believe this guy, who was such a hustler, such a self-destructive, thickheaded guy, would ever stop. He may have moved out of New York, but he wouldn't *stop*."

Scorsese's intent was to turn Eddie Felson into a kind of Jake La Motta of *Raging Bull* and put his own personal stamp, appropriately or otherwise, on the picture. He hired screen-writer Richard Price to turn his vision into words, and the two met often with Newman to throw ideas around. Before long both Scorsese and Price realized that *The Color of Money* was going to be a star vehicle and that Newman was the ultimate boss. Scorsese became frustrated at the way they would just be arriving at some decision when Newman would rush off to go racing. All Newman did was talk about sports, and Scorsese, no big athletic fan, had trouble bonding with him. Price was nearly driven crazy at the number of times Newman would point out to him that he was missing some opportunity in the script. Newman told Price that the screenplay was too grim and had to be lightened. "I myself didn't care if it was grim," Price said. "But the reality is, you've got to write for Paul Newman, because he's got to *play* it, and if he won't play it, there's no movie!" Newman also thought Felson should have a girlfriend, so a male bar owner was turned into a female played by Helen Shaver.

Price had to rework the screenplay so often that he said, "I had a vision of myself spending the rest of my life rewriting *The Color of Money*. I'd get gray. My child would grow up and go to college, and still I'd be doing revisions." Part of the trouble was that Price at first had written the dialogue for a character instead of specifically for Paul Newman, not realizing that Newman was the kind of technically limited actor who needed total control over what he said and did because anything outside his range would make him look bad. The Eddie Felson of both *The Hustler* and *The Color of Money* is a combination of Newman and a fictional creation of Tevis, Price, and Scorsese's, which is probably why Newman's performance is so effective.

Scorsese had seen Tom Cruise in *All the Right Moves* and contacted him while he was filming *Top Gun*. Cruise humbly said he'd be delighted to work with Newman and Scorsese. Cruise told me he found Newman "galvanizing, exciting to play with; he certainly enhanced my performance." By the time *The Color of Money* was released, *Top Gun* had already become a megahit and Cruise the prime sex symbol of his generation—as well as a more bankable star than Newman.

Cruise and Newman bonded while making the picture. In some ways Tom was a substitute for the late Scott Newman, although both Paul and Cruise claim their friendship is more like that of equals, buddies, rather than father and son. Newman got Cruise interested in racing, making future wife Nicole Kidman speedway widow along with Woodward. As with Robert Redford, unsubstantiated rumors about Newman's relationship with Cruise circulated at all the bars and cocktail parties of Hollywood and New York. In reality, Newman and Cruise, busy with so many projects and their respective mates and children, have hardly had time to carry on a friendship, let alone a torrid affair.

While most of the poolroom sequences were carefully storyboarded beforehand, there was a little more leeway in other sequences. Scorsese and cinematographer Michael Ballhaus always had a pretty good idea of what they wanted, but unfortunately Newman also had his much less focused ideas, and the other two men had to handle him carefully to keep him from screwing things up. "Marty knew exactly what he wanted," said Ballhaus, "and I knew what he wanted. So what we did, we just tenderly and slowly pushed [Newman] in the direction—from both sides, from my angle and from [Marty's] angle—to do what we wanted. And he did every-thing; he was wonderful." One day Newman came in and said he felt Eddie should be eating something during the scene they were about to shoot. Scorsese took twenty min-utes to explain the whole set up to him and why eating something probably wasn't such a good idea. Newman finally saw it his way.

Newman and Cruise did all of their own pool shots, except for a very complicated shot Cruise's character does at the end of the tournament. He would have needed another week or so to learn the shot, and the production would have fallen behind. Whenever Newman started falling back on inappropriate mannerisms, Scorsese would "creep over" to him "like a crab," as Newman put it, and shout at him to spit it out. "He's on you *like a hawk*," Newman said. But then, Newman had asked Scorsese early in preproduction if he was good at holding actors' hands, and Scorsese had told him he was. Part of the "holding hands" process is to keep the actor from going astray, and Scorsese generally did a marvelous job of keeping Newman from doing so.

In the script concocted by Scorsese and Price, by way of Newman, "Fast" Eddie Felson takes a cocky, young pool player (Cruise) under his wing and tries to guide him to the top. Eventually Felson himself winds up playing pool again and even enters a competition in Atlantic City. His re-emergence, and his realization that he's not quite a has-been, is actually the core and theme of the picture. *The Color of Money* is for obvious reasons very much a Hollywood concept movie, but it's still effective, surprisingly riveting filmmaking from Scorsese. The trouble is that the screenplay lacks depth and the characterizations are mostly one-dimensional. In particular one never gets a handle on the female characters, the men's respective girlfriends, played by Mary Elizabeth Mastrantonio (who seems too smart to hang out with these fellows) and Helen Shaver, who really gets short shrift. Newman is terrific, as is Cruise, who offers an incredibly charismatic performance and one that might have made him a major player if *Top Gun* hadn't already done so (and if *The Color of Money* had made more money).

Tom stayed at Paul and Joanne's house in Connecticut so he could attend a sneak preview of the picture with them in Paramus, New Jersey. Audience reaction convinced everyone to move the release date up. *The Color of Money* premiered at Manhattan's Ziegfeld Theater, followed by a benefit for the Actors Studio at the Palladium nightclub, where over one thousand guests paid $250 a ticket for the

privilege of attending the soiree. The dance club was dec-
orated like the world's largest pool hall for the occasion.
When Cruise walked in wearing sharp-looking cowboy boots,
Newman gave him a wolf whistle. *Life* magazine ran a special
dual cover featuring head-to-head shots of the two male stars
of the movie: one cover had Newman right-side-up, the other
had Cruise in that position. And Newman did virtually everything the publicity department asked of him to help pub-
licize the movie.

In spite of all this, *The Color of Money* did respectably
but not outstanding business, which surprised just about
everyone concerned considering the star power involved
and the pure entertainment value of the movie. (The participants certainly did their best to make it sound as if *The
Color of Money* was a great work of art, however, giving out
interviews in which they pretentiously dissected every aspect
of the film as if they had just mounted an opera by
Mascagni.) There was less surprise, however, when Newman
received his seventh Best Actor nomination for the movie.
Publicly Newman stated that he thought there was no such
thing as a best actor or best performance, even though he
wanted this real Oscar very badly. He was sure there was no
way he'd win after just receiving the honorary Oscar. He
had no intention of attending the ceremony and asked director Robert Wise, who'd worked with him so many years
ago, to accept it if by any chance his name was announced
at the end of the evening.

There was no high-powered competition for Newman
that year, except perhaps for the vastly overrated William
Hurt, who'd won the previous year for *Kiss of the Spider Woman*
and this year was up for *Children of a Lesser God*. The other
nominees included such talented competition as James
Woods for *Salvador*, Bob Hoskins for *Mona Lisa*, and the
relatively unknown (an as actor) Dexter Gordon, better

known as a real-life tenor sax, for the French-American coproduction *'Round Midnight*. Woods and Hoskins were certainly more Oscar deserving than ol' Blue Eyes, but once again the Newman Luck and the unpredictabilities of Hollywood had their way and our boy Paul was finally given the grand nod he'd been awaiting for over thirty years.

That was *all* he got, however. Robert Wise was supposed to read a tribute to him once he'd accept the statuette, but presenter Bette Davis took so long telling the audience who Wise was that the time ran out and the flustered director never got to say a word. Davis marched off on her spindly legs and went to smoke a cigarette. But what can one say about a dame (and Connecticut neighbor) of the Newmans who once replied "Why?" when Joanne Woodward asked her if she'd like to come over to see them some time.

Another offshoot of his appearance in *The Color of Money* besides his Oscar was a new feud with the *New York Post*. The *Post* objected to a sentence in a *New York Times Magazine* profile that stated Newman stood five feet, eleven inches tall. Richard Johnson, the *Post*'s "Page Six" columnist, pledged to pay $1,000 to Newman's favorite charity for every inch he measured over five-foot-eight, barefoot. On *Live at Five* with Liz Smith, Newman upped the ante to $100,000 per inch. The controversy continued for some weeks, even months, with other papers and even European publications getting into the act, and although the *Post* eventually played the whole business down, they stuck to their $1,000 an inch without going any higher.

How tall is Paul Newman? His official bio says that he is five feet, eleven inches tall, but I have stood right next to him and would have to say that Mr. Newman is no more than five-feet-nine on a good day—but I wouldn't bet $1,000 on it.

21

GLASS HOUSES

NEWMAN DECIDED THAT ALL OF THE PROFITS FROM THE assortment of Newman's Own products would go to charity, and there was a lot of profit to be distributed. In making generous donations to various charities, Newman was no different from many other wealthy celebrities, but somehow the press always got wind of his do-gooder activities despite his claim that he was reticent to be mentioned in connection to same. With the exception of Bob Hope, no other celebrity has gotten as much press mileage out of his charitable contributions as Paul Newman.

Some of the millions made selling bottled dressing and spaghetti sauce went to Catholic Relief Services, New York Hospital Burn Center, groups for the homeless, hungry, and mentally retarded, the Fresh Air Fund, *The New York Times* Neediest, Flying Doctors, and even such quasi-political groups as African Medical Researchers. Contributions were also made to the cultural sector, with checks sent to PBS and the Actors Studio. The Scott Newman Center got plenty of money, of course, as did the College of Atlanta's science wing where daughter Nell was studying, of all things, falconry. While all of this was money from Newman's Own, it's debatable as to whether or not this could be considered Newman's own money. In any case, he must be credited with doing something worthwhile with cash he could have easily blown.

With profits in the millions, a free summer retreat was built for children from approximately ages seven to seventeen, who had been diagnosed with such illnesses as leukemia and AIDS. Associated with the Yale-New Haven Medical Center, the Hole-in-the-Wall Camp, as it would be called, was constructed on three hundred acres in northern Connecticut. To see the project through to completion also required donations from individuals and corporations. "It's a Paul Newman no one recognizes when he's at the camp," Hotchner said. "When he gets there, there is a transition to almost being a kid again himself. The children react to that and he gets down to their level. If they're painting their faces, he paints his face. If they're sitting around the fire telling stories, he does that." Hotchner told *USA Today*'s Susan Wloszczyna that when his friend saw just how big the profits of Newman's Own were going to be, he was "jolted" into becoming an "accidental philanthropist." He wanted to give something back to all of the people who had made him a star.

As of now, Newman's Own brings in about $55 million a year. "Better than my last flick," Newman quipped to Leslie Stahl. Newman is also involved in a variety of other charities and causes, such as the Save the Children Foundation, which he and Joanne actively support by adopting seven children and doing many print ads; the Seaside Environmental Alliance, which is concerned with oil spills; and even the comparatively frivolous effort, spearheaded by Jacqueline Onassis around 1987, to keep a tower out of Columbus Circle that would block the view of Central Park from many celebrities' luxury condos (although the official reason for the protest was that the tower would block sunlight from the park with its mothers and babies).

Also in 1987 the wealthy owner of a Westport deli, Julius Gold, claimed that Newman had promised to cut him in on the profits of Newman's Own, apparently because he had given Newman some advice on how to proceed as well as stocked the products before they had taken off around the country. Newman said he had never promised Gold any such thing, and it wasn't long before the two men were having their day in court. At the courthouse Newman was on his worst behavior, spitting like a cobra at reporters as Joanne, always ready to stand by her man, stood silently at his side. Newman was even more angry when a mistrial was declared, but the judge promised to set a new trial date as soon as possible.

Newman embarked upon two new projects that year, involving his old friend and screenwriter, Stewart Stern. First he asked Stern if he would begin work on an "autobiography" of the actor, not for publication, but a record of his life that he could leave behind when he was gone. Stern agreed to do so and set about interviewing those people Newman suggested. This memoir got sidetracked when Stern asked if he could write a journal of Newman's work on his next film project, a new adaptation of Tennessee Williams's *The Glass Menagerie.* Joanne had played Amanda in a production at Williamstown in 1985, with John Sayles as her son, Tom. She then repeated the role the following year in New Haven with Treat Williams instead of Sayles. Stern figured the bio project might never see the light of day, but he could probably get a book deal for the journal, which he did. The slender volume was published in 1989; Newman gave his approval but reportedly was not at all pleased, although the book, even if occasionally frank about his working methods, was full of Stern's love and admiration for his friend.

Once again Newman would be directing a sensitive, highly emotional drama of the sort that usually embarrassed him and that he had difficulty playing in, on or off the screen. Stern noted in his journal that Newman is "reticent to show just how sensitive he is. Ever since I wrote *The Rack* for him, Paul has been kidding me for what he calls my 'Daddy Never Kissed Me' scenes, and I've always wondered why he's had to scoff at them when they've provided the basis for some of the loveliest work he's done." In 1957 I had lunch with Tennessee Williams in Philadelphia during an out-of-town tryout of his *Orpheus Descending*, when the subject of Newman came up. "Larry," he told me, "I'm surprised Paul can act as well as he does considering how self-inhibited he is."

The Glass Menagerie tells the story of a pixillated, faded beauty, Amanda Wingfield, who lives in a small apartment with her shy, delicate, somewhat mentally off daughter, Laura, and her resentful son, Tom, who wants to escape to the merchant marines and a more exciting life. Amanda begs him to bring home a date, a "gentleman caller" for Laura, chosen from the men he works with. He does so, but although the evening goes better than expected, it turns out the young man has a fiancée and can never see Laura again. The implication is that she will never find love or happiness or have any kind of normal life. In the play's final monologue, Tom tells how he fled home but was never able to erase the memory of his sad sister. "I was more faithful than I intended to be," he says.

Newman's public reason for directing the movie was that he felt there should be a definitive record of Williams's great play, but privately he knew Woodward wanted her performance captured permanently for the camera; he took on the task himself out of love for her. There weren't many other people who would have wanted to helm this adaptation of a play that had already been filmed twice and seemed rather gentle (only on the surface, however) as far as 1980s audiences were concerned. Cineplex Odeon put up a modest but workable $3.2 million for the production, and rehearsals were held at the Kauffman Studios in Astoria, Queens, where filming would also take place. An East Harlem tenement was chosen to show the Wingfield apartment many, many years after Tom has left home, where actor John Malkovich would deliver some of the plays several monologues.

The participants included actors Karen Allen as Amanda's daughter, Laura, and James Naughton as Laura's gentleman caller, both repeating their stage roles. Michael Ballhaus from *The Color of Money* would be cinematographer. When they gathered together at Kauffman Studios, there was tension almost from the outset, and it only got worse as time went on. Three of the four actors in the cast were already locked into a certain way of performing their roles, but Newman wanted to set all of that hard-earned technique aside and start completely fresh for the camera. The newcomer, Malkovich, who was also an experienced director, showed up with a chip on his shoulder and made it clear with his very body language that he had his own ideas—not just for the character of Tom, but about the play itself. Woodward, perhaps sensing a threat to her husband, took a dislike to Malkovich at first and wondered why she always got stuck with troublesome Toms.

Matters weren't helped by Paul's horrendous cold, which had him packed in towels and Vick's Vapo-Rub, or Joanne's bad permanent, which she swore was making her hair fall out in clumps. When she read about Reagan's plans to initiate Star Wars, she got so mad she took it out on everyone on the set. Newman wasn't able to bond with Naughton or give him satisfactory direction until he'd invited the latter to the races—naturally—played pool and other minor sports with him and decided for himself that the actor was an okay Joe.

As rehearsals proceeded, Newman worried Naughton

and infuriated Malkovich by suggesting he might eliminate all of Tom's monologues except for the ones at the very beginning (in which Tom sets up the story by looking back into the past) and end of the play. His theory was that Williams had only written them to cover costume changes, and they would only slow the picture down (so much for being entirely faithful to Williams). This disturbed Naughton because the background to his character was explained in one of those monologues, and without it he would just show up in the scene all at once like a cipher. Newman's feeling was that if the audience didn't get a sense of who Jim O'Connor, the gentleman caller, was just from his dialogue and actions in this scene, something wasn't right.

Naughton and Malkovich would have hasty, whispered conferences while Joanne knitted, Allen picked at the buffet, Stewart Stern scribbled, and Ballhaus tried impatiently to get Newman's attention over some cinematographic matter or other. Over the next few days, there would be many tiresome dissections and much second-guessing of Williams's play, with the participants foolishly acting as they though they could go the great playwright one better.

As the time for the actual shooting of the film approached, most of the cast and Ballhaus were frustrated by Newman's inability to articulate what he wanted them to do, as well as his refusal to make a final decision on whether those monologues were to stay or be scrapped. During the first week of rehearsals, Newman had constantly put Ballhaus off whenever the cinematographer wanted to discuss important filmic approaches with him, and now the actors found him in conference with Ballhaus when they needed his help in crafting the final approaches to their roles. In truth, each of these experienced cast members could have probably come up with the right approach, as three of them did for the stage productions, but Newman had them in circles trying one thing after another after another. "You find out what gives the actors confidence," Newman said about his directorial approach, "and when you do that it liberates them to try different things." Unfortunately, none of the actors felt particularly confident.

Newman finally decided to keep all of the monologues, but a new crisis emerged when Newman decided that he wanted Malkovich to look like his present-day self for each of them. Malkovich and Ballhaus argued that once Tom went back into the past (in his memory) after his opening monologue, he should deliver the subsequent monologues (except perhaps the final one) as the Tom he used to be. Anything else would jar the audience too much and disturb the fragile delicacy of what Williams had called a "memory" play. Newman was adamant about this, however, and filmed it his way over Ballhaus's objections.

Ballhaus also had strong opinions about how to handle the opening scene and how to make that initial switch from the present to the past, but Newman found it all too technical, too reliant on special effects, and wouldn't use it. Ballhaus, who'd been quietly simmering for days, exploded all at once and walked off in a snit. He felt as if Newman were treating him like a mere cameraman or boom operator when he was a distinguished cinematographer who had solid, educated ideas about how to film a picture, ideas that dithering, indecisive Newman kept dismissing. For his part, Newman was deeply troubled by what he called this "contretemps," but as the director, his opinion had to take precedence. Eventually the two men settled their differences.

Another problem was Malkovich's desire to play Tom gay. At first Newman had reacted with what his adoring assistant Mary Bailey described as "mock shock" to Malkovich's suggestion that Tom Wingfield was a homosexual, but the trouble had more to do with Malkovich's

apparent homophobia than any discomfort Newman may
have felt. *The Glass Menagerie* was based on Tennessee
Williams's (née Thomas Lanier) own family, so there was no
question that Tom was gay or that Amanda was Tennessee's
mother and Laura was his sister, Rose (who wound up institu-
tionalized in real life). But just because Tom was gay didn't
mean he was an obvious, stereotypical queen, and that's how
Malkovich wanted to play him. He had an extreme dislike of
the character, calling him "a spoiled little shit-ass," and saying
that when he went to the movies, "he got drunk and found
some fifteen-year-old boy to have sex with." There is nothing
in Williams's play or in the playwright's own life to suggest
Tom was a pederast, but neither Newman nor anyone else on
the set challenged Malkovich's assertion that Tom would have
sex with minors.

Malkovich was also unfair in thinking Tom a "shit" because he leaves home in the end. In the play, Tom doesn't
even have his own bedroom (Newman gave him one in his
"faithful" adaptation), and his blathering, nagging mother
would drive anyone to distraction. Tom was too old to be
living with his mother in any case. While Tom may indeed
have shown some selfishness in abandoning Laura and
Amanda, Malkovich should have understood his character's
desperation and sense of entrapment and recognized that the
whole play is about Tom's feelings of guilt. (Decades later
Williams would sort of catch up with the character in a seedy
New Orleans boardinghouse in his brilliant and underrated
Vieux Carré.) Malkovich could never get past the character's
homosexuality and played him almost like an outrageously
campy figure in rehearsals and in the first takes. It got so bad
that Joanne referred to her and John as (a notoriously gay
character actor) Clifton Webb and (his mother) Maybelle.
Newman's instincts were entirely right in getting Malkovich to
tone it down and to use the straighter take every time. Be-

cause of this, Malkovich's performance is much better than it would have been.

Unfortunately, in spite of, or perhaps because of, all the weeks of preparation, it is generally agreed that *The Glass Menagerie* is a good picture but not a great one. The only opening up Newman does is to show Malkovich walking around the abandoned apartment during the opening monologue, a sequence between Laura and Tom on the staircase outside the apartment, and a scene when Amanda invades Tom's bedroom while he's listening to *Pagliacci*. As noted earlier, only this last bit is a directorial misstep because the fact that Tom has only a nook to sleep in, instead of his own private room to escape to, is one of the paramount reasons he leaves home.

Newman muffs it in other areas also. For instance, he allows Woodward to be too literal and too unemotional for too much of the movie, the prime exception being the superbly delivered speech when she remembers her younger days when she was the belle of the ball. Otherwise, Woodward fails to get across the character's desperation with enough intensity even though, conversely, she gives many of her lines too much emphasis. Malkovich delivers his early monologues rather badly but improves as the picture progresses, delivering his final speech with great expertise and poignancy. Karen Allen is a little too strong as the hopelessly fragile Laura, but Naughton hits exactly the right note as Jim O'Connor.

In addition to appearing over rehearsed, the cast often holds back in an attempt to reduce their stage effects for the movie screen, but Newman has them holding back too much. Newman also allows Allen and Woodward to muff one of the play's most pivotal moments, the revelation that Laura, who was supposed to be attending business school so that she would have some chance to support herself in the likelihood that a marriage partner failed to appear, secretly dropped out of the college months before. Laura's lines, "I couldn't go back. I threw up on the floor," are supposed to be an outcry of abject humiliation that in a sense sums up her whole existence. Allen just delivers them in a matter-of-fact fashion. And Woodward simply doesn't register enough despair and anger at the realization that her hopes for Laura will never come to fruition.

In general, critics felt Newman had captured some of the play's poetry and poignancy but none of its magic or fire. It had little impact at the box office, despite the fact that Newman's public relations people engineered a publicity campaign, and Joanne was even encouraged to do television commercials for Audi. (These ads garnered her a lot of criticism because the previous year the Audi 5000 had received a lot of negative publicity alleging the car was unsafe and causing accidents.)

Newman himself was also coming under attack, from the Actors Studio, of all places. Newman had been made its president, and things were going along smoothly until a disagreement broke out between Paul and artistic director Ellen (*The Exorcist*) Burstyn, who didn't see eye to eye with Newman on any number of items. Reportedly, Burstyn felt the group's power and prestige would be enhanced by having big names, such as Madonna, admitted to the Studio, while Paul felt, ironically, that admittance should be limited primarily to the lesser known. Finally Burstyn, who was rumored to be tense at times due to frustration over the short circuiting of her once high-powered career, had it out with Newman, and losing the battle, she decided to resign her post. Newman wasted no time calling an old friend, director Frank Corsaro, to fill in for Burstyn. There were many who believed that that had been his goal all along because Newman always found it easier to work, and argue if he had to, with friends rather than with acquaintances. More important, for the first time the artistic director was a full-time salaried employee of the Actors Studio. "Corsaro needed a steady income," said a source. "Newman got it for him, one way or another. He wanted Burstyn to quit. That's really all there is to it." Newman covered up by having the "wonderful job" Burstyn had done mentioned in the press release regarding Corsaro's appointment.

Meanwhile, Newman continued his battle for privacy with reporters and especially photographers. In 1987 Newman was sixty-two years old, and although he looked much younger, he still did not like to be caught by shutter-bugs when his famous blue eyes were bloodshot or he was in any way less than his handsome self. Returning drowsy-eyed from the theater one night, Paul and Joanne had just entered the lobby of their building when a group of photographers followed them in and started flashing pictures. Paul and Joanne reacted as if they were being threatened by muggers and lashed out with both verbal and physical abuse. After hitting two male photographers with her handbag, Joanne then had to practically pull her husband off a terrified female photographer. Reportedly, the two women nearly got into a slap-and-scratch cat fight after the woman photographer told Paul she thought he was getting fat and that Joanne was going bald. The whole incident was laughed off by most people, although it made a lot of the columns, and many agreed that Newman should learn to handle the press, however invasive, with a little more tact and diplomacy.

In his next film project, Newman would team up with director Roland Joffe of *The Killing Fields*. Both men were dedicated antinuclear types and wanted to make a film that would demystify the atom bomb, as Joffe put it. *The Killing Fields* was based on a true life memoir, and Joffe's previous films were all documentaries. His project with Newman, *Fat

Man and Little Boy (1989), was sort of a docudrama fictionalizing events surrounding the making of the atom bomb but
using mostly actual historical figures as characters.

In the film, Newman plays Major General Leslie Groves,
who oversaw from the military end the research into and
construction of the bomb at Los Alamos. Paramount Studios
wanted his co-star, the actor who would play the project's
scientific chief, Robert Oppenheimer, to be another powerhouse along the lines of Harrison Ford or even Bob Redford.
But Joffe wanted stage actor Dwight Schultz, best known for
his work on television's *The A Team*, to play the part, not only
because his slighter build was more like Oppenheimer's but
also because he could bring the proper, almost neurotic
intensity to the role. "Joffe went to the wall for me," Schultz
said. "I understand the studio wanted anyone but me." Even
after they began shooting, however, Schultz was getting calls
from Paramount—via his manager, who'd heard from his
agent, who'd heard from the studio—that he was playing
it too villainously and should tone it down. Apparently
Paramount's commitment to nuclear disarmament was not
quite as high as Newman's or Joffe's.

Neither was Schultz's, who styled himself a conservative
on geopolitical issues if more liberal on domestic social
concerns. Right away this caused some stimulating friction
between him and Newman, which added to the tension
between their characters, possibly what Joffe had hoped for
all along. Newman spent a lot of time baiting Schultz, but
otherwise was, according to Schultz, "sweet and helpful and
competitive in a very interesting way."

In fact, there was much debate on the film set—a $2
million full-scale reproduction of Los Alamos on a plateau
near Durango—about the veracity of what they were shooting, debate that trickled over into the newspapers once the
film was released. Newman and Joffe had only one goal in

mind: to convince people that the bombs should not have been made, let alone dropped on Japan. They were convinced that Groves knew the Germans were finished and was aware of Japanese peace overtures long before the bombs were dropped. In fact, they felt that the bombs were dropped to send a message about the United States's power to the world in general and Russia in particular. When they weren't, according to their critics, twisting the facts to make their point, they were anxiously trying to convert everyone on the set to their cause.

There were two particular sequences that got the film's critics in a dither. One sequence suggests that unsuspecting humans were used as guinea pigs by the government and injected with plutonium to test the effect of radiation poisoning during the making of the bomb and that the Los Alamos scientists were aware of it. One of the scientific advisers for the film told *The New York Times* that Joffe made the offending substance plutonium when he was told that polonium, which Joffe claimed was the actual material injected into people, wouldn't have the dire effects the screenplay called for. Another pivotal scene has a fictional character, a scientist played by John Cusack, involved in an irradiation accident at Los Alamos, an accident that never actually took place while the bomb was being constructed. (Two such accidents did occur afterward, however.)

Joffe responded to these critics in part by producing a thirty-eight-page congressional report entitled "American Nuclear Guinea Pigs: Three Decades of Radiation Experiments on U.S. Citizens," which stated that unsuspecting terminal patients were injected with polonium in 1943 and plutonium two years later. Tony Garnett, the film's producer, claimed *Fat Man and Little Boy* was "a work of the imagination" concentrating more on the emotions of the participants than on every single factual detail."

Newman is very theatrical as Leslie Groves, playing him as a one-dimensional hard ass who hasn't the remotest moral qualms over what he's doing. In spite of this, he almost manages to lose himself in the character under a variety of mumbles and hoarse whispers. Newman wore some padding under his uniform to give him more heft and make him seem as if he could muscle his way through. "I think an actor can play somebody like that and some of the enjoyment of being superior has got to rub off on him," he commented.

Schultz noted that Newman seemed to be in charge no matter who the director was. "He dictates how the film is shot," Schultz said. "Somehow he has control. He has a sense of how it should be. He's passionate like a tiger behind the scenes but on the set it all just happens around him."

Newman's best line comes when Oppenheimer asks Groves about he morality of it all and Groves tells him off. "Was Pearl Harbor moral?" he thunders. It's Newman's best scene in the picture. Schultz is good as Oppenheimer, although his jittery acting style (appropriate for Oppenheimer) sometimes makes him seem like the poor man's Tony Perkins. His best scene has him reacting to news of his mistress's suicide during an early test. The use of the "Dance of the Reed Flutes" from Tchaikovsky's *Nutcracker Suite* during a later, much more explosive test is an inspired touch, the beauty man is capable of producing alongside the basest ugliness.

To be fair to *Fat Man and Little Boy*, it is not a bad picture, and it does attempt to include all points of view but ultimately it fails both as drama and propaganda. John Cusack's radio-active accident seems dragged in just to create some excitement, and one wonders why, if Joffe and Newman really wanted to bring home the pathos and horror of the atomic bomb, they didn't show one dropping through the air from the cargo bay doors of *Enola Gay* as charming, innocent

Japanese women and children in Hiroshima went about their business—and *boom!* Instead the dates and number of deaths are simply recorded on the screen at the end. Being subtle isn't always the best way to drive a point across, but Newman probably argued that a more dramatic finish would be, as usual, too emotional.

Although the controversy over *Fat Man and Little Boy* generated much discussion in print, the film came and went without causing much of a ripple at the box office or in the public's consciousness. Part of the problem was the title, too obscure for a youth-oriented industry. Joffe and Newman didn't take into account that the activism of the seventies had pretty much dissipated by the time a new generation had arrived at the dawn of the nineties. If Newman had mounted the whole thing as a television movie, it might have been seen by the millions of viewers who stayed away from the theaters.

Another problem was that Paul Newman, although hardly a has-been, was not a major bankable star anymore, at least not in thought-provoking pictures like *Fat Man and Little Boy*. Newman and Joffe do have to be congratulated for at least trying to make a picture in 1989 that was about something, a movie that despite its many flaws and false propagandistic aspects, made some people talk, debate, read, and think.

22

SOMEBODY'S FOOL

FANNIE BELLE FLEMING FROM TWELVE POLE CREEK, WEST
Virginia—better known as the stripper Blaze Starr—was down
in the dumps when a call from Hollywood perked her up
again. Blaze had once been notorious as the beautiful
stripper who became the mistress of politician Earl Long,
whose career was ruined by the affair. "I never *used* Earl," she
said. "I was making twice as much as he was." She used to tell
her lover that he had "Paul Newman eyes." Now her home,
known locally as Belle's Little Acre, had been wiped out by
flooding, her burlesque savings were gone, and she'd had to
finally give up stripping after over thirty years as a showgirl.
To make ends meet, the rather hard-looking, somewhat
chunky fifty-seven-year-old brunette was selling custom-made
jewelry in a mall near Baltimore.

Director Ron Shelton, who had helmed the hit *Bull
Durham* with Kevin Costner, had read Starr's memoirs and
wanted to make a film of them. He went to Baltimore to meet
with Starr and took an immediate liking to her. "Blaze is an
American original," Shelton said at the time. "I've been in

love with her since I was thirteen and clipping out newspaper articles about her. It was, in fact, meeting her, riding around Baltimore with her, that actually decided me about making [the film] because she was such a fascinating character." A needy Starr gave Shelton permission to film her story. She was hired as a production assistant and told she'd receive a percentage of the profits.

It wasn't until the grosses for *Bull Durham* were counted that Shelton was given the go-ahead for *Blaze* (1989), the film about Starr and Long that he wanted to make. The script was shown to Newman, who liked it but wasn't crazy about playing a seventy-year-old man (he was six years younger at the time). Shelton then went after Gene Hackman, who was all set to step into the role when Newman reversed his decision and told Shelton he would do it.

The next step was to get a gal to play Blaze. Melanie Griffith was Shelton's first choice, but Newman had to be paid so much that there would be little left to give Griffith what she'd require. Another problem was that she was pregnant, and there was no guarantee filming would be over before it started to show. Michelle Pfeiffer expressed interest in the part, but she didn't quite have the shape Shelton was looking for. After a casting director looked at approximately five hundred actresses, Shelton personally auditioned eighty of them (a dirty job, no doubt). A pretty, curvaceous unknown named Lolita Davidovich was signed for the part.

As far as Newman was concerned, "I'm not so sure what happened to Earl is much different than what happened to Gary Hart. I don't think whether Earl was screwing around made him a better or worse public servant. His personal life should have had nothing to do with the politics of the state of Louisiana." Shelton's attitude toward Long: "I'll allow for a little corruption here and there for the greater good. All this ethics crap . . ."

The film crew shot much of the movie in and around Winfield, Louisiana, where Long was buried. Starr and Shelton worked on the script together, also referring to A. J. Liebling's biography of Long for added details. Starr felt the movie should be even spicier than her memoirs. She did her infamous act on a jerry-rigged platform for the cast and crew when Lolita Davidovich asked if she could see how Blaze had done it. Blaze would give Davidovich pep talks and tell her how to play the part whether she wanted to hear it or not. Before long, Lolita, who felt as if she were torn between two directors, froze Blaze out and refused to even pose for photographs with her. (In truth, both on and offscreen, Davidovich is more ladylike than the more vulgar Starr.)

Blaze was consoled by a scene in which she was cast as an aging showgirl who gets kissed on the shoulder by Newman. "I'm so glad they didn't use a body double for me!" she laughed. "When I first saw Paul act in a scene, I was amazed to see how he walked and talked like Earl. He must have really studied him. It's as if Earl Long's spirit is inside of that man's body."

The real on-the-set battles were between Newman and Shelton, not the two ladies. Newman had his own ideas on how to play Long and how the picture itself should proceed. Roland Joffe may have allowed Newman to get away with largely shaping *Fat Man and Little Boy*, but Shelton was made of sterner stuff and told Newman he would be calling all the shots. "I guess it took a lot of chutzpah on my part to tell Paul Newman how I wanted things done, but right or wrong, the director always has to be the one to make decisions." Of course Newman appreciated this opinion on the set of *The Glass Menagerie*, but not *Blaze*. Newman and Shelton didn't always see eye to eye on political issues, either, which didn't help matters.

For Newman a happier part of the filmmaking process

was working with gorgeous Davidovich, particularly on an erotic scene involving a melon and a barely dressed Blaze. About that scene Newman quipped: "I gave Disney back a week's pay. There was no reason for me to collect any money for that." Reportedly, Davidovich, although she liked Newman, was not as impressed with his physical appearance. But then she was the kind of beauty who could have any young man she wanted; Newman must have seemed a bit superannuated by her standards.

Although the studio could not be faulted for its publicity—they launched a massive campaign for *Blaze*—word of mouth sunk the picture at the starting gate. Here was a movie about two of the most colorful characters in political history, and the picture Shelton had served up was dull, dull, *dull*. Part of the problem was that the script didn't add a whole lot of real drama to the relationship between Long and Starr, who as depicted were neither sympathetic nor interesting. Attempts to punch up the script with contemporary flavoring by focusing on Long's controversial support of black voting rights didn't provide enough compensation. Newman was miscast as Long but got by with charisma and the same kind of gravelly (often unintelligible) voice he used in his previous film, *Fat Man and Little Boy*.

As soon as it got out that the not-so-sexy *Blaze* was as short on entertainment value as it was on substance, very few people bothered to see it. Blaze Starr was soon on her way back to the mall and her homemade jewelry, a small, rather unimportant piece of human Americana that flared again briefly before fading once more into obscurity.

Newman's next project, *Mr. and Mrs. Bridge* (1990), did not fare much better with the public or critics. His fiftieth appearance on film, and the tenth time he appeared on camera with Joanne, was to be a prestigious item from the team of Merchant-Ivory. It grew out of a dinner party where director James Ivory found himself conversing with the

Newmans. Joanne had long been an admirer of author Evan S. Connell's fictionalized accounts of his parents' marriage, *Mr. Bridge*, and the sequel, *Mrs. Bridge.* Joanne wanted to mount the latter for television and already had a deal with a certain producer, but they were having trouble attracting interest from the networks.

Ivory identified with the background of the novels—"The world of Mr. and Mrs. Bridge is the world I grew up in," he said—and told Joanne it might be better to combine both of the books into one theatrical feature. Joanne discussed it with her producer, who agreed it might be the smarter route. Ivory then enjoined his partner Ismail Merchant to produce the feature while he took on the directorial reigns. Newman told his wife and Ivory that he would consider playing Mr. Bridge to Joanne's Mrs. Bridge if he liked the script when it was ready for perusal. Ultimately Newman liked what he read and agreed to do the picture.

He admitted that on the surface the story seemed to be about nothing. "But it really is about absolutely everything, life and love and the family." One of his main reasons for doing the film was that he liked the way the story would unfold, "By splashing essences of scenes, telling a story with a head-on impression followed by a glancing impression, and in the end coming away with a whole painting."

For her part Joanne was most intrigued by the generational differences between her and her character. "There was a time in my generation when you framed your home life around your boyfriend or your father or a husband. It had always been that way, and it was very hard for women of my generation to get out of that. In Mrs. Bridge's generation, there was simply no hope at all." Her fascination with the story was that it looked at a marriage from two distinct viewpoints that bore "absolutely no relationship one to the other."

Merchant-Ivory got a modest $7.5 million from Cineplex

Odeon to make the film, but it was higher than their usual budget. Part of the reason was the stars, although Merchant noted that Paul and Joanne were taking much less money than they usually got. Merchant economized every way he could, borrowing tiffany lamps, paintings, and desks from law firms, museums, and relatives to dress up the set. "Ismail can talk museums into lending us things no one in his right mind should lend to a movie company," said the prop man, Sandy Hamilton. Merchant gleefully accepted donations of everything from paint to clothing in exchange for screen credit and got author Evan Connell to cannibalize his and his sister's homes of every item that could possibly be used as a prop in the house the fictional Bridges lived in.

Alas, to no avail. The exceedingly minor drama, which follows the quaint married couple and their children through the decades, has only three notable scenes: the son (Robert Sean Leonard) is the only boy who won't kiss his mother at a kind of mother-son awards ceremony; the Bridges remain seated calmly at a table in a restaurant after everyone else flees as a tornado approaches and the wind rushes menacingly past them; and the secretary who has secretly loved Mr. Bridge for many years finally confronts him. Unfortunately there is no follow-up to the first and third scenes, making each appear as an oasis in a desert. The impression one gets is that the film's best moments have been left on the cutting room floor, assuming they were ever even scripted. The head-on, then glancing approach Newman admired didn't work at all.

A director like William Wyler might have been able to take this script, rework it for its dramatic potential, and craft a film that made its points clearly and emphatically, but Ivory has no talent for knowing how long to let a scene go on or which scenes should be lengthened or shortened and so on. His pictures always look very pretty with lots of lovely period detail, but everything else is just off.

This time the critics weren't fooled, and *Mr. and Mrs. Bridge* garnered Merchant-Ivory some of their worst notices. Audiences stayed away from the movie also. As the cold, emotionally distant Mr. Bridge, Newman was right in his element, although he was out-acted by his wife as Mrs. Bridge.

Newman was now sixty-five years of age, and the movies meant even less to him than they ever had. "There was a time when I could read ten scripts and find a film I wanted to do," he said. "Now I have to plow through at least one hundred fifty. I'm a dinosaur. I'm on my last legs. Spaghetti sauce is outgrossing my films." The truth was there weren't that many good parts for a man his age, and it had long been ascertained that his appearance in a film did not guarantee that anyone would show up. He concentrated on his Newman's Own business, visited the Hole-in-the-Wall Camp, went to the races, and spent a lot of time resting in his private riverside retreat at the Connecticut estate.

Four years later Newman took what amounted to a supporting role in another bad picture, entitled *The Hudsucker Proxy* (1994). (Some Hollywood wags wondered what the hell a "*Hud*-sucker" was supposed to be.) In this bizarre comic story, the board of directors of the Hudsucker Company promotes a mailroom boob (Tim Robbins) to president after the real president commits suicide. The board hopes that Robbins's ineptitude will cause a panic so that they can buy company stock at greatly reduced prices. But the boob fools them all by coming up with a fantastic money-making gizmo that every kid in the country has to own—the hula hoop! Newman was cast as Sid Musberger, a sinister member of the board.

Director Joel Coen is considered by many to be an "inventive" filmmaker, but if *The Hudsucker Proxy* is what "inventive" filmmakers turn out these days, Hollywood is really in trouble. A parody of old-fashioned movies of the type Frank Capra used to excel in, *Hudsucker* is more busy and stylized than actually amusing. It gets off to a good start but quickly degenerates, despite the occasional interesting scene. The whole business with the hula hoops captures the fun that the movie in general completely misses.

Newman proved that he still hadn't developed a light touch after all these years, although he manages to get into the spirit of things in several scenes, such as when he finally gets the chance to tell the hated Robbins that the board is going to fire him. Still, Newman clearly has trouble with the kind of material that Lloyd Bridges or Leslie Neilsen could probably do better in their sleep. (In the golden age of Hollywood, Charles Coburn would have made the Musberger role really tingle.) Robbins only proves that he is no Bob Hope or even Steve Martin, and as Amy Archer, the reporter-love interest, Jennifer Jason Leigh does a Kate Hepburn imitation that captures Hepburn's surface but none of what makes her great.

A visually oriented director, Coen made sure that *Hudsucker* looked wonderful, but he was not able to direct actors and pushed them into the wrong approach time and again. Wanting to prove he wasn't an old fogy, Newman leaped at the chance to do the picture, but it was perhaps a leap too far. Coen was too intimidated to give him much direction, not that it would have done any good.

A much happier movie experience for Newman that same year was his project with director Robert Benton, *Nobody's Fool* (1994), in which he had the starring part, one that seemed tailor-made for his abilities. Newman and Benton had nearly worked together twenty years earlier when Newman was mulling over the possibility of directing one of Benton's screenplays. Since that time Benton had directed such acclaimed films as *Kramer vs. Kramer* (1979) with Meryl Streep and Dustin Hoffman, for which he won an Oscar. By 1994, however, Benton had been superseded in Hollywood by Young Turks like Joel Coen and, as was the case with

Newman, was no longer as bankable as he used to be. In a sense, *Nobody's Fool* was to be an outcry against the mindless youth mind-set of Hollywood. The stately—and very old—Jessica Tandy was signed for a role, but Benton wasn't above hedging his bets. Younger superstar Bruce Willis would appear unbilled in a supporting role, and Melanie Griffith, who'd had a small part years earlier in *The Drowning Pool*, would play Willis's wife, an improbable kind of love interest for Newman.

In the likable if flawed *Nobody's Fool*, Newman played a sixty-year-old (he was actually sixty-nine at the time) named Sully, who ran out on his family many years ago and now occupies a room in Tandy's boardinghouse. He's in the midst of a dispute with his former boss, construction chief Willis, when Newman's son and daughter-in-law come to town to visit Sully's ex-wife (Elizabeth Wilson). After an argument, the daughter-in-law leaves with the kids, and Sully's son eventually goes into business with his father. As the two men begin to bond after years of distance and neglect, others in the small town drop in and out of their lives.

Newman offers a good, un-self-conscious performance in *Nobody's Fool.* He is generally quite solid and arresting and at nearly seventy still exudes his trademark charm and charisma. He gets across Sully's tiredness and lack of caring very well, and he has several notable scenes, such as when he's telling off Willis (who's quite good) with barely restrained fury, and an especially fine moment when he stands in his father's old house where he grew up years ago and lets all the memories wash over him. Sully is a likable old coot, but in many ways (such as the abandonment of his family), a thoroughly reprehensible character. One imagines Newman and Benton thought they had a parable about redemption on their hands. In any case, they deserve credit for daring to make a film in the 1990s that contains hardly any obligatory sex or violence.

There are a lot of problems with the picture, however.

Newman's romance—if that's what you'd call it—with Willis's wife, Melanie Griffith, is pure Hollywood and never believable. A foolish small-town cop who keeps getting into altercations with Sully comes off like a bleeding-heart liberal's view of an officer of the law. The movie has a lot of oddly poignant scenes. It's warmly human and sentimental (in the right way), but the parts don't quite add up to a whole. There's not enough drama or desperation in these characters' lives. Still, it somehow works as an effective, if disappointing, low-key slice-of-life study.

This was Jessica Tandy's last picture before her death, and *Nobody's Fool* is dedicated to her. Her line, "God's getting closer; I think this is the year he lowers the boom," is poignantly prophetic. Many years ago Tandy told me, "Any artist has just so much to give. The important thing is to give it all. Sometime it's more than you think." She was talking about actors in general, but she could have just as easily been talking about Paul Newman.

Many people noted that Dylan Walsh, the actor who plays Sully's son, has a slight resemblance to the late Scott Newman. It's fair to say that whenever Newman does a scene that focuses on a relationship—particularly a difficult, distant relationship—between father and son, he's inevitably haunted by what might have been had he been a different kind of father, a different kind of man. "I don't think anybody will ever know what Paul Newman is really like," Melanie Griffith said after doing this picture. "I think he's very mysterious. And that's so cool." Cool? Maybe.

After making the film, Benton and Newman attended a special screening at the Actors Studio where they answered questions for the young students afterward. The young women in the audience giggled and stared at Newman as he and the director walked in. Newman advised the students that when he directed, he refused to let the actors use such techniques as pauses or tears or anger all the time because it would quickly lose effectiveness. "I let them do it three times and no more." Benton told them how they had to erect a house used in *Nobody's Fool* around a big rock because the town wouldn't let them blow it up, and that a scene that takes place in a snowstorm (when Newman keeps stealing Willis's snowblower) was entirely improvised because the snowfall caught the film crew unawares.

At a special question-and-answer session in front of a more celebrated audience, including Ellen Burstyn, Newman told an interviewer that if he couldn't act, his least favorite job would be professional greeter. His favorite? He surprised everyone by saying a writer instead of a race car driver. When he expressed disappointment in how his old film *The Left-Handed Gun*, which is a cult film in limited quarters, turned out, Ellen Burstyn shouted out that he should look at it again.

Nobody's Fool didn't break box-office records, in spite of a heavy promotional campaign in key cities, but it did get respectful reviews. Many in the industry were surprised, however, when Newman was nominated for an Academy Award for his work in this picture. His performance was certainly nothing he should have been ashamed of, but it was hardly of Oscar-winning caliber. Although this is often not the case with the nominations, many feel Oscars should only go to actors who show evidence of stretching their talent, and nothing that Newman did in *Nobody's Fool* was outside of his usual range. Most of the voters must have agreed, because Tom Hanks won the Oscar for his work in *Forrest Gump*. (Joanne Woodward played Hanks's mother in *Philadelphia*, for which he won the Best Actor Oscar the previous year.)

Newman has been off the screen since *Nobody's Fool* but he has not decided to retire. One likely project as of summer 1996 was *The Magic Hour*, in which he would be teamed with Susan Sarandon in what has been described as "a contemporary detective story set in Los Angeles." As a director, he may be at the helm of a Western entitled *The Homesman.* Newman has often said that he does not enjoy looking at his old movies. "I see the actor working too hard, and I don't have to do that anymore." As for his old feeling that he is a cerebral as opposed to emotional actor, he says, "I hope I've fallen into the other river."

His wife, who remains very active in the theater, regrets that her husband has not done the same. "He was a wonderful theater actor," she has said. "It was too bad he got involved in films so totally. I think it would have been a more interesting career for him if he had been able to move back and forth. I don't think there ever is the satisfaction of doing a film that there is from a play."

Newman has kept his hand in politically. In November of 1995, he bought the 130-year-old leftist magazine the *Nation* as one of a group of buyers billed as the Nation Company, which include the *Nation*'s editor Victor Navasky and novelist E. L. Doctorow. At the time Navasky said, "Years ago there was a consensus among writers on virtually everything, from South Africa to nuclear freeze to the contras. This week, on Bosnia the magazine was split fifty-fifty. There is no more consensus in this community." Apparently the purpose of the buy-out was to correct all that. On a more physical note, Newman would occasionally pitch in and help in such projects as the Habitat for Humanity's house-building marathons, in which an entire house for a family would be constructed by volunteers in five days.

As of 1996 Newman was still getting in car wrecks, although not necessarily at the racetrack. In March he was driving Joanne back home from a dinner party when an oncoming car swerved into his lane. First this other vehicle hit the car in front of Newman, then collided with his Volvo station wagon. The oncoming car then slammed into a telephone pole. All three cars had to be towed away. In the night Newman's hand swelled up and an X ray revealed that it was broken. "All the competitive races I've been in," Newman said. "Then to be hurt while driving on a back road!"

A few weeks later there was more bad news as a blood vessel burst in his eye. Sporting a bandage on his hand and a rather weird pair of sunglasses over his eyes, Newman attended a benefit for the City Center with Joanne at the Pierre Hotel in New York in April. It wasn't long before he learned that Rupert Murdoch, the owner of the hated *Post,* was also at the benefit, and he nearly broke more blood vessels until Joanne exerted a calming influence. Murdoch and Newman never came to blows.

Newman does not like growing old. He worries about the cancer that claimed both parents, worries about what life might be like without Joanne, or vice versa, worries about being washed up and dried out, an ancient, forgotten casualty of Hollywood. "Bette Davis said it as well as anybody," he says. "Old age ain't for sissies." On balancing a marriage with a career, political interests, racing interests, and so on, he says, "It was impossible at the beginning, impossible halfway through, and it still is impossible."

But weep not for Newman. One hopes that he is well aware of the charmed life that he leads, even if it is in its twilight, a twilight some people are never even lucky enough to reach. "Somewhere along the line," he once said, "somebody took a lot of votes. They voted that public people were public people whether they wanted to be private or not. I was not around when they voted. I was denied my vote. Since I was denied, I will object loudly."

On this issue Newman is as out of touch with reality as he is with his own feelings and with the common man. He decries his loss of privacy as a public person but has absolutely no problem using his public persona to try to garner votes for candidates or for publicizing his assorted political causes. He wants to have his cake and eat it, too. He wants to be Paul Newman: Movie star but only when he feels like it. After seventy-two years of existence, nearly fifty of those years as a public figure, he has yet to understand what most everyone else does: It doesn't work that way, and life isn't fair.

Paul Newman gets flashbulbs in his face because he's a good-looking actor who's made millions of dollars as he's risen to the top of his profession. He eagerly pursued a career in pictures and was perfectly aware, as all would-be celebrities are, that it would inevitably result in a certain loss of privacy, a loss that came about not because he lost his family in an air crash or was mugged or wrongly accused of a crime, as too often is the case, but because his greatest dream came true.

ACKNOWLEDGMENTS

With sincere thanks to my colleague, William Schoell, author and editor, who went above and beyond the call of duty as a research assistant and whose suggestions and opinions helped immeasurably in shaping this manuscript. Also with deep appreciation to my editor, Michael Emmerich, and Anita K. Edson and Jim Green. And with continuing warm thanks to my agent and lawyer, Dimitri Nikolakakos.

With continued thanks to the many who crossed paths with Paul Newman over the years, who offered quotes and material for this book, some of whom did not wish to be named, some deceased, and others who are quoted and mentioned throughout the text and notes.

Thanks also to Jerry Ohlinger's Movie Material Store; Howard and Ron Mandelbaum of Photofest; Ed Maguire; Mary Atwood; the James R. Quirk Memorial Film Symposium and Research Center, New York; the Lawrence J. Quirk Collection; the British Film Institute, London; the Margaret Herrick Library of the Academy of Motion Pictures Arts and Sciences, Hollywood; the Billy Rose Theater and Film

Collection/New York Public Library of the Performing Arts at Lincoln Center, New York; and the Museum of Modern Art, New York.

Also thank to Jim Runyan (to whom this book is dedicated), Harry Alexander, Joe Bly, Robert Dahdah, Don Koll, John Cocchi, Jim McGowan, Dr. Rod Bladel, Arthur Tower, Doug McClelland, Barbara Barondess MacLean, Gregory Speck, Douglas Whitney, Barry Paris, Lou Valentino, Ernest D. Burns, Mike Snell, Frank Rowley, and Albert B. Manski.

ENDNOTES

Chapters 1 to 4

Much of the material on Newman's early days, his attitude toward acting in general, and his acting ability in particular—not to mention his attitude toward running his father's business—came from my interviews with Paul Newman in 1959 and on other occasions. Ditto for his recollections of high school and wartime experiences, as well as summer stock, college (including the laundry business), the various panics he underwent in his younger days, and also Yale and the Actors Studio. The incident with the chaplain was record in Gore Vidal's memoir, *Palimpsest*, as were some other mentions of Newman's attitude towards and experiences with homosexuality. Some material on Jackie Witte was from confidential sources. Material on *Picnic* and Newman's early relationship with Joanne Woodward came from conversations with Newman, Josh Logan, Joanne Woodward, William Inge, Paddy Chayefsky, Lee Strasberg, and confidential sources.

Also consulted were the following: *Cleveland Plain Dealer*, *The Player* by Lillian and Helen Ross, *Paul Newman* by Charles Hamblett; *Paul and Joanne* by Morella and Epstein, *Paul Newman* by Elena Oumano, *The Films of Paul Newman* by Quirk, and *Josh* by Joshua Logan.

Chapters 5 to 7

Sources for material on *The Silver Chalice* included Paul Newman, Victor Saville, Pier Angeli, Virginia Mayo, and William Schoell. Sources on Newman's marital troubles and his relationship with Joanne Woodward were confidential; some information came from Josh Logan. James Dean's bisexuality was an open secret in Hollywood, later discussed not only in books but also in television films about the actor. Sources for his crush on Paul Newman included Anthony Perkins, who also had a relationship with Dean, and other confidential sources. Robert Montgomery was the primary source for material on *The Desperate Hours*.

Sources for material on *Somebody Up There Likes Me* included Paul Newman, Pier Angeli, Sal Mineo, and Everett Sloan. Newman, Walter Pidgeon, and Edmond O'Brien spoke to me about *The Rack*, as did Charles Drake and Newman about *Until They Sail*. Newman's arrest on Long Island was documented in newspapers at the time. Michael Curtiz provided information on *The Helen Morgan Story*. Some *Long Hot Summer* material was provided by interviews with Lee Remick and Orson Welles, as well as correspondence with Richard Anderson. Gore Vidal's friendship with Newman and Woodward, his engagement to the latter, as well as details of her pregnancy and such, are in Vidal's memoirs. Books consulted were Hamblett, Morella and Epstein, Quirk, *Player*, *Palimpsest*, also *This Is Orson Welles* by Welles and Bogdanovich, other Welles biographies (see bibliography), and *Shelley II* by Shelley Winters.

Chapters 8 to 10

Material on the Newman-Woodward honeymoon, early married life, and marriage in general, as well as Jackie and children's reaction to same, came from confidential sources and from published and private interviews with Newman and Woodward. Gore Vidal discussed *The Left-Handed Gun* and Newman's involvement in the film in his memoirs. Sources for material on Woodward's Oscar included Joan Crawford and published interviews.

Sources for *Cat on a Hot Tin Roof* material included Richard Brooks, Paul Newman, Burl Ives, and Jack Carson. Material on *Rally 'Round the Flag, Boys*, *The Young Philadelphians*, and *From the Terrace* came from Newman, Jack Carson, Robert Vaughn, and Myrna Loy. Source for Newman's confrontation with Jack Warner was Newman himself. Otto Preminger and Peter Lawford were sources for material on *Exodus*. Sources for *The Hustler* included Robert Rossen, Jackie Gleason, and Don Koll.

Sources for her backstage behavior at the Academy Awards and her marriage to Newman included Woodward herself, Joan Crawford, and other confidential sources. Jack Garfein and Newman's struggle to get *The Wall* made was detailed in Morella and Epstein. Sources for *Paris Blues* included Newman, Woodward, and confidential sources. Elia Kazan, Geraldine Page, and Paul Newman talked to me about Newman appearing in the stage play *Sweet Bird of Youth* (and the film adaptation). Other sources were Richard Anderson and Richard Brooks. Books consulted were Hamblett, Elena Oumano, Quirk, and *On Being and Becoming* by James Kotsilibas-Davis and Myrna Loy. Also helpful were Tennessee Williams's and Otto Preminger's memoirs and Gene D. Phillips's *The Films of Tennessee Williams*. The Elizabeth Taylor and Jackie Gleason biographies consulted are listed in the bibliography.

Chapters 11 to 13

Sources for Newman's political activities were Newman himself, news reports, and published interviews. Sources for *Hud* and for Newman's other film activities discussed in chapter 11 included Newman, Joanne Woodward, Richard Beymer, Melvyn Douglas, Patricia Neal, Pandro Berman, Shirley MacLaine, A. Ronald Lubin, and Edward G. Robinson. *Baby Want a Kiss* material was from confidential sources and published reports, as well as published and private interviews with the Newmans. The Newmans' cruise with Gore Vidal was described in Vidal's autobiography. Sources for *Lady L* included Peter Ustinov and David Niven. Sources for *Torn Curtain* included Newman, Hitchcock, William Schoell, and other confidential sources. Sources for material on Newman's home life, marriage, children, and the filming of *Rachel, Rachel* included published and private interviews with Newman, Woodward, Susan Newman, as well as confidential interviews. Information on real-life "Cool Hand Luke," Donald Graham Garrison, came from newspaper reports. Sources for *Hombre* included Fredric March. Books consulted included Hamblett, Morella and Epstein, Oumano, Quirk, as well as memoirs by MacLaine and Neal. For Alfred Hitchcock biographies consulted, see the bibliography. Also helpful was Carlton Jackson's *Picking Up the Tab: The Life and Movies of Martin Ritt.*

Chapters 14 to 16

Newman's racetrack activities—wins, losses, accidents, and so on—were well documented in newspaper reports. The feelings of Newman, Woodward, their friends and associates (and competing drivers) on Newman's racing and his motives came from private and published interviews, as well as from confidential sources. Ditto for details on the Newmans' marital problems and their attitudes toward fans. Sources for *Winning* included Robert Wagner. Newman's business dealings and partnerships have been well documented in the press, as has his interest in the Center for the Study of Democratic Institutions and other political interests. Sources for films discussed in chapter 15 included Newman, Woodward, Katherine Ross, Anthony Perkins, Laurence Harvey, Bruce Cabot, Henry Fonda, Richard Jaeckel, Lee Remick, Lee Marvin, and confidential sources. Paul Zindel's experiences with the Newmans were recounted in Morella and Epstein. Sources for films discussed in chapter 16 included Newman, Anthony Perkins, John Huston, James Mason, Robert Shaw, George Roy Hill, and confidential sources. Sources for Newman's alleged homosexual activities were confidential. Anthony Perkins spoke frankly with me about *Judge Roy Bean*, his homosexuality, and his relationship with the Newmans. Books consulted were Hamblett, Oumano, Quirk, Neal memoirs, and John Huston memoirs. For the John Huston biographies consulted, see the bibliography.

Chapters 17 to 19

Sources for pictures discussed in chapter 17 include Steve McQueen, Burt Lancaster, and William Holden. Newman and Woodward's relationship with his son, Scott, and daughter Susan came from published and private interviews, as well as confidential sources. Scott's troubles with alcohol and drugs were well documented by the press, as was his run-in with the law at Mammoth Lake. Details of his death were from the numerous press reports and confidential sources. Newman has discussed his periods of heavy drinking in numerous interviews. Newman's behavior toward Nancy Reagan and Charlton Heston was reported in the press. Sources for *Quintet* and *When Time Ran Out* included Vittorio Gassman, William Holden, and James Franciscus. Joanne's relationship with the Dancers company, Dennis Wayne, and Dylan McDermott came from confidential sources as well as published reports, as do the various public quarrels between Joanne and Newman. Sources for material on *The Front Runner* included Patricia Nell Warren, published reports, and private interviews. The protest of *Fort Apache, the Bronx*, as well as the assorted controversies over *Absence of Malice* and *The Verdict* and the airing of *The Shadow Box*—and Newman's reactions to same—were all well documented in the press. Confidential sources were also consulted. Books consulted included Hamblett, Morella and Epstein, Oumano, Quirk, and *On Being and Becoming*.

Chapters 20 to 22

Information on Newman's Own products, their marketing and profits, and the charitable organizations receiving contributions were from newspaper sources and business reports, as were Newman's battles with the press and photographers and his activities with various political and charitable causes, including the Save the Children Foundation and the Hole-in-the-Wall Camp. Newman's reactions to his honorary Oscar and subsequent Oscar nomination and win, as well as problems at the Actors Studio, were from published and confidential sources. The controversy over Newman's height was reported in several newspaper and magazine articles. Julius Gold's lawsuit against Newman was covered in the press and in court documents. Sources for films discussed in these chapters included Tom Cruise, Jessica Tandy, and published and private reports and interviews. Books consulted include Stewart Stern's *No Tricks in My Pocket*. For the Martin Scorsese biographies consulted, see bibliography.

Periodicals and newspapers used throughout include *The New York Times, New York Post, New York Daily News, Us, People, TV Guide, Variety, New York Newsday*, and *Chicago Sun-Times*.

SELECTED BIBLIOGRAPHY

Bacon, James. *How Sweet It Is: The Jackie Gleason Story*. New York: St. Martin's, 1985.

Brody, Frank. *Citizen Welles*. New York: Scribner's, 1989.

Frishchauer, Willi. *Behind the Scenes of Otto Preminger*. London: Michael Joseph, 1973.

Grobel, Lawrence. *The Hustons*. New York: Charles Scribner's Sons, 1989.

Hamblett, Charles. *Paul Newman*. Chicago: Henry Regnery, 1975.

Henry, William A, III. *The Great One: The Life and Legend of Jackie Gleason*. New York: Doubleday, 1992.

Heymann, C. David. *Liz: An Intimate Biography of Elizabeth Taylor*. New York: Carol/Birch Lane, 1985.

Higham, Charles. *Orson Welles: Rise and Fall of an American Genius*. New York: St. Martin's, 1985.

Huston, John. *An Open Book*. New York: Alfred A. Knopf, 1980.

Jackson, Carlton. *Picking Up the Tab: The Life and Movies of Martin Ritt.* Bowling Green, Kentucky: Bowling Green State University Popular Press, 1994.

Kazan, Elia. *A Life.* New York: Alfred A. Knopf, 1988.

Kelley, Kitty. *Elizabeth Taylor: The Last Star.* New York: Simon and Schuster, 1981.

Kelly, Mary Pat. *Martin Scorsese: A Journey.* New York: Thunder's Mouth Press, 1991.

Keyser, Les. *Martin Scorsese.* New York: Twayne/Macmillan, 1992.

Kotsilibas-Davis, James, and Myrna Loy. *On Being and Becoming.* New York: Alfred A. Knopf, 1987.

Logan, Joshua. *Josh: My Up and Down, In and Out Life.* New York: Delacorte Press, 1976.

McGilligan, Patrick. *Robert Altman: Jumping off the Cliff.* New York: St. Martin's, 1989.

MacLaine, Shirley. *My Lucky Stars: A Hollywood Memoir.* New York: Bantam, 1995.

Morella, Joe, and Edward Z. Epstein. *Paul and Joanne.* New York: Delacorte Press, 1988.

Neal, Patricia. *As I Am.* New York: Simon and Schuster, 1988.

Oumano, Elena. *Paul Newman.* New York: St. Martin's, 1989.

Phillips, Gene D. *The Films of Tennessee Williams.* East Brunswick, New Jersey: Associated University Presses, Inc., 1980.

Phillips, Julia. *You'll Never Eat Lunch in This Town Again.* New York: Random House, 1991.

Preminger, Otto. *An Autobiography.* New York: Doubleday, 1977.

Quirk, Lawrence J. *Fasten Your Seat Belts: The Passionate Life of Bette Davis.* New York: William Morrow, 1990.

—. *The Films of Fredric March.* Secaucus, New Jersey: Citadel Press, 1971.

—. *The Films of Myrna Loy.* Secaucus, New Jersey: Citadel Press, 1980.

—. *The Films of Paul Newman.* Secaucus, New Jersey: Citadel Press, 1971 and 1981.

—. *The Kennedys in Hollywood.* Dallas: Taylor, 1996.

—. *Robert Francis Kennedy.* Los Angeles: Holloway House, 1968.

Ross, Lillian, and Helen Ross. *The Player.* New York: Simon and Schuster, 1961.

Schoell, William, "Anthony Perkins: The Mirror Image of Norman Bates?" *Filmfax,* September/October 1995.

Spoto, Donald. *The Dark Side of Genius: The Life of Alfred Hitchcock.* New York: Little, Brown and Co., 1983.

Stern, Stewart. *No Tricks in My Pocket: Paul Newman Directs.* New York: Grove Weidenfeld, 1989.

Taylor, John Russell. *Hitch: The Life and Times of Alfred Hitchcock.* New York: Pantheon, 1978.

Thompson, David, and Ian Christie, editors. *Scorsese on Scorsese.* London: Faber and Faber, 1989.

Thompson, Frank. *Robert Wise: A Bio-Bibliography.* Westport, Connecticut: Greenwood Press, 1995.

Truffaut, Francois. *Hitchcock.* New York: Simon and Schuster, 1966.

Vidal, Gore. *Palimpsest: A Memoir.* New York: Random House, 1995.

Weatherby, W. J. *Jackie Gleason: An Intimate Portrait of the Great One.* New York: Pharos Books, 1992.

Welles, Orson, and Peter Bogdanovich. *This Is Orson Welles.* New York: HarperCollins, 1992.

Williams, Tennessee. *Memoirs.* New York: Doubleday, 1975.

Winters, Shelley. *Shelley II.* New York: Simon and Schuster, 1989.

Wloszczyna, Susan, "A Legend with a Soft Heart and Sharp Wit," *USA Today*, March 27, 1995.

FILMOGRAPHY

The Silver Chalice. 1954. Director: Victor Saville.

Somebody Up There Likes Me. 1956. Director: Robert Wise.

The Rack. 1956. Director: Arnold Laven.

Until They Sail. 1957. Director: Robert Wise.

The Helen Morgan Story. 1957. Director: Michael Curtiz.

The Long Hot Summer. 1958. Director: Martin Ritt.

The Left-Handed Gun. 1958. Director: Arthur Penn.

Cat on a Hot Tin Roof. 1958. Director: Richard Brooks.

Rally 'Round the Flag, Boys. 1958. Director: Leo McCarey.

The Young Philadelphians. 1959. Director: Vincent Sherman.

From the Terrace. 1960. Director: Mark Robson.

Exodus. 1960. Director: Otto Preminger.

The Hustler. 1961. Director: Robert Rossen.

Paris Blues. 1961. Director: Martin Ritt.

Sweet Bird of Youth. 1962. Director: Richard Brooks.

Hemingway's Adventures of a Young Man. 1962. Director: Martin Ritt.

Hud. 1963. Director: Martin Ritt.

A New Kind of Love. 1963. Director: Melville Shavelson.

The Prize. 1963. Director: Mark Robson.

What a Way to Go. 1964. Director: J. Lee Thompson.

The Outrage. 1964. Director: Martin Ritt.

Lady L. 1965. Director: Peter Ustinov.

Harper. 1966. Director: Jack Smight.

Torn Curtain. 1966. Director: Alfred Hitchcock.

Hombre. 1967. Director: Martin Ritt.

Cool Hand Luke. 1967. Director: Stuart Rosenberg.

The Secret War of Harry Frigg. 1968. Director: Jack Smight.

Rachel, Rachel. 1968. Director: Paul Newman.*

Winning. 1969. Director: James Goldstone.

Butch Cassidy and the Sundance Kid. 1969. Director: George Roy Hill.

WUSA. 1970. Director: Stuart Rosenberg.

Sometimes a Great Notion. 1971. Director: Paul Newman.

Pocket Money. 1972. Director: Stuart Rosenberg.

The Effects of Gamma Rays on Man-in-the-Moon Marigolds. 1972. Director: Paul Newman.*

The Life and Times of Judge Roy Bean. 1972. Director: John Huston.

The Mackintosh Man. 1973. Director: John Huston.

The Sting. 1973. Director: George Roy Hill.

The Towering Inferno. 1974. Director: John Guillermin.

The Drowning Pool. 1975. Director: Stuart Rosenberg.

Silent Movie. 1976. Director: Mel Brooks.

Buffalo Bill and the Indians. 1976. Director: Robert Altman.

Slap Shot. 1977. Director: George Roy Hill.

Quintet. 1979. Director: Robert Altman.

When Time Ran Out. 1980. Director: James Goldstone.

The Shadow Box. 1980. Director: Paul Newman.* (Note: This was a made-for-television movie.)

Fort Apache, the Bronx. 1981. Director: Daniel Petrie.

Absence of Malice. 1981. Director: Sidney Lumet.

Harry and Son. 1984. Director: Paul Newman.

The Color of Money. 1986. Director: Martin Scorsese. (Note: Newman won Best Actor Oscar.)

The Glass Menagerie. 1987. Director: Paul Newman.*

Fat Man and Little Boy. 1989. Director: Roland Joffe.

Blaze. 1989. Director: Ron Shelton.

Mr. and Mrs. Bridge. 1990. Director: James Ivory.

The Hudsucker Proxy. 1994. Director: Joel Coen.

Nobody's Fool. 1994. Director: Robert Benton.

* Newman directed but did not appear in these films.

INDEX